Mystical Encounters, Miracles, and Divine Love

Mystical Encounters, Miracles, and Divine Love

True Stories of Faith and Stumbling through God's Plan

KM Wohnoutka Books

KATHRYN M. WOHNOUTKA, OFS

KMWohnoutka Books, LLC
PO Box 466, Katy, Texas 77492
https://kathrynmwohnoutka.com/
https://www.facebook.com/KMW.Books
kmwohnoutka.books@gmail.com

ISBN: 978-1-7348728-4-2 (print)
ISBN: 978-1-7348728-5-9 (e-book)
Library of Congress Control Number: 2024908888

Cover and Interior Design: Inspire Books
Rose illustration by RJ Christensen
First Paperback Edition

Dedication

To the Triune God who manifested mystical encounters, miracles, and divine love in my life and the lives of others.

To my mom, who taught me that divine love makes it possible to communicate beyond the grave.

To my husband, George, with gratitude and love for his constant support and encouragement.

To all my family and friends who have prayed for and supported me throughout my life! Thank you. You are a blessing.

What I say to you in the darkness, speak in the light;
what you hear whispered, proclaim on the housetops.
—Matthew 10:27

CONTENTS

Introduction: My Mystical Call to Write 1

Chapter 1: Exploring Mysticism 5
  What Is Mysticism? 7
  Are You a Mystic? 9
  Embracing Mystical Experiences..12

Chapter 2: Observing from the Top of the South Tower..........19
  September 11, 2001...21
  Back to New York City 28
  First Anniversary of 9/11 31

Chapter 3: Bringing Me to My Knees 33
  Growing in Spiritual Direction School................................40
  Returning to St. Justin's Retreat Team 43

Chapter 4: Traveling with Companions on a Journey 45
  To Forgiveness 48
  The Mystery of the Cross 51

Chapter 5: Starting a New Life 63
  Starting My New Life on the Road......................................67
  God Guiding Me 73
  Lost and Found...74
  Surgery Stress...75

Showing Up for Work..76

Presenting on the Main Stage 77

Chapter 6: Teaching on the Road 81

Overnight in Rome..82

Snow and Ice!...84

More Travel with God 85

The Golden Aspen of Fall 89

God's Surprises 92

Hurricane Rita...94

Following God to a New House............................97

Chapter 7: Changing Directions 101

From Ashes to Joy..102

Susan's Growing Pain..108

Surviving the Tax Class and More 108

A New Beginning 111

George's Close Call...112

The Lights Were Getting Dim 116

Retirement...118

Chapter 8: Hannah Means Grace 119

Moving to my Second Daughter Chapter...........122

The Holy Spirit Moves 123

God Leading Me to Obedience..........................128

Starting Hannah Chapter 130

Grace Junior DOK Chapter...............................131

Sharing the Divine Mercy Chaplet....................132

Little Daughters of the Good Shepherd Chapter 134

The Cindy Olsen Chapter 135

Adventures with the Juniors 138

My Girls Move On 140

Chapter 9: Moving from Background to Center Stage 143

Triennial 1997: Philadelphia 144

Triennial 2000: Denver.................................... 145

Fraud and God's Saving Grace............................. 146

One More Job! 150

Surviving Financial Shortages............................ 151

Triennial 2003: Minneapolis.............................. 153

Chapter 10: Enjoying the Calm Before the Storm.................. 155

A Train Wreck 156

Solving Problems 158

A Unified National Council............................... 159

Standing for the National Council........................ 160

Triennial 2006: Orlando.................................. 162

Chapter 11: Surviving Persecution and God's Plan 165

Hiring Goodman Financial Corporation 168

The Bologna in the Sandwich.............................. 169

Visiting Mercy Center.................................... 173

Triennial 2009: Anaheim.................................. 175

Well Done, My Good and Faithful Servant 185

Chapter 12: Trusting in Jesus 189

Diana's Discovering the Divine Mercy 192

Belinda's Baby... 197

Off to Eastern Europe 199

Divine Mercy Day of Reflection........................... 203

Mystical Glimpses from the Diary 204

Chapter 13: Leaving the Desert for Perfect Joy 207

    Searching for Answers 211

    My Franciscan Pilgrimage 213

    The Story of Perfect Joy 215

    The End of My Desert Time 219

Chapter 14: Growing into Community 223

    Preparing the ACTS Team 225

    Spreading ACTS 227

    The Color Purple 228

    My Last Two ACTS Teams 230

Chapter 15: My Stumbling Continues 235

    Continuing My Quest 242

    My Pilgrimage to Iona 243

    Adventures in the Caribbean 247

Chapter 16: Surviving Harvey and the Pandemic 251

    Surviving Hurricane Harvey 253

    Encountering the Empty Church 257

    The Miracle of Technology 259

    A Healing Miracle 261

    The Light in the Darkness 262

Conclusion 265

    My Dreams Coming True 267

Resources and Other Stories 271

    Merton's Example of Mysticism 272

    St. Faustina and Divine Mercy Story 279

    A Radical Idea 282

Bibliography 287

About the Author 293

MY MYSTICAL CALL TO WRITE

For my thoughts are not your thoughts,
nor are your ways my ways – oracle of the Lord.
For as the heavens are higher than the earth,
so are my ways higher than your ways,
my thoughts higher than your thoughts.
—Isaiah 55:8–9

God used a near-death experience to convince me that I am an author. He told me to write my first book for over eighteen years. I had written several stories and given many talks about my first abusive marriage, divorce, and recovery. I even had a friend sit me down and convey God's desire for this book directly, but a book was still a distant dream.

When I attended a retreat in June 2011, the verse that was prayed for me by my prayer partner was John 15:16: "It was not you who chose me, but I who chose you and appointed you to go and bear fruit that will remain." Wow! I knew the verse was another nudge from God. He expected me to bear fruit that would last and affect people's lives while adding good to the world. At the same retreat, a team member gave me this beautiful reading called "A Spiritual

Goal Will Give Your Life Purpose" by Father John Catoir, which was undoubtedly another nudge to write my book.

> God has a job for you to do in this world that nobody else can do. Fulfill your spiritual goal, and you will find your joy. God's will for you is your destiny. Dear Lord, show me Your plan for my life and help me to follow it.[1]

Despite these clear messages from God, my life continued. Then came the strongest nudge—or I should say God hit me between the eyes with a powerful mystical encounter. I could no longer ignore His nudgings. This powerful mystical encounter came on a Saturday morning. I had just taken the last dose of the antibiotic I had been on for nine days. Suddenly, I felt my face and throat start to swell. I told my husband, George, to put on his shoes because I thought we needed to go to the Emergency Room. When he left the room to get his shoes, my throat continued to close, so I dialed 911.

The dispatcher asked me questions, told me to get my Epi-Pen and use it, and take some Benadryl while she dispatched an ambulance. Nothing was helping, and my breathing was getting more and more difficult. The ambulance arrived in just seven minutes. Soon, I was on the stretcher, out the door, an oxygen mask placed over my nose, and we were off to the ER. While en route, I was struggling more and more to live, fighting for each breath. I remember the young paramedic trying to get a vein where he could inject medicine to help me breathe, but all he got was blood running down my arms as my veins broke with each try.

---

[1] John Catoir, "A Spiritual Goal Will Give Your Life Purpose," in *Uplifting Thoughts for Every Day* (NJ: Catholic Book Publishing Corp., 2007), 105

Then, suddenly, I was somewhere else talking to God. I told Him, "If You want me to write my book You told me to write years ago, You must let me live. The book is a jumbled mess of notes. I'm the only one who can write the story". Just then, a faraway voice told the driver to stop the ambulance, and the paramedic gave me a shot directly into the artery in my neck. After that, my breathing improved; long story short, I lived! As my husband took me home, I knew this wasn't just an allergic reaction. My almost-death experience was a powerful message from God that I needed to take being an author seriously.

That specific mystical encounter spurred me to finish my book, but I was still confused about how to do it. God started putting people in my life to guide me, beginning with Father Michael Gemignani. He was one of my spiritual directors, and we became prayer partners at a meeting. Father Mike needed prayer, so I thought I was there to help him, but when I shared my confusion about my book, Father Mike offered to help me. He had written several books. Then God led me to a company that helped with all the editing and finishing process while educating me along the way. Thank you, God! *Whole, Single, Free, ME! An Escape from Domestic Abuse* is the story of my escape and recovery from my abusive first marriage, which I wrote to help other women.

God didn't have to push me as hard to write this, my second book, although many mystical encounters, miracles, and His divine love filled me as I stumbled through three false starts before the book finally started to be on His track. And God again provided many people to help me with the second book: my editors Rachel Penate and Beth Lottig, my marketing advisor Geoff Affleck, my brother Jim Willis, who added his artistic talent and advice; and many friends and family who read my drafts, verified my stories, and gave me moral support along the way. Thank you to all! To my readers, I hope God will be inspired and blessed as you walk with me through my many stories.

CHAPTER ONE

EXPLORING MYSTICISM

Living as a Mystic

In the beginning was the Word, and the Word was with God,
and the Word was God.
He was in the beginning with God.
All things came to be through him, and
without him nothing came to be.
What came to be through him was life,
and this life was the light of the human race;
the light shines in the darkness,
and the darkness has not overcome it.
And the Word became flesh
and made his dwelling among us,
and we saw his glory,
the glory as of the Father's only Son,
full of grace and truth.

—John 1: 1–5, 14

Cartagena, Columbia! Oh God, you are giving me a mystical encounter here in a place that seems so far from You. It was 1999. George and I celebrated our fifth wedding anniversary with a cruise. Cartagena, Columbia, was one of our stops. First, we visited a few markets where the vendors kept freaking George out by putting hats on his head and touching him, and I embarrassed him by haggling over the price of a few souvenirs. We then boarded an old, rickety bus for a drive up a narrow, winding dirt road to an old Spanish church atop a hill. It was a beautiful day, so I walked outside into an open courtyard and saw the city of Cartagena's beautiful, sparkling skyscrapers against the blue sky.

I heard children's voices calling out in Spanish from the other side of the courtyard. When I walked and looked over the short brick wall, I saw dirty, half-dressed, barefoot children below with long poles they created by tying straws, pieces of bamboo, and other bits of trash with cans or paper cups tied on top. They were yelling for us to throw coins for them to catch. Beyond the children were miles and miles of the most abject poverty I have ever seen. Dirty, naked children, not a green plant in sight, lean-tos falling over. God stopped me right where I stood. I'll never forget the radical difference—the modern city and the terrible, heartbreaking poverty. God embraced me and let me see these precious children through His eyes—as beautiful, beloved, and happy, embraced by His divine love. God touched my heart permanently with this mystical encounter. He called me at that moment to give more to each of His beloved children He put in my path, whether they needed food, water, shelter, a listening ear, a kind word, a hug, or a smile. To live out what Jesus said: "Amen, I say to you, whatever you did for one of these least brothers of mine, you did for me" (Matthew 25:40). I smiled and waved down at the children as I threw all the coins George and I had with us.

Over the years, God has stopped me in the middle of my day or awakened me in the night to write His messages or explain my life experiences. So I'm obedient and always get up or out of the shower, dripping wet, or stop whatever I'm doing to write on the nearest piece of paper or in my journal I always carry when traveling. I have learned that I will lose the message if I don't write down what He is saying. Such is my life as a mystic.

I have learned to live each moment and stop to recognize when God gives me a mystical encounter, a miracle, or an embrace with His divine love. Sometimes, He reveals more of His plan for my life. Sometimes, He wants my attention.

WHAT IS MYSTICISM?

Many great mystics have explained mysticism and how becoming a mystic happens. One of my favorites of the great mystics is Brother David Steindl-Rast. He is a ninety-six-year-old author, scholar, and Benedictine monk. He has traveled the world and shared his message of gratitude as a way to lasting joy. Brother David explains the suddenness of the mystical experience.

> The mystical experience is an [often sudden] awareness of being one with the Ultimate—a sense of limitless belonging to God . . . Suddenly, for a brief moment, you feel no longer "left out," as we so often

do, no longer orphaned in the universe. It feels like
a homecoming to where you belong.[1]

And that has been my experience. A few months ago, I was returning to my seat after serving the Precious Blood of Jesus during
Holy Communion. As I looked at the Divine Mercy Image[2] in the
back of the church, I stopped because the Image was looking at me.
The Image has been there since 2007, and I have never seen it look at
me before. My mystical encounters happen when I least expect them,
and I was totally unprepared for this one, but I became His beloved,
belonging to God and feeling Him embrace my whole being. And I
want to remain in His embrace forever. I took my seat and rested in
His embrace for a few minutes until the concluding prayer of Mass
interrupted my mystical time with God.

David B. Perrin further defines the heart of mysticism,
explaining:

> The core of mysticism is the radical surrender of
> self to the loving embrace of the Other who is at
> the foundation of all life, the One to whom we owe
> our very existence . . . to enter into the depth of the
> human experience known as mysticism is to enter
> into the story of the passionate love affair between
> humanity and the divine.[3]

---

[1] David Steindl-Rast, OSB, *The Way of Silence: Engaging the Sacred in Everyday Life* (Cincinnati, OH: Franciscan Media, 2016), 20-21.

[2] Divine Mercy Image is a symbol of charity, forgiveness, and love of God, referred to as the "Fountain of Mercy."

[3] David B. Perrin, "Mysticism," in *The Blackwell Companion to Christian Spirituality* edited by Arthur Holder (West Sussex, UK: Wiley-Blackwell, 2011), 443.

Yes, it is a passionate love affair between the Triune God and me. Sometimes, I surrender to God the Father, who created me and enter into His loving embrace or listen to His answers to my questions. Other times, Jesus, my companion and beloved, rescues me from loneliness or uncertainty and often brings me joy. The Holy Spirit gives me peace and mystical guidance when needed and helps me follow God's plan for my life.

ARE YOU A MYSTIC?

Brother David teaches us we are all mystics and have the capacity for mystical experiences, which he calls glimpses:

> We all have had these moments, even if we shy away from calling them mystical. Rightly understood, the mystic is not a special kind of human being; rather, every human being is a special kind of mystic. At least, this is our calling . . . All of us are challenged by the glimpses we catch in our best moments. Those who rise to that challenge become mystics."[4]

Recognizing the mystical in my life has been a learning process. At first, I wanted to deny anything extraordinary happened. Still, as the consequences became too obvious to ignore, I saw God directing my life after my divorce. I began journaling and pondering my mystical encounters. As they happened, I tried to understand them. I became more open to the change God brought into my life

---

[4] Steindl-Rast, *The Way*, 21.

and trusted Him to know where we were going as I stumbled along, hoping I had the correct understanding.

In *God in the Dock*, C.S. Lewis said, "The miracles are, in fact, a retelling in small letters of the very same story which is written across the whole world in letters too large for some of us to see."[5] God has done huge miracles from the start of creation, such as creating our world from nothing, making our human body, which works with such complexity, and so on. So the everyday miracles we experience are small by comparison, but still miraculous, and help build our faith and lead us closer to God. Miracles have been a reinforcing point in my life to recognize mysticism—to see the incredible and impossible become possible through God's divine love. In embracing mysticism, I have grown in my understanding of what miracles God can accomplish, which gives me a continuing desire to deepen my relationship with Him.

In early 2003, one such glimpse happened to me at an airport while traveling for work. Sitting in the waiting area before my flight, I watched the ebb and flow of people arriving on planes. I became aware of God's presence and His divine love for all of us. At that moment, I felt oneness with God, and as the waves of people walked toward me, I wanted to holler, "God loves you! Do you know that?" But they hurried to their gates or baggage claim, unaware of me or my mystical experience.

In the busy airport, my heart overflowed with God's divine love for humanity. The God of the Universe loved all of us so much that He gave His Son to save us. Gratitude filled my soul. But I also felt, in that mystical moment, God's sadness at the human tendency to

---

[5] C.S. Lewis and Walter Hooper, editor, *God in the Dock: Essays on Theology and Ethics* (Grand Rapids, MI: William B. Eerdmans Publishing, 1970), 29.

be distracted by the world's busyness. I, too, am often distracted, and conversing with God becomes a distant goal. As I watched the crowds, I realized the importance of rising to the challenge to embrace these glimpses of God's divine love.[6]

In my experience, awareness of Jesus' presence in my life and trust in God requires love and action based on that love. For example, Bible study, prayer, attending Mass, serving others, and openness to listening in silence to hear God's still, small voice are a few ways to live out my love for Him. Dan Burke further explains in his article *A Mystical Encounter with God*:

> This doesn't mean that we seek these experiences, but that we recognize and acknowledge that what Jesus promised in John 14 is true; if we love Him and live in a covenant of love with Him, He will "manifest" Himself to us; and that He and the Father will "abide" with us. This is mysticism, the real and tangible encounter with God in time, space, and experience.[7]

Living in a covenant of love with God means surrendering my self-will and embracing God's will. This surrender helps me see God's plan in my life and the manifestation of mystical encounters, miracles, and, most importantly, His divine love. A favorite prayer

---

[6] *Conjectures of a Guilty Bystander*, by the great mystic Thomas Merton, beautifully describes a similar example of the mystical encounter I experienced at the airport. See the *Resources* chapter at the end of the book.

[7] Dan Burke, "A Mystical Encounter with God," *SpiritualDirection.com*, November 14, 2014, https://spiritualdirection.com/2014/11/14/a-mystical-encounter-with-god.

of mine to start the day is, "I surrender my will, my life, and my all to You, Lord." Sometimes, I repeat the prayer throughout the day, as the busyness of my life causes me to lose myself in the world's distractions. This awareness of the importance of being open to His plan has helped me to look beyond the mystical encounter and find God's message in each occurrence.

EMBRACING MYSTICAL EXPERIENCES

My mystical encounters began long before I could name them. As a teenager, I felt alone and isolated—searching for something or someone but unsure what. My grandmother had a cabin in Estes Park, Colorado, on the Big Thompson River, the site of family gatherings. Even surrounded by family, I felt isolated as the oldest and the only girl, with four brothers and many male cousins. So I would sit in silence on the rocks, watching the beautiful flowing water of the river racing in and out of the stones, reading poetry, and talking to God for hours, slowly embracing the feeling of not being alone. I began to recognize the sense of belonging to God, to coming home to His divine love. God was there, and His presence comforted me and helped me through my teen years. At the time, as I rested in His love, one of my favorite poems by Helen Steiner Rice, "On the Wings of a Prayer," helped me understand that God always held me securely in His divine love.[8]

It would be years before I fully understood the mystical nature of God and why entering into silence with Him was so powerful. I learned through practice that silence leads us to prayer, faith, and

---

[8] Helen Steiner Rice, "On the Wings of Prayer," from *A Collection of Love Gifts* (Uhrichsville, OH: Barbour and Company, Inc., 1995), 54.

love. Silence helped me come closer to Jesus and let go of the world with its noise and concerns. I let the Divine energy, found in silence, fill me. Prayer and silence became my constant dialogue with God.

Unfortunately, my constant dialogue with God stopped when I became pregnant in my teens and married my baby's father. My husband was abusive, and to survive, I pretended everything was okay and shut down my feelings, including my relationship with God. I went through the motions for twenty years and showed a false self to everyone, including myself. I had two children, and eventually, God rescued us through the prayers of members of my DOK prayer order,[9] friends, Al-Anon,[10] and a set of circumstances God orchestrated. It took me seven years to recover and become a single, free, whole person.

As I recovered, a tiny spark of spirituality began to grow, and as I grew closer to God, I realized I needed to connect honestly with all who crossed my path. I started seeing God in every part of my life, being awake to the Holy Spirit's guidance, being authentic, living my faith, facing the truth, and exploring life, becoming a person who had fallen in love with God. During my abusive marriage, I had become a robot going through life locked inside a protective covering, but I started breaking out of the shell and letting people see the real me—hugging, talking, smiling, and sharing the truth of who I was becoming. One man who worked with me in our local civic association said to me one day, "It was like you had a facelift. You are a new person." And I was.

---

[9] The Order of the Daughters of the King, Inc® (DOK) is a women's prayer order started in 1885 in the Episcopal Church. A Daughter pledges herself to a lifelong program of prayer, service, and evangelism.

[10] Al-Anon is twelve-step program that helps members come to understand that problem drinking is a family illness that affects everyone in the family.

A simple Bible verse perfectly defined my passionate love affair with God: "But seek first the kingdom [of God] and his righteousness, and all these things will be given you besides" (Matthew 6:33). I continued to grow in my love and gain an understanding of God's mystical encounters and divine love by living out that verse and constantly saying to myself, "Simply: Jesus." The motto helped me stay centered through my life's adventures and trials.

After my divorce, I embarked on a whole new life. I went to college, gave back by serving in many ministries, eventually joined the working world, and grew in many ways. Then God put another surprise in my life—a second marriage to George. A man I could pray with who became a much-needed father and grandfather to my family. George was deeply spiritual. He worked in healing ministries and attended charismatic[11] events.

George was a breath of fresh air, allowing me to show my true self. Years earlier, during a temporary split with my first husband, I attended a charismatic prayer group in a friend's home. One night at a meeting, I had sinned and refused to keep my nose out of something God had told me to leave alone three times. My interference caused a firestorm. But worse than the firestorm, I felt that God had left me. My sin of disobedience put a wall between God and me. I repented in front of the group with tears and genuine regret. As I left the prayer meeting, I began praying in tongues for the first time. It was a mystical reunion with God, and I was relieved to find forgiveness. As I continued in my knowledge of my charismatic gifts,

---

[11] Catholic Charismatic Renewal (CCR) is a spiritual movement within the Catholic Church that emphasizes the availability of the power and the many gifts of the Holy Spirit in the life of every believer, and the need for a personal relationship with God through Jesus Christ in order to live life to the fullest.

I felt I had the gift of healing but was afraid to say it aloud, just like I kept my talking in tongues secret. George was a blessing in helping me find the real me and accepting my charismatic gifts.

Then, one night, shortly after we were married in 1994, George and I were on a prayer team at a charismatic healing service. It was my first time to serve on a healing team. I was scared because I wasn't sure I had the gift of healing. A woman came to us for prayer. We started to pray for her, but George said we should go to the chapel as she was very agitated. I didn't understand what was happening, but George did. One of the other prayer ministers walked behind us and prayed for us.

As we sat in the chapel, I held the woman in my arms, rocking her and trying to calm her. I prayed in tongues. George was sprinkling her with holy water and praying for her to be released from whatever possessed her. We prayed with her for some time, and then she went limp in my arms and fell asleep. I held her until she woke, and we helped her return to her husband. We continued praying for others. Later, after the service, she came to me and said that I had the gift of healing. She was grateful that through my prayers God had set her free from the demons possessing her. I was speechless and just hugged her. But a part of me was overjoyed by this confirmation from God that I did have the gift of healing. George and I continued to serve in healing ministry for many years.

Then, in 1998, God called me to become a spiritual director through several mystical encounters that surprised me. During the program's second year in 2000, one assignment was to write about a person who exhibited deep spirituality. Our instructors gave us a list of people to choose from, and I chose a thirteenth-century mystic, Marguerite Porete. Through her writings, I finally put a name to my mystical encounters. I found her writing moving and inspiring, taking me deeper into God's divine love.

Her book, *The Mirror of Simple Souls,* is written as a love letter to her beloved, Jesus. Marguerite teaches that total union with God comes through love and annihilation of the will. In her book, Marguerite paints beautiful images of the connection between her soul, love, and reason. These images helped me understand my earlier mystical experiences and why I embrace Jesus as my beloved. As I explored my mystical encounters while reading Marguerite's book, I experienced a profound intimacy during prayer that surpassed any earthly experience. I felt a complete merging of my whole person with Jesus. Marguerite's writing also gave me the knowledge that uniting with God through divine love requires more suffering on my part, humbling both my body and will to God's will to become entirely spirit:

> "And when is the soul completely spirit?" says Reason. Love [says]: When the body is completely mortified, and the will delights in dishonor, in poverty, and in tribulations, then it is completely spirit."[12]

I also learned from St. Francis, who taught me how a soul becomes completely spirit by denying self, living for the other, embracing poverty, and serving the poorest of the poor, the lepers. But even more, St. Francis was also a contemplative who went into the mountains alone, fasted, and prayed for many days until God's

---

[12] Ellen L. Babinsky, translator, *The Mirror of Simple Souls by Marguerite Porete: The Classics of Western Spirituality,* (Mahwah, NJ: Paulist Press, 1993), 147.

divine love pressed the stigmata[13] on his body as a sign that helped St. Francis identify himself as entirely spirit. St. Francis's example helped me learn to let go of earthly possessions and center on God's plan for my life. I have followed the nudging of the Holy Spirit to serve others at every opportunity. These actions have brought me closer to God and inevitably removed the layers of false self that kept me from closeness with God.

Bernard McGuinn describes another image—the symbolic nature of the mirror, which helped Marguerite see her true self:

> The mirror, a medieval and modern image of women's vanity and narcissism, and of the superficial and false self, becomes transformed in this [book] . . . into a symbol of the honesty and depth of the true self before, in, and becoming [united with] God.[14]

Like Marguerite, I, too, have found that honesty and depth of my true self are necessary to draw closer to God, when I surrender my will to live and entirely trust in God's divine love, an all-encompassing love. I only see God's image when I look in the mirror of my soul and continue to strive toward total surrender, day by day.

---

[13] The stigmata is the spontaneous appearance of the wound marks of our crucified Lord on a person's body. These marks include the nail wounds at the feet and the hands, the lance wound at the side, the head wounds from the crown of thorns, and the scourge marks over the entire body, particularly the back. From Catholic Straight Answers website: https://catholicstraightanswers. com/what-is-the-stigmata//.

[14] Bernard McGuinn, editor, *Meister Eckhart and The Beguine Mystics: Hadewijch of Brabant, Mechthild of Magdeburg, and Marguerite Porete* (New York: Continuum, 1997), 76.

Sadly, Marguerite's book was condemned, and she was burned at the stake in 1310 because of political and ecclesiastical tensions. She taught that the soul only depends on God's divine love. At the time, church authorities viewed her teaching as heresy. She refused to recant what she had written and continued distributing her book. Like Jesus, Marguerite didn't speak or defend herself during her trial. Many who watched were moved to tears by her dignity and grace.

Now for the stories of how I stumbled through God's plan for my life and recognized the mystical in each encounter. The stories show how God led me closer to Him and how I learned to recognize God's plan through trials, suffering, mystical encounters, miracles, and His divine love. Being a mystic has led me to times when I was amazed to see how God has changed me into His beloved daughter; as Merton said: "This little point of nothingness and of absolute poverty is the pure glory of God . . . blazing with the invisible light of heaven."[15]

---

[15] Thomas Merton, *Conjectures of a Guilty Bystander* (New York: Image, 1965), 155.

CHAPTER TWO

OBSERVING FROM THE TOP OF THE SOUTH TOWER

Experiencing God's Divine Love through 9/11

O God of love, compassion, and healing,
look on us, people of many different faiths and traditions,
who gather today at this site,
the scene of incredible violence and pain . . .
God of peace, bring Your peace to our violent world:
peace in the hearts of all men and women and
peace among the nations of the earth.
Turn Your way of love to those whose hearts
and minds are consumed with hatred.
God of understanding, overwhelmed by the
magnitude of this tragedy, we seek Your light and
guidance as we confront such terrible events.
Grant that those whose lives were spared
may live so that the lives lost here
may not have been lost in vain.

Comfort and console us, strengthen us in hope,
and give us the wisdom and courage to work tirelessly
for a world where true peace and love reign among
nations and in the hearts of all. Amen.[1]

My 9/11 story began fifteen years earlier, in September 1986, when I ran away to New York on a fictitious business trip looking for freedom, joy, happiness, and a new life. I couldn't take the pain of abuse anymore and was so beaten down I didn't believe I could make it alone. Thanks to several friends God put in my life, I finally dared to say, "No more!"

During this trip, my friend had planned for us to tour the Statue of Liberty, but it was closed for renovations, so he brought me to the observation deck of the South Tower of the World Trade Center. Here, from this extraordinary view, blue skies as far as I could see—New York City and the Statue of Liberty far below. "Lord, I'm happy, joyous, and free," I thanked God as I gazed down upon this stunning scene. Little did I know then that God directed my steps even when I was unaware of His presence. He brought me to this place to declare my freedom from my abusive marriage and to prepare me for future events. *Oh, Lord, help me build a new life.* It was a simple prayer, but God's answer would be beyond any life I could imagine.

Fifteen years later, in April 2001, I found myself in awe of the Statue of Liberty again as I looked down from the ninety-eight floor in the South Tower. *It is so small from up here,* I thought, *another blue sky, just like so many years ago.* My new life consisted of a remarkable

---

[1] Pope Benedict XVI, "Prayer at Ground Zero," *EWTN*, New York, April 20, 2008, https://www.ewtn.com/catholicism/library/prayer-at-ground-zero-6613.

career teaching accounting software for Oracle Corporation[2] and traveling the world. I married the most wonderful man, my sweet George—Porgie, to me. *Thank you, Lord, for rescuing me and bringing me here fifteen years later with a whole new life.*

The South Tower of the World Trade Center was a beautiful building with a spectacular view! I was excited to be there and to teach a General Ledger class for a new client. The project manager took longer with his previous meeting, so I had more time to stand there and look down at the sprawling city of New York beyond the Statue of Liberty. I thought, "Lord, this world of Yours is so awesome."

The project manager finally called me into his office. He wanted me to help him solve a reporting problem. The young Oracle consultant joined us, and I quickly helped them with the problem and returned to the ninety-seventh floor to the class of the employees I was training.

SEPTEMBER 11, 2001

On September 11, 2001, I was home in Houston, putting my suitcases in the car to go to the airport to teach a class for a company located north of New York City. The *Today* show was on, and the channel showed footage of the first plane hitting the North Tower. Then the second plane came out of that clear, blue sky and hit the South Tower! I couldn't believe what I was watching. The horror overwhelmed me.

---

[2] Oracle Corporation is an American multinational computer technology corporation headquartered in Austin, Texas.

This can't be happening, I thought as I rushed out to the car. I had to get to my doctor's appointment and the airport. I stopped at a traffic light. My thoughts were fragmented. *What did the news say? The South Tower collapsed? How could it collapse? I stood on top of that building earlier this year. I enjoyed the breathtaking view. Oh, Lord, send Your angels to help those people, to help all of us—armies of angels, Lord. The building and so many of the employees are gone!* In my mind's eye, I saw all the people I'd worked with and interacted with on my last visit to New York City.

My doctor and I watched in horror as the North Tower collapsed. All those people. My thoughts continued to race as I cried for the rescue workers, clients, coworkers, and many more trapped in the rubble. Something that seemed so strong was now a pile of rubble in a matter of seconds. *Lord, this can't be real. This can't be happening.*

The airports closed. I called the client to tell him I couldn't fly to New York to teach the class. I drove home in shock. I continued pleading with the Lord to send angels to help those trapped in the rubble or caught on the top of the building with no way down. Tears filled my eyes as I remembered the faces of my students, making it hard to drive. I asked what many were asking: "Oh, God, how could this happen?"

Two weeks passed, and I experienced sadness, fear, grief, and helplessness as I watched the blur of TV images like many others around the world. At the end of the two weeks, I attended the DOK Diocese of Texas Fall Assembly, including a tenth-anniversary celebration of the Glory Bound Singers.[3] One of the Glory Bound

---

[3] The Glory Bound Singers are Daughters of the King who through the ministry of music proclaim that Jesus Christ is Savior and lead music at all levels for The Order of the Daughters of the King.

Singers began to read the names of people lost in the World Trade Center as the others played and sang softly the song *You Called Me by Name.*[4] As they sang, I felt drained and empty from the tragedy. I let the music soothe my tired soul as my mind floated back to memories of my last class in New York City. I saw my class laughing, eating, and learning together. They were excited about the efficiency the new software would bring to their jobs. Now they were gone.

Then, suddenly, my thoughts shifted to a vision. I saw golden staircases and an army of glowing, golden, and smiling angels helping people—no, not people, but beautiful spirits—out of the rubble of Ground Zero. The angels were assisting the spirits up the stairs to heaven. The spirits were smiling, chatting, joyful, glowing souls. The scene felt holy and continued for several minutes as the music played far in the background. All I could think was, *Oh God, I'm an accountant; why am I having this vision?* as it was so unexpected. The vision was extraordinary, unreal, and mystical. More and more people kept coming, accompanied by angels climbing the staircases that reached into the clouds.

As the vision continued, I asked the Lord, "Where are the hijackers? I can't find them. Are they in hell? Why aren't they climbing the staircases too?" I could hear God's answer with a power and surety that only God could give me: "They remain below in the rubble and can't rise." The vision continued; the beautiful spirits kept coming, so joyful, happy, and free—free from the rubble, the pain, the worry. The vision was a fantastic and comforting answer to my prayers for God's presence to comfort those who had died and those of us still here grieving.

---

[4] *You Called Me by Name.* Words and music by Daniel Charles Dawson, 1989.

Later in the week, God woke me in the middle of the night, as He often does, to write my 9/11 memories and the story of the vision. I didn't want to lose His words, so I got up to write the story and realized God protected me on 9/11. All the classes I taught for the last four years had always started on Monday, occasionally on Tuesday, but never on Wednesday. I traveled the day before the class. During the week of 9/11, the client at another location in New York City couldn't get a room for the class to start on Tuesday. He had to schedule a four-day class in three ten-hour days to begin on Wednesday. So I was still in Houston on 9/11 instead of stranded in New York City with no way to fly home. Thank You, God, for always caring for me as I traveled.

As I continued writing my memories, I realized that the souls in the vision were joyful, happy, and free, just like I dreamed of being when I stood on top of the World Trade Center in 1986, declaring freedom from my abusive marriage. Oh, wow! Tears formed in my eyes as I realized God was here with me, holding me, talking to me, and giving me clarity and peace—another mystical encounter. As it says in John 14:27: "Peace I leave with you; my peace I give to you. Not as the world gives do I give it to you. Do not let your hearts be troubled or afraid." Joy and happiness started to return to my life that night as I gained a greater trust in God's providence and plan for my life. Both encounters taught me that God was and continues to be there. Although I still grieved the loss of so many lives and prayed for all the others this tragedy deeply affected, I was able to rest in the peace only God can give. Thank You, Lord, for waking me to experience your divine love tonight.

A month after 9/11, Bill Jacobs[5] published a poem that circulated and spoke volumes about how many felt, including me.

Bill Jacobs said: "A friend sent the message below to me this week. The author is unknown, but I think this piece makes a significant statement about the unity the September 11 attack brought to this country. The job now for us as a nation is to build on that unity and not let it crumble."

On Monday, we were talking about heroes as being athletes.
On Tuesday, we relearned who our heroes are.
On Monday, we were irritated that our
rebate checks had not arrived.
On Tuesday, we gave money away to people we had never met.
On Monday, people were fighting against praying in schools.
On Tuesday, you would have been hard-pressed to
find a school where someone was not praying.
On Monday, people argued with their kids
about picking up their room.
On Tuesday, the same people could not get
home fast enough to hug their kids.
On Monday, people were upset that they had to wait
six minutes in a fast-food drive-through line.
On Tuesday, people didn't care about waiting up
to six hours to give blood for the dying.
On Monday, we waved our flags, signifying our cultural diversity.
On Tuesday, we waved only the American flag.
On Monday, people were trying to separate each
other by race, sex, color, and creed.

---

[5] Bill Jacobs, *The Daily Leader*, 2 Oct. 2001. https://www.dailyleader.com/2001/10/02/one-day-what-a-difference-its-made/.

On Tuesday, they were all holding hands.
On Monday, we were men or women, black or white, old or
young, rich or poor, gay or straight, Christian or non-Christian.
On Tuesday, we were Americans.
On Monday, politicians argued about budget surpluses.
On Tuesday, grief-stricken, they sang *"God Bless America."*
On Monday, the President was going to Florida to read to children.
On Tuesday, he returned to Washington to protect our children.
On Monday, we had families.
On Tuesday, we had orphans.
On Monday, people went to work as usual.
On Tuesday, they died.
On Monday, people were fighting the Ten
Commandments on government property.
On Tuesday, the same people all said, "God help
us all," while thinking, "Thou shall not kill."
Sadly, it is ironic that it takes horrific events to
place things into perspective, but it has.
The lessons learned this week, the things
we have taken for granted,
The things that have been forgotten or overlooked,
Hopefully will never be forgotten again.[6]

Three lines especially touched my heart: First, "Get home fast enough to hold their kids." I, too, just wanted to hug my kids and grandkids. Second, "On Tuesday, we were Americans." I was

---

[6] This set of comparisons, often dubbed "What a Difference a Day Makes," circulated anonymously via email following the terrorist attacks of September 11, 2001.

amazed at how 9/11 united the country. American flags were flying everywhere. The third line that affected me was, "God help us all," which was what I and many others were praying for at the time. God showed me He did help and was there through my mystical encounters at the World Trade Center and my vision afterward.

Year after year, I continued to pray for all who died and for the rescuers to be surrounded by God's divine love and a spirit of hope. I used one of my favorite ways to pray, magic penning, which is writing everything in my head quickly until I have nothing more to write. This journaling technique helps me release thoughts circling in my mind to open up space to listen to God's still, small voice.

I use this technique to write love letters to God. I start the page with "Dear God" and write until I have nothing else to say. I sign the letter "Love, Kathy." Then I write "Dear Kathy" and listen. I write whatever comes. Sometimes, I don't hear anything, but sometimes, very profound thoughts come from deep within my heart, and I continue to write until the thoughts stop. Then I sign the letter "Love, God." I know God is talking because God says things I never expected to hear in a language different from mine! Following is my journal writing I did a few weeks after 9/11:

> *Dear Jesus, Heal my sad heart, O God. Why did those people do this terrible thing? So many people were hurt and killed, lives changed forever. The poor rescuers—hours of searching with no results. Please let them find some people alive to give them hope. Guide our president to make the right decision. Your decision. Oh, Lord, I feel so helpless. Love, Kathy.*

I listened and heard God saying:

Dear Kathy, I love you. I am here. Let Me take care of things and quit worrying. You have My work to do. I care for you, your family, and the people of New York City. I am still in charge. I love you! Rest in My divine love. Your Father God.

BACK TO NEW YORK CITY

The following Sunday, the airports reopened, and I flew to New York City to teach the rescheduled class. The usually full airport parking garage, however, was empty, strange, and unreal. As I walked to my gate, the typically crowded passageways were also empty, with people few and far between. The flight had primarily empty seats, but the flight attendants were kind and happy to have passengers. My hotel was lovely, and the staff was friendly and excited to have people staying with them.

After I settled in, I called a friend who was working in one of the buildings near the World Trade Center on 9/11. We discussed how she ran like many others in the chaos after the planes hit the building. Shocked and confused, she wandered the New York City streets, trying to find her way home. Kind strangers found her and took her to their hotel room, where she finally contacted her frantic husband. I empathized with her grief and losing her job, the office she worked in, and all she knew of that part of Manhattan.

I told her about my vision. She told me about a memorial service she watched at Yankee Stadium that afternoon, where a Jewish rabbi had talked about Jacob's Ladder. As I shared my vision, she expressed the feeling that it was an extension of the Rabbi's message. The image of Jacob's Ladder[7]comes from the Hebrew Bible [the Old Testament] when the Patriarch Jacob dreams about a stairway reaching heaven and God's messengers going up and down the ladder. What a perfect image and explanation for my vision with the angels going up and down, escorting those who had died out of the rubble.

After I hung up, I began writing in my journal, processing all she had told me and asking God to clarify my vision. I wanted to know if my vision was only to give me peace or for others, such as my friend. Then I listened, and God's answer started flowing onto the paper:

> *Dear Kathy, your vision was meant to bring peace to you and others. The vision is a sign to you and others that I was there, that I heard your prayers and others' prayers to send My legions of angels to rescue the people. To take the souls of the innocent home. To immediately wrap them in divine love and not let Satan win. I am still in charge. Good will come from this tragedy. It saddens Me when My children don't know Me. When they are so deceived by the evil one. Stay grounded in Me, where your peace and joy come from. Love, God.*

I continued to journal my feelings but just wanted to rest in His presence. I was tired and ready to go home. I found it challenging to be in New York City. My students were also grieving 9/11, so they were distracted from the course material, making teaching difficult. The loss was still too real for all of us, so we shared our stories during our breaks.

---

[7] Genesis 28:10–22.

I wish I could have gone to the World Trade Center site, but it would have been physically and emotionally challenging. The site was still smoldering and closed off to visitors. God continued reassuring me and encouraging me to share my story as His words appeared on the page.

> *Dear Kathy, I love you. I am proud of you and all you have done to change, love, and help your family. Serve Me each day wherever I send you, listen to My voice, and see Me in people. You are My daughter. I will lead you beside still waters, and though you walk through the valley of the shadow of death, I will be with you and the people lost in the World Trade Center. You saw the vision I gave you of My angels helping them up the stairs, Jacob's Ladder, as your friend called the mystical staircases. Please share that those souls are okay. I am still in charge. I AM! I have always been and will always be. Trust Me, today, tomorrow, always. I love you. GOD.*

I hold 9/11 as a special day in my heart as I remember those innocent souls escorted by the angels that day. My World Trade Center experiences have melted together to become what Murray Bodo called "The Mysticism of the Historical Event."[8] Bodo teaches that I can take a Scripture passage and make it as vivid as possible as I meditate and learn a lesson to apply to my daily life. In much the same way, I took my 9/11 experience and reflected on it often during

---

[8] Murray Bodo, OFM, *The Road to Mount Subasio: Spiritual Pilgrimage as a Path to God.* (Phoenix: Tau Publishing, 2004), 84.

the coming months. I remembered the people and events as vividly as possible, which brought healing and taught me lessons. Some of the lessons I reflected on were never knowing when we will go home to Jesus, the importance of family and telling them you love them often, how people are good and want to help, how some give their lives to help others, and, most importantly, that God is there for us.

Father Mychal Judge, a Franciscan priest and chaplain to the New York Fire Department, rushed into the North Tower and prayed for firefighters who ran past him and office workers escaping down the stairs. He was killed when the nearby South Tower collapsed by the tsunami of rubble that burst into the North Tower lobby. Father Judge's prayer was always:

> Lord, take me where You want me to go; Let me meet who You want me to meet. Tell me what You want me to say. And keep me out of Your way.[9]

His prayer has become my prayer, another lesson learned from 9/11.

FIRST ANNIVERSARY OF 9/11

On the first anniversary of 9/11, which felt like such a long year, I experienced God's peace at a small church in Orlando. I was attending an Oracle course in Orlando to learn how to teach another product

---

[9] Mike Kelly, "9/11's First Casualty Mychal Judge Is a Legend—Can He Be a Saint?" *NorthJersey.com*, September 10, 2021, https://www.northjersey.com/in-depth/news/columnists/mike-kelly/2021/09/10/father-mychal-judge-911-attacks-fdny-catholic-saint/4939813001/.

with several other instructors and students. Our manager wanted us to go to Downtown Disney for the evening of 9/11 to spend the night partying.

Instead, I took at cab to a small church and attended their memorial Mass. I tipped the cab driver more than needed so he would return when Mass was over. It was a beautiful, old church, small and quiet, with a sparse crowd on a Wednesday night. As I slid into the pew and knelt to pray, I thought back over the past year—the pictures and specials that replayed the events of 9/11 over and over. I was tired of the reminders and feelings as I relived the 9/11 event many times during the year, experiencing the incredible grief, sadness, and hopelessness others were also feeling. There were other stresses in my life during the year, including a manager change at work and my daughter's accident that required back surgery. This anniversary reminded me of the light of hope God gave me with my vision, His constant presence, and His encompassing divine love comforting me throughout the year amid my grief. Going to Mass and praying was my way of honoring all who died and were affected by 9/11.

The quiet church helped me find the strength to go forward where God was leading me. Let's return to 1998, when a mystical surprise drove me to my knees. God's plan was amazing when I realized why He pushed me in a new direction and prepared me to serve others and help them grow spiritually.

CHAPTER THREE

BRINGING ME TO MY KNEES

Training in Spiritual Direction

Light of the Soul

Dear Jesus, help me to spread Your fragrance everywhere I go.
Flood my soul with Your spirit and life.
Penetrate and possess my whole being so utterly,
That my life may only be a radiance of Yours.
Shine through me, and be so in me
That every soul I come in contact with
May feel Your presence in my soul.
Let them look up and see no longer me, but only Jesus!
Stay with me, and then I shall begin to shine as You shine,
So to shine as to be a light to others;
The light, O Jesus, will be all from You; none of it will be mine;
It will be You, shining on others through me.
Let me thus praise You the way You love best,
by shining on those around me.

Let me preach You without preaching,
not by words but by my example,
By the catching force of the sympathetic influence of what I do,
The evident fullness of the love my heart bears to You. Amen.[1]

God showed His sense of humor when He started me on a trans-formative journey in 1998, four years after George and I were married. Our new married life, joining the Roman Catholic Church and then changing parishes a year later, had left me in limbo for a few months, not knowing how God wanted me to serve Him. I was slowly learning that my view of God's purpose for me was limited. As it states in 1 Corinthians 13:12: "At present we see indistinctly, as in a mirror." Stumbling my way through God's plan sometimes feels like I'm seeing indistinctly, like I only have a vague view of where He is taking me and am sometimes very unsure of which way to go. The day before the June 1998 St. Justin's Women's Retreat at Camp Tejas,[2] I was looking through my daughter's Episcopalian newspaper when I saw an ad for a personal growth seminar the following week-end at Camp Allen[3] featuring one of my favorite Christian authors, Claire Cloninger. I called the contact, hoping she would tell me it was too late. Instead, she graciously encouraged me to come. I debated not attending the St. Justin's retreat, but I had promised several friends. The personal growth seminar sounded more stimulating,

---

[1] Saint John Henry Newman, "Light of the Soul," in *Meditations and Devotions of the Late Cardinal Newman* (New York: Longmans, Green, and Co., 1893), 500.
[2] Camp Tejas Retreat Center is in Giddings, Texas.
[3] Camp Allen, Episcopal Diocese of Texas, is a year-round facility located northwest of Houston. Camp Allen accommodates a variety of spiritual, social, corporate, and educational events.

and meeting Claire Cloninger, whose book *A Place Called Simplicity* had a powerful influence on my life years ago, sounded exciting. To do both would mean being gone two full weeks from home since I travel for my job during the week. And how about the laundry I needed to do for week two? After praying, I got my family's blessings and arranged with Camp Allen to use their laundry facilities.

With suitcases packed for five destinations—Camp Tejas to Denver and Dallas, week one, then Camp Allen and Philadelphia, week two—I went to the retreat, hoping to receive spiritual guidance from God for next steps in my life. As I drove up alone with God as my companion, I enjoyed the Texas bluebonnets in bloom and sang praise music with the Christian radio station. As the radio station faded, I loaded an inspiring CD. Again, my soul was filled with the Holy Spirit's presence.

The evening started with me resting in my cabin, journaling a letter to God expressing how tired, weary, and weighted down I felt. My desires were for a quiet place of serenity and simplicity. To not be so driven. When I'm at home, I feel pulled apart by everyone's needs. At least when I'm on the road, I only have my class and me to take care of, with a simple hotel room, quiet, alone time, and no clutter or demands. My schedule and life are my own, but I miss my family, holding my grandson Isaiah, and hugs from my husband, Porgie, and daughter, Susan.

Now, it was time to go to the evening session. Lucy Chemalack, the team's spiritual director, talked about spiritual direction. I was so tired and only partially listening. As she spoke, something inside of me went "ping." A small flame seemed to leap up in my spirit. I looked up at God and said, somewhat irritated, "What?! God, spiritual director? Really? I was thinking of a small way to serve you.

My life is already busy with work!" I was uncertain what God had in mind, but knowing it was best to be obedient, I signed up for spiritual direction, as Lucy suggested.

When I walked into the session the next day, I was unsure what to say to the spiritual director. I told her I didn't know why I was there, but I thought God was calling me to be a spiritual director. I explained that the night before, as Lucy was talking, a flame leaped up in my spirit, and I felt God wanted me to be a spiritual director. I listened to people all my life, and my strong faith from childhood helped me share Jesus with others. Serving others has always been a priority in my life, so helping people hear God would be an awesome calling. I couldn't tell her more than that, but having other mystical encounters, I knew in my heart the flame was from God. She suggested I pray on the message and said I might want to call the Cenacle Retreat Center[4] next week and gather information on their spiritual direction program.

As I returned to my cabin, I passed the room of our director of religious education. She was alone, so I shared my feeling that I was being called to be a spiritual director. She encouraged me to explore my feelings and discern if being a spiritual director was a call from God. Later that day, one of my friends said she thought of me when Lucy discussed spiritual direction. She said I already listened to others and walked with people on their spiritual journeys. Ironically,

---

[4] The Cenacle Retreat House offered a three-year class on becoming a spiritual director. The Houston Cenacle was a welcoming, peace-filled place, a sanctuary for prayer, discernment, and spiritual growth. The original Cenacle Retreat House (building and grounds) in Houston, where I spent many wonderful days at retreats and in spiritual direction, was destroyed by Hurricane Harvey in August 2017. The school continues with a group of spiritual directors. See their website: https://emmausspiritualitycenter.com/.

I spent that night with another retreatant who needed someone to listen, a premonition of my future.

I went to the airport from the retreat to fly to my two classes that week, one in Dallas and the second in Denver. However, I called the Cenacle that week to get information on their spiritual direction school. When I returned to Houston, I went from the airport directly to the Episcopalian personal growth seminar with Claire Cloninger as the speaker at beautiful Camp Allen.

On the first day of the growth seminar, I met two women interested in becoming spiritual directors. After our conversations, I believed that God meant for me to be a conduit to introduce them to one another and pass on the spiritual direction school information I had just learned of earlier in the week. I thought, *I'm off the hook!* I was definitely in denial of what God was trying to tell me.

The following day, I shared with my small group the confirmations God had given me to become a spiritual director. Yet doubt reentered my mind when I was done sharing, and I sat down. I thought, *What if being a spiritual director isn't God's message for me, only my misplaced desire?*

I have often been a healing prayer team member, so I volunteered to help on Saturday night. I was standing there alone, singing praise and wondering if anyone would come up for me to pray for them. I felt awkward because I usually prayed in a team. Then, a woman came up and asked if she could pray for me. She asked my forgiveness for calling me a token Catholic Daughter of the King earlier. I didn't remember the incident, so I didn't take offense but forgave her anyway. [This interaction is funny to me now, so many years later. As you will see later in this book, my life as a "token Catholic" in The Order had just begun and continued for many years!] Then she continued and said God had told her that He wanted to confirm me in my ministry. God said, **"There will be tough times, bringing you to your knees, but I will send people, just as I did for Moses, to hold you up."** The woman thought the message was related to my work in The Order of the Daughters of the King, but I knew instantly this was God's message to confirm His desire for me to become a spiritual director. It's funny how God sends messages, but the messenger may not know the whole story.

The message filled me with dread and fear. And the part of the message about being brought to my knees wasn't comforting. That evening, when I returned to my room, I called my sweet husband, George, and asked him how many confirmations I needed before knowing God was leading me to something. He said three. I told him I was in deep trouble because I already had six! He said matter-of-factly: "Kath, you need to do it."

The following day, my doubts started returning: *Do I have time to make this commitment? Am I holy enough to be a spiritual director? As a relatively new Catholic, can I help people with their Catholic faith? Part of me would like to take on the challenge of learning something new and serving God, but the other part is afraid that maybe I wasn't hearing God.* I asked God to give me a sign. The song "I Am the Bread of Life"[5] had been sung at important spiritual times in my life, so I asked God to have that song sung during the closing service. We had sung modern Christian music all weekend, songs that were new to me. I had no input on what was to be sung that morning. The

---

[5] *I Am the Bread of Life* is a Christian hymn composed by Sr. Suzanne Toolan in 1966. It is based on the Bread of Life discourse in the Gospel of John chapters 6 and 11.

service began. I thought I was home free after Holy Communion when the song wasn't played.

Then, the song leader put the words on the overhead for the recessional hymn. You got it! It was "I Am the Bread of Life"! I paused for a moment, looking at the words. Then, as if in slow motion, I realized the song was my sign and began to shake. I had to sit down. Tears rolled down my cheeks as I sang praises to my awesome God. I felt God's Spirit overpowering me, confirming that I was to become a spiritual director. I suddenly realized that deep down, I wanted this new challenge. It was a beautiful mystical encounter, a glimpse of how much God loved me. All my doubts and fears melted away. I felt the training as a spiritual director would enhance my service in any ministry in the future. Listening to people and the Holy Spirit's messages for them is critical to being a good servant. I would also grow deeper in my relationship with God through the training. I left immediately following the service, not speaking to anyone and still shaking. My car automatically headed toward the airport for my next work trip as I sang His praises.

After I had digested everything, I wrote: "What an awesome God You are. I have been in limbo for the last few months, not knowing what You had planned for me. Now, this! Another new beginning." I applied for the Episcopalian Formation in Direction (FIND) program because the training schedule fit my traveling work life. I wanted to attend The Cenacle Spiritual Direction Catholic program, but they only met on Tuesday mornings. When I talked to the Sister at The Cenacle, she encouraged me to go to FIND as some of the sisters helped as teachers and resources for that program. Even as a new Catholic, she assured me it would be okay and I would still get good training as a spiritual director.

GROWING IN SPIRITUAL DIRECTION SCHOOL

My first year of the FIND Spiritual Direction program was challenging. Our group met on Saturdays starting in the fall of 1999, sometimes in Houston and other times in Austin, almost three hours from Houston. I would arrive home from work on the road late Friday night, exhausted. My dear husband would drive me to Austin for class and then tour the city for hours until it was time to pick me up. God's prophecy given to me by the woman who prayed for me a year earlier had come true. She told me God said there would be tough times, bringing me to my knees to pray for forgiveness, strength, and wisdom, but He would send people to hold me up just as He did for Moses. My sweet George was one of those people.

One faculty member was an example of how God used others in my spiritual direction program to help me grow in my journey. He made me very angry when he badmouthed the Roman Catholic Church. He had been a Roman Catholic priest. At every chance, he made negative comments about his interpretations of the teachings of the Catholic Church. I thought he was judgmental and critical. Being the only Catholic in the program, I felt out of place, so his comments made me even more uncomfortable. I wondered if I made a mistake selecting this program.

For months, I was angry with him and tried to avoid him. But God kept putting him in my path! Finally, after sharing my feelings with a fellow student and praying, I realized God showed me some of my sins through him. How could I be angry with him when I was judgmental and critical? I had to forgive him so God would forgive me. And I had to concentrate on correcting my behavior, not his. I had known this in my mind for years, but God had implanted the truth in my heart so I could grow and be further transformed through another spiritual lesson.

This transformation was necessary in my path to being a spiritual director. I was learning that the role of the spiritual director is to walk with the directee as they explore their relationship with God, and this was exemplified in my relationship with this instructor. We were taught that good spiritual direction is done by respectfully listening to the directee's experiences and helping the directee recognize and listen to their own experiences of God. The director doesn't tell the person what to do but may offer suggestions for reflections and prayer. My instructor was entitled to the same respectful listening as my future directees.

As the days continued, so did my lessons in spiritual direction from both my teachers and God. One of those lessons came through a prayer exercise involving a canvas labyrinth.[6] The labyrinth felt like some "New Age" idea without a solid spiritual history. Being Roman Catholic in an Episcopalian spiritual direction school, I often stopped and prayed about activities we were doing. I wasn't sure about this one. I walked slowly around the outside of the labyrinth several times, praying and determining whether I was to participate. Finally, I decided to enter the labyrinth with Jesus and trust Him. As I walked slowly in and out, following the path to the center, I felt Jesus' presence. I began letting go of my stress, tiredness, and doubts. As I reached the center, I paused and prayed for several

---

[6] Labyrinths are prayer tools made of canvas, stone, grass, or other materials that involve walking or following a path with your fingers or stylus. Many modern-day labyrinths are replicas of the path found in the Cathedral of Notre Dame in Chartres, which originated as a symbolic pilgrimage to the Holy City (the New Jerusalem) commissioned by Pope Innocent III.

minutes—resting in silence with Jesus and breathing in the essence of the Holy Spirit. As others joined the center, I started walking out quicker than I had walked in, feeling entirely embraced by Jesus, and we started dancing. I was light and weightless in His arms and filled with joy, and all my stress and doubts disappeared. I was surprised to feel like I was in His arms. It was a fantastic feeling to be the beloved—what a beautiful mystical encounter. I was thankful I took the risk and entered the labyrinth.

This experience moved me so much that I immediately began researching the labyrinth to learn more about this prayer tool. I found that the labyrinth had a Roman Catholic history. Dr. Lauren Artress, in her book *Walking a Sacred Path*, explains that:

> Christians in the Middle Ages made a vow: to make a pilgrimage to the Holy City of Jerusalem once during their life. However, by the twelfth century . . . travel had become dangerous and expensive . . . [So Pope Innocent III] appointed seven pilgrimage cathedrals to become "Jerusalem" for pilgrims [by creating labyrinths inside their cathedrals].[7]

I was so relieved to find the Catholic connection. Walking the labyrinth is one lesson I took forward into my life by teaching the labyrinth to my attendees on retreats or in workshops as a different way to pray that involved the whole person.

---

[7] Lauren Artress, *Walking a Sacred Path: Rediscovering the Labyrinth as a Spiritual Tool* (New York: Riverhead Books, 1995), 32.

RETURNING TO ST. JUSTIN'S RETREAT TEAM

Three years later, in June 2002, I graduated as a spiritual director and returned to the St. Justin's Women's Retreat Team as spiritual director. I wanted to give back to the retreat that started me on a new path. And how poignant it was that during that weekend, there was a moving tribute to Lucy Chemalack, who spoke at the retreat four years earlier and started me on the path to becoming a spiritual director. Now, I was here to serve in her place after her recent death from cancer. As I learned from John Graham's book *Graham Crackers & Milk*, God takes our tragedies, heals our wounds, and sends us out to bring healing to others.[8]

God continued to amaze me with His divine love, forgiving grace, and plan for me to serve Him. My hope in answering God's call to be a spiritual director is, as one of my favorite saints, St. Catherine of Siena, said, "Be who God meant you to be, and you will set the world on fire." Little did I know that God's amazing plan was just the beginning of the mystical experiences and miracles I would stumble through while being a spiritual director for the St. Justin's retreat team, with my hope of setting women's hearts on fire.

---

[8] John K. Graham, *Graham Crackers & Milk: Food for the Heart and Soul* (Nashville: Dimensions for Living, 2003).

CHAPTER FOUR

TRAVELING WITH COMPANIONS ON A JOURNEY

Ministering to St. Justin's Women's Retreats

With love for the God who has so loved us, we pray:
Teach us Your ways, O Lord!
You made us in Your image:
Reveal Your love to the world through our love for one another . . .
You showed the depth of Your love in the mystery of the Cross:
Grant us the wisdom to seek forgiveness rather than vengeance . . .
You taught us that all peoples are neighbors:
Remove all the false boundaries that set limits on our love.
Teach us Your ways, O Lord! Amen.[1]

In 2002, I assumed the role of spiritual director for the St. Justin Martyr's Companions on a Journey annual women's retreat; my mind flashed back to a powerful mystical experience on my first St. Justin's retreat years ago. That experience was something that helped

---

[1] Author Unknown.

a beautiful young woman heal from a significant loss and something I will never forget.

During the year of that first retreat in 1996, I was preparing to start the Hannah Chapter of The Order Daughters of the King at St. Justin's. God had rescued me from my abusive first marriage, just as God saved Hannah from her inability to have children. And through this new chapter, God gave me a child who needed an earthly mother after the sudden death of her mother, just like God gave Hannah children. She was a beautiful young woman called to serve as my vice president. Many years earlier, her mother had been a Daughter of the King in the Episcopal Church, and she was following in her mother's footsteps by joining our Catholic Daughters of the King (DOK) chapter.

Months after the chapter formed, we were alone, setting up the meeting room before anyone else arrived. She asked me if I knew her mother. I asked, "What was her name?" When she told me her mother's name, I burst into tears as I realized she was my dear sister in Christ, who had been murdered many years ago by her abusive second ex-husband. Feelings of grief and guilt flooded back. I had attended her mother's funeral. While watching her first husband and the grown children I had never met, I started questioning God. Why did she die and I didn't? We divorced our abusive husbands about the same time and began new lives. Then, two years later, her ex-husband broke into her apartment and killed her, her new boyfriend, and himself. At the funeral, I felt guilty about being spared, so I promised to serve God for both of us. Now, her daughter needed me, so I started fulfilling my promise. We hugged, and I told her, "I'll always be here for you."

A few weeks later, I was asked to give a talk at the church's annual women's retreat. I found it strange since I was new to the church, had healed, and moved on from my abusive marriage. As I began writing my talk, I prayed about what I would share. God placed on my heart to tell the story of my friend who had died, along with my own story. I also included how her daughter came into my life through the new DOK chapter. I had never written about my friend's death. I warned her daughter before the retreat that I would share part of her mother's story.

From the moment I walked into the meeting room that Saturday morning, I could feel God's power. The priest started the day with Mass and shared a story on the importance of Baptism. We each went up and confirmed our Baptism, a moving renewal. I felt my friend's presence. I looked at my friend's daughter, who was crying, and wondered if she also felt her mother's presence.

As I began my talk that evening, over 100 women sat on the floor on blankets in their pajamas. The room got quieter and quieter as I read my story of abuse and recovery, except for my friend's daughter. She began to cry, not softly, but with sobs that grew louder the longer I talked. Finally, her sobs reached a climax when I told her mother's story and revealed our connection. Everyone in the room realized I was talking about her mother. As I finished and the strains of the closing song began to play, I looked up.

Over the door across from me was my friend's spirit. She smiled at me and left. Tears filled my eyes, and gratitude mixed with joy filled my heart. I then knew I wasn't there to tell my story but to help her daughter heal. When I talked to her daughter later, she said she felt her mother's spirit there all day. I confirmed her feelings by saying, "Yes, she was." Then, she told me that the retreat date was the seventh anniversary of her mother's death. Wow! God does work in mysterious ways! She also told me the song I chose to close the talk was her mother's favorite. Her mother and I found the strength to trust God during our struggles to be freed from our abusive marriages with a special song, "Learning to Trust,"[2] by David Meece.

TO FORGIVENESS

I continued to serve as spiritual director on St. Justin's women's retreat team for many years. The theme of the next retreat was Companions for the Journey: To Forgiveness. Forgiveness is a tough one for many of us. When our leader first suggested that I do a talk on the retreat, I was getting ready to board a plane for work. As I sat at the plane reviewing my life and thinking about when I had forgiven others, past hurts began running through my mind: my first husband's abuse, a job layoff during a downtime, a friend's betrayal, and a supervisor's excessive verbal abuse. Had I forgiven these people? Yes—a little book, *Forgiveness & Inner Healing* by Betty Tapscott and Father DeGrandis, helped me forgive those who had hurt me throughout my life. I followed the book's advice and prayed the Forgiveness Prayer[3] for thirty days. Each day, new people or events were brought to mind by the Holy Spirit. I went deeper and deeper into my heart. At the end of the thirty days, I felt I had taken a huge step in healing my past. My spirit felt lighter and cleansed. I have learned to repeat this prayer every two to three

---

[2] "Learning to Trust," lyrics by David Meece and Michael Hudson and music by David Meece, Star Song Records, 1989.
[3] "Forgiveness Prayer" in *Forgiveness & Inner Healing*, 5-10. See the Resources for the prayer.

years, usually during Lent, to clean out any unforgiveness hiding in the depths of my heart.

Despite my mystical experience of forgiving others, I struggled with what to share. I prayed and wrestled with the topic of forgiveness all afternoon and through the night, waking up with still no inspiration or direction. Then, during my morning devotional, God led me to three basic questions from the last chapter of the book, *The Purpose Driven Life*, by Rick Warren. The book states, "Most people struggle with three basic issues in life. The first is *identity*: 'Who am I?' The second is *importance*: 'Do I matter?' The third is *impact*: 'What is my place in life?'"[4] Finally, God was leading me to what He wanted me to share about my journey by deeply exploring my answers to these questions.

I turned to a new page in my journal and wrote: "Who am I?" and then: "A forgiven child of God!" came almost immediately. I continued, "Do I matter?" An emphatic "YES" appeared in bold letters across my page. I was sure of God's forgiveness and divine love at that moment. I hadn't always believed that I mattered, but God's amazing love restored my life, and Jesus' gift of forgiveness convinced me that I was important in His plan. "What is my place in life?" was the last question I needed to answer. I wrote: "I see God's plan in the hurtful times in my life when I needed His guidance and divine love." As Henri Nouwen shares on the cover of his book *The Wounded Healer: Ministry in Contemporary Society*: "In our own woundedness, we can become a source of life for others."[5] I'm called

---

[4] Rick Warren, *The Purpose Driven Life: What on Earth Am I Here For?* (Grand Rapids, MI: Zondevan, 2002), 312.
[5] Henry Nouwen, *The Wounded Healer: Ministry in Contemporary Society* (New York: Image Books, 1979).

to share my wounded times with people God puts in my life to show them His amazing love and forgiveness. Without forgiving others, it is impossible to entirely heal the hurts caused by others. I also have to forgive myself for mistakes, hurts I have inflicted on others, and sins against God. Forgiveness was the basis of the answers to all three questions and the key to my growing into a beloved child of God.

A passage that helped me accept losses in my life and forgive my bad decisions as a teenager that led to marrying an abusive man was from the book of Joel:

> Return to me with your whole heart, with fasting, weeping, and mourning. Rend your hearts, not your garments, and return to the LORD, your God, for He is gracious and merciful, slow to anger, abounding in steadfast love, and relenting in punishment . . . The LORD said to his people: . . . Do not fear . . . delight and rejoice, for the LORD has done great things . . . I will repay you double what the swarming locust has eaten . . . (2:12, 13, 19, 21, 25)

The words, "Rend your hearts . . . and return to the Lord . . . I will repay you double what the locust has eaten," ran through my mind. I had felt for years that I lost many life experiences during my abusive marriage. Losses like going to college, having a career, enjoying a blessed marriage with a partner I could pray with, and enjoying life without constant fear. I missed visits with my family because my husband isolated me. I was heartbroken when my first husband wouldn't let me go home when my mom called and asked me to come home to be with her during a possible cancer scare. I didn't realize until years later that my lack of support had deeply hurt her. I missed my brother's wedding. I'm still sad I wasn't there to celebrate with them. I missed many other events, funerals, weddings, and family reunions.

I praised God for restoring my life, forgiving me, being merciful, and giving me many opportunities and experiences I thought I would never have. I went to college at the age of thirty-eight, belonged to college fraternities, dated, and won many awards. In the process, I forgave my first husband and saw how my twenty years of abuse made me a strong, empathetic, knowledgeable woman who helps others. I concluded my story on the retreat with my answer to question three, "What is my place in life?" God continues to reveal His plan for my life by giving me more opportunities to help others while wrapping me in His divine love and forgiving grace.

THE MYSTERY OF THE CROSS

The next retreat's theme was Companions on a Journey: Building Community through the Mystery of the Cross. I again struggled with what to share when I received my talk assignment. God eventually gave me an image but nothing more. "What am I supposed to do with this image?" I asked. God finally filled in the blanks three months before the retreat by changing my plans at the last minute and giving me an extraordinary mystical encounter.

I planned to attend a Daughters of the King event with our national president in Dallas. Unfortunately, my daughter had back surgery, and I didn't want to be far from her, so I attended a silent retreat at the Cenacle Retreat House in Houston instead. I was amazed when the speaker, Brother Robert Lentz,[6] started talking about the mystery of the Cross of Christ. We were all sitting in a circle as Brother Lentz reverently laid a large wrought iron cross with a heart in the middle on a napkin in the center of the floor. Wow! The cross was the exact image God gave me for the theme of my talk—a cross with a large heart in the middle.

I was surprised but knew I needed to take notes. I was immediately aware that God was speaking to me through this man and giving me the words to use in my talk. But even more, I felt it was Jesus talking. I didn't want Brother Lentz to stop. I could have sat there all night at his feet like Mary of Bethany sat at Jesus' feet. As Brother Lentz diagrammed the cross, he placed Christ at the top with creation at the bottom. His point was that all creation comes from God. So then, the horizontal arms of the cross embrace all creation and bring it into the center of the cross, the heart of God. Within the heart of God is the Holy Spirit that flows into the center of each of us, helping to heal our sufferings and empowering us to bring light to the world.

Although the image of the cross with the heart in the center was the same, the teaching for my talk, which God led me to after much prayer, was different. The image God gave me is pictured below. The completed image below summarizes how compassion and suffering unite our lives around our center, the Holy Spirit. The Holy Spirit empowers us to use our compassion to endure our sufferings, and our sufferings help us to grow in compassion, enabling us to reach out to others.

---

[6] Brother Robert Lentz is a Franciscan brother whose innovative icons are known throughout the world. Besides writing icons, he teaches apprentices, writes, and conducts workshops on art and spirituality throughout the United States.

The Mystery of the Cross

As you can see, at the top of the cross, I placed compassion, which means being motivated to relieve another's suffering. Jesus showed great compassion when He came into the world to relieve us from the suffering caused by sin. His compassion helped Him endure suffering and was brought to fruition with His death on the Cross. The Bible reflects this divine love in a powerful verse: John 3:16: "For God so loved the world that he gave his only Son, so that everyone who believes in him might not perish but might have eternal life."

I experienced compassion when I sat by my dad alone during the night while he was dying, holding his hand and speaking gentle words to him to help relieve some of his suffering. The blessing of my compassion was that other family members got some sleep, and Dad could also sleep peacefully for a few hours. Christ suffered even more. His unlimited compassion empowered Him to endure the suffering of the Cross for us poor sinners.

The next truth is that suffering teaches compassion. Years ago, I suffered from depression for many months, and I experienced a breakdown that taught me compassion for others with depression. Before having experienced depression, I didn't truly understand how hard it is to move on, help yourself, and deal with life. I now have both compassion and empathy for others. I can walk with them in their pain and depression. Nouwen's book *Life of the Beloved* says it this way:

> Our first, most spontaneous response to pain and suffering is to avoid it, to keep it at arm's length, to ignore, circumvent, or deny it. Suffering—be it physical, mental, or emotional—is almost always experienced as an unwelcome intrusion into our lives, something that should not be there. [Our] first response, then, to our brokenness is to face it squarely and befriend it.[7]

My experience with suffering was helped by facing each episode and befriending the suffering. I have found healing and a closer relationship with God by living through the dark times of my life. For example, when I was newly divorced, the pain was devastating. I joined a support community, and as I healed, I reached out with compassion to help those suffering from losing a spouse. As Edwina Gateley states in *Christ in the Margins*:

> The kind of empathy that spills out in such compas-
> sion and sacrifice for others is what will change us

---

[7] Henry Nouwen, *Life of the Beloved: Spiritual Living in a Secular World* (New York: The Crossroad Publishing Company, 1992), 92–93.

and our world. It is God's unceasing invitation to each of us, no matter what burdens we bear, to allow compassion to flow through our broken places into others who need to feel God's gentle kiss through the touch of our caring. We are not called to transcend our suffering—we are called to absorb it into compassion [to be a community to each other].[8]

My suffering taught me compassion, leading me to the next truth: Compassion relieves suffering. By walking with others in a grief support community, my suffering was relieved by their compassion, the compassion of Christ. I, in turn, became a group facilitator to help alleviate the suffering of others who came after me. Henri Nouwen tells us in *Life of the Beloved*:

> I cannot do it on my own. I need someone to keep me standing in it, to assure me that there is peace beyond the anguish, life beyond death, and love beyond fear . . . Nonetheless, real care means the willingness to help each other in making our brokenness into the gateway to joy.[9]

Many years ago, I helped start a prayer blanket ministry while a parishioner at St. Justin's, supported by my Daughters of the King chapter. Like old-fashioned quilting bees, we had sewing sessions to make prayer blankets. These small squares of cloth were made with love and prayer and blessed by our priest. Our group knew it was

[8] Robert Lentz and Edwina Gately, *Christ in the Margins* (Maryknoll, NY: Orbis Books, 2003), 78.
[9] Nouwen, *Life*, 95-96.

God who heals, but as humans, we often need something tangible to hold during suffering. These blankets offered hope and comfort to the receiver and reminded them of God's compassion and our prayers for them. And for those of us creating the blanket, the time together became a community environment of compassion that helped us grow closer to God and each other.

A few months into our ministry, I gave a prayer blanket to a young coworker. She was trying to have a baby but couldn't get pregnant. So I told her to sleep with the blanket over her stomach at night. The blanket signified that our group was praying for her. A few months later, she was pregnant and had a beautiful baby boy. God answered our prayers.

As I have worked in the prayer blanket and other ministries, helping to relieve others' suffering, I have grown stronger in my compassion. My heart has softened, and my empathy has increased. Through this ministry, I learned the next point: Suffering strengthens compassion to help us carry our crosses into our communities.

Years ago, I worked in a job where I did payroll for consultants. One of the young men had just lost his mom to cancer. He didn't get his time sheet turned in because he had been at her bedside and funeral. My coworker harassed him and was insensitive to his suffering. Having lost my mother, I had compassion for the young man. I tried to ease her harshness and explain his situation. I prayed for her heart to be softened and for her to understand his suffering. The following week, her father died suddenly of a heart attack. We were all supportive and walked with her during this challenging time. She later commented how our kindness had surprised her and how she appreciated our compassion. She now understood the suffering of the young man she had harassed. And her grief opened her heart to compassion. In *The Mystery of the Cross*, Cardinal Basil Hume says:

> Suffering is so often a mystery . . . Frequently we are left with the question, "Why?" . . . You know suffering? So did He [Jesus]. Have you felt abandoned, even by God? So did He. Perhaps you have been misunderstood, vilified. So was He. He [Jesus], too, walked in the darkness, entered the tomb lifeless and defeated, vanquished . . . love [compassion for us] is His reason . . . only this inspired His deeds [sacrifice].[10]

Each of us has unique experiences with suffering and responds differently to our times of suffering. My world suddenly stopped in 1993 when my mother died at sixty-four after a heart attack followed by a stroke. When my brother called me to tell me she had a heart attack, I took the stack of tax returns due in a few days into my manager's office with a note on top that I would call her later and walked out of the office. I went home and threw a few things in a suitcase, including a dress for a funeral. At some level, I already knew she wouldn't make it. One of my other brothers and I flew to Albuquerque. When we arrived, we called my brother at the hospital from a pay phone (yes, this was before cell phones). He said to hurry! We drove eight hours to the hospital in Montrose, Colorado, often in the dark. Rushing was out of the question. My job was watching for deer that liked to hang out on the highway, making driving too

---

[10] Cardinal Basil Hume, *The Mystery of the Cross* (Brewster, MA: Paraclete Press, 1998, 2000), 99, 108, 109.

fast dangerous. It was a tough trip with much suffering, sharing, and wondering if we would make it in time. As we walked in, Dad told Mom we were there. She squeezed my hand and had a massive stroke. She had just been waiting for us and then let go and went home to Jesus.

I put my suffering on hold as I watched my four brothers and Dad each experience their unique suffering. As the only girl and the oldest, I had to prepare a funeral, notify family and friends, and take care of food and housing, among many other details, for twenty-eight family members who arrived for the funeral in a small town with only four motel rooms. No time to grieve. I stayed on after the funeral to teach Dad how to run the washer and dispose of Mom's things.

Later, I grieved in my unique way with many tears, anger, and regrets. My mother and I hadn't been close, partly because of my abusive marriage and partly because of distance and my dad's desire not to travel to visit his children. I regretted not knowing her better. I hungered for any small writing that showed me who she was, but I found little in her things. I was angry at her untimely death and the loss of her presence at special times as our family grew. In *Life of the Beloved*, Nouwen beautifully explains the value of our suffering:

> Our sufferings and pains are not simply bother-some interruptions of our lives; rather, they touch us in our uniqueness and our most intimate individuality. The way I am broken tells you something unique about me. The way you are broken tells me something unique about you . . . Our brokenness

is always lived and experienced as highly personal, intimate, and unique.[11]

Nouwen's perspective on suffering taught me to give my suffering the respect it deserved. I can then share my pain with others to reveal myself, a way to heal my hurts and reach out with compassion, to turn those feelings of anger and rejection into love within a community.

I have grown to understand that the suffering from my mother's untimely death came with many blessings. I found a new life. I supported my husband through losing his mother a few months later, and I had wonderful, supportive friends who listened and hugged me as I cried. Even my boss was sympathetic when I had an inappropriate outburst of anger that wasn't about the job but my grief. Most importantly, my suffering helped me grow stronger and more compassionate toward others' suffering regardless of the cause.

To summarize one last example from Nouwen's book, *Can You Drink the Cup?*

> Still, the Cross of Jesus is often presented as a glorious throne on which the King is seated. There, the body of Jesus is portrayed not as racked by flagellation and Crucifixion but as a beautiful, luminous body with sacred wounds.
>
> The Cross of San Damiano that spoke to St. Francis of Assisi is a good example. It shows the crucified Jesus as a victorious Jesus. The Cross is surrounded

---

[11] Nouwen, *Life*, 87.

by splendid gold; the body of Jesus is a perfect, immaculate human body; the horizontal beam on which he hangs is painted as the open grave for which Jesus rose, and all those gathered under the Cross with Mary and John are full of joy. At the top, we can see God's hand, surrounded by angels, drawing Jesus back into heaven.

This is a Resurrection Cross in which we see Jesus lifted up in glory. Jesus' words, "When I am lifted up from the earth, I shall draw all people to myself" (John 12:32), refer not only to His Crucifixion but also to His Resurrection. Being lifted up means not only being lifted up as the crucified one but also being lifted up as the risen one. It speaks not only about agony but also about ecstasy, not only about sorrow but also about joy, [compassion and community].[12]

Nouwen helps us realize that the Cross wasn't only a source of suffering and resurrection. The Cross leads us to ecstasy and joy. The Cross lifted Christ for His death, later symbolizing Jesus being raised from the dead. A powerful conclusion of Jesus overcoming death, the ultimate victory over Satan, revealing to us the true mystery of the Cross.

After my talk on the mystery of the Cross, the group had Adoration,[13] including healing prayer. Several team members prayed

---

[12] Henri Nouwen, *Can You Drink the Cup* (Norte Dame: Ave Maria Press; 10th Anniversary Edition, 2012), 47–48.

[13] The Adoration of the Holy Eucharist is an opportunity for Catholics who wish to express and deepen their love of Christ to pray to Jesus Christ before the Eucharist at their local parish.

in twos or threes for those who were suffering and in need of healing. Father Roy Ogero, the priest for that weekend, moved around the room, blessing those needing healing with the monstrance[14] where the Blessed Sacrament was exposed. The most powerful healing was for a young woman who had suffered from years of incest by her father. She was so traumatized that she had blocked much of the memories of those instances. As we prayed for her, the Holy Spirit flowed through her, healing took place, she was released from the evil she had endured, and tears flowed. I accompanied her back to her room, and we quietly talked for some time, bringing closure to the healing. Eventually, she became joyful. A beautiful miracle that reminds us that God still heals in our world today.

I have attended many retreats, but the one with Brother Lentz remains the most powerful and life-changing mystical encounter. Not just because he confirmed that the picture of the cross God gave me was what I was supposed to talk about but also because, in a private session, Brother Lentz sent me on two quests. First, he confirmed my internal calling to follow St. Francis, and second, he challenged me to find my Celtic roots. I did accomplish both of these quests, but those stories come later. Now, step back in time to see how God's plan turned this accountant's life upside down and sent me to travel the country each week.

---

[14] A monstrance is used during eucharistic adoration. When priests or deacons bless the people with the monstrance, they cover their hands with the ends of the veil so that their hands don't touch the monstrance as a mark of respect for the sacred vessel and as an indication that it is Jesus' presence in the Eucharistic species who blesses the people and not the minister.

CHAPTER FIVE

STARTING A NEW LIFE

Joining Oracle Corporation

A New Beginning

O generous and loving God, guide me on the journey of my life,
light the path before me, which is often doubtful and uncertain.
When I am confused and struggling,
I look for You; I seek Your direction.
I wish to know Your will for me as I begin again each day.
Bless my life with meaning and purpose.
Open my eyes to see that every ending
is an opportunity for a new beginning.
Refresh my mind and my heart, O God.
Heal me of life's painful disappointments.
Give me the courage to start anew.
Strengthen me to trust that You are with me in
each new beginning in my life. Amen.[1]

---

[1] Capuchin Franciscan Friars, "A Prayer of New Beginnings."

After my late-in-life college degree at forty-two, I got an exciting job in the tax department with Houston's largest and most sought-after Big Six accounting firm, Arthur Andersen. I never dreamed I would get a job with a Big Six accounting firm at my age. I interviewed with all six accounting firms twice, right before I graduated with my bachelor's degree and then again while studying for my master's degree. I received eleven rejection letters. At that time, the major accounting firms preferred attractive, intelligent, and young employees straight out of college. This offer was indeed a miracle. I thanked God for opening the door for me.

In January 1993, just before I began my new job, I got a call from an Andersen partner telling me there would be a news story about them settling an age discrimination lawsuit the next day. He told me my hiring had nothing to do with the lawsuit. I didn't believe him. I was deflated and brokenhearted. I thought I got the job on my merits, not as proof they didn't discriminate.

After working hard for a year, it became more apparent each day that I was facing age discrimination. I wasn't promoted or given work to do. Instead, I was assigned to do tax returns in the payroll department for employees in the sister organization, Andersen Consulting. It was a humiliating demotion after graduating at the top of my class with many honors. But as a single mother with a daughter to support, I did what was needed to keep a roof over our heads and food on the table. This job was important.

During my time in the payroll department, I also confirmed that my salary was considerably lower than that of my younger peers hired at the same time. I was angry. I had work experience, energy, and skills that my younger counterparts lacked. It felt like a knife in my back. I was also very frustrated as I struggled to keep my bills paid.

I got acquainted with the Andersen Consulting employees as I performed my job. I helped with their payroll and taxes. I solved several payroll problems for the Consulting human resource manager, who was assisting employees who were on out-of-town assignments. She saw my age and life experiences as assets. I approached her when Andersen Consulting won a large contract to set up an accounting center for British Petroleum (BP) Company in Houston. I informed her of my previous work experience in accounts payable and receivables before I went to college. That previous accounting experience, plus my Certified Public Accounting (CPA) License, helped me get the job. When the Consulting HR manager offered me a transfer, I felt valued for the first time since coming to Andersen.

I immediately said yes and crossed over the "Chinese Wall," the nickname given to the division between the two Andersen firms. Few people were able to cross over. I felt blessed to have established the right connections. The consulting side of the company had varied and challenging work, plus a relaxed dress code. Many others would have crossed over if transferring had been easy. But, again, God's hand was there as I became the General Ledger administrator for BP Oil Company's Oracle Financial accounting system. The job involved managing all the accounting entries imported into the General Ledger from the many sub-ledgers, including payables, receivables, assets, and payroll, to name a few of the thirty-two systems, and submitting timely reports to the parent company in Great Britain.

After a year and a half with Andersen Consulting, God opened another door in August 1997. BP Oil was going to upgrade the

Oracle accounting system. Interested to learn more and grow in my career, I asked to go to Oracle training in Dallas. My manager agreed to pay for the training, but I had to pay my expenses, so I drove up and stayed with my husband's son and his family. On the first day of class, I got lost and arrived late. I hate being late and was very upset as I entered the room after the class had started. Only one seat was open in the very back row. I'm a front-row person, and an extra Oracle employee sitting in the back annoyed me with his chatter. He rolled his chair up during lab times and joined my partner and me. He talked a lot, which was distracting and frustrated me as I tried to absorb all I could. Over the week, most of the class had lunch together, and I discovered he was a new manager at Oracle. I learned his name was Kim, and despite my interest in learning more about Oracle, I still found his constant talking distracting. When class ended, I was relieved and ready to start using my new knowledge to help BP Oil have a successful upgrade—hopefully even resulting in a raise and promotion. I felt terrible about failing to grow my career at Arthur Andersen, even though I knew I was never given a chance to succeed.

As I was leaving, Kim surprised me by offering me a job. I was flattered by the offer, but the job involved traveling 100 percent, leaving little time at home with George, so I said no. We had only been married three years, so we were still newlyweds. I just wanted to go home, and I had a long, arduous, four-hour drive ahead of me.

Kim continued to call me about the job after I returned home. I was flattered but kept saying no. Then, my boss at Andersen Consulting called me into his office and told me the promised promotion wouldn't happen. My boss said everything was running so well that they eliminated the position. Yes, everything was running smoothly because I had been doing all the work of my previous boss plus my job for several months. Eighty-hour weeks! I was furious and very disappointed. I had been out of college for over three years and still was a staff consultant. No promotions and no raises. I ranted, "God, this isn't fair. I worked hard and did a good job."

I was in tears when I walked in the door at home. George consoled me as he listened to my hurt and anger and advised me to call Kim from Oracle. I thought for a moment and said a small prayer. I realized I didn't have to accept the job; I could check out the opportunity. What did I have to lose? With hope in my heart, I called Kim.

STARTING MY NEW LIFE ON THE ROAD

It took two months of interviews and a trip to Denver before Kim's manager made the official job offer. George and I had prayed about the job and salary I would accept. I didn't tell them how much I was making because I knew my salary was low. I just said, "Make me a fair offer." When they offered me a 65 percent raise, I took the job— surprising the senior manager who made the offer by immediately saying yes. I told him I had prayed about the job, and the decision was made when the offer met my salary needs.

I may not have seen it on the first day of Oracle training when I was forced to sit in the last row, but God guided me to a new job. Kim was my manager for four years and supported me as I grew into my new job. In a very real way, I learned the value of Matthew 20:16: "Thus, the last will be first, and the first will be last."

My new life as an Oracle University instructor teaching accounting software classes began on December 8, 1997, as I entered my first Oracle class in Seattle, Washington. Yes, I started my new job on the road, and living on the road became my life for the next ten years. (Little did I know then that I would spend twenty-four years at Oracle.)

Living on the road taught me to cherish my brief family time, alone time, and classroom time with my students. These three parts of my life corresponded with the ideas expressed in *Radical Hospitality: Benedict's Way of Love*. The lessons in this book helped me recognize the importance of not spreading myself too thin, keeping the focus on my whole life, and being gentle with myself. The following passage made it clear that balance was the key to not burning out in my new job:

> Balance gives us freedom, it eases anxieties, and it makes room in our lives. Cloister [solitude], community, and hospitality represent this balance . . . By gently and gradually gathering up the strands of your fragmented life into one whole, you will become one in skin that can distribute yourself to others and still have something left to take into the great solitude of your vast soul and rest in God.[2]

Resting in God became vital to my soul and required solitude. I did have more privacy on the road. I spent time alone while eating meals, in my room, and on the plane. I began to cherish the solitude and missed it when I returned home for an extended period.

---

[2] Lonni Collins Pratt and Father Daniel Homan, OSB, *Radical Hospitality: Benedict's Way of Love* (Brewster: Paraclete Press, 1952), 106–107.

In my new job, I learned to set boundaries and focus on the areas of my life that were being neglected. When one of my life's areas demanded too much, I had nothing left for the others. Often, that was my family. Gently, God taught me to say no and have faith that the world wouldn't stop if I weren't running everything. I tried to clarify what was essential and gather up, as Pratt calls, "the strands of [my] fragmented life."

I offset the solitude and community with my days of teaching accounting software. These classroom moments were beautiful opportunities for hospitality as I listened to my students' needs and reached out to them with kindness, understanding, and excitement for the positive changes Oracle software made in their jobs. Changes were often scary and stressful to my students. Easing their fear with reassurance that the software would work and teaching them how their work would be more accessible brought me joy. I was doing a job I genuinely loved and did it passionately as I sprinkled in God's divine love at every opportunity. I enjoyed refining my teaching skills and felt God was preparing me for more chances to teach in spiritual venues someday.

During the early years, management cared about the instructors' welfare and arranged our schedules so that we had some downtime at home every five or six weeks to rest and reconnect with our families. It was such a blessing. My new job helped me clarify what was necessary by simplifying my life. I ate my meals alone and lived on the road in a sparsely furnished hotel room five days a week. I learned only to pack what was necessary. I minimized my packing by wearing the same outfits each week. I was constantly training new customers, so they didn't notice my standardized wardrobe, which consisted of summer or winter outfits with scarves and inter-changeable jackets.

God went with me everywhere and was in charge of my sched-ule. In January 1998, six weeks after I started my new job, I had to attend an internal training at Oracle Headquarters in Redwood Shores, California. I had booked an early flight in the midafternoon, packed my best suits, and was off to the airport. I had never been to Redwood Shores and wanted to arrive in San Francisco early enough to get to my hotel for a good night's sleep, or at least I thought that was the plan. However, all the flights to San Francisco Airport (SFO) were canceled or delayed that afternoon and early evening due to a bad storm. Being new to business travel, I prayed and went to Continental Airlines' customer service desk, hoping to get to my training session on time.

Many travelers had gone home from the airport, believing that the San Francisco Airport wouldn't reopen, leaving empty seats on later flights. I waited and trusted God. Sure enough, the airport reopened, and I got a seat on the last flight out of Houston. I was so relieved! Thank you, God! I gave God my trust, and He helped me—even arranging for my rental car to be waiting for me, ensuring a safe arrival at my hotel (no cell phones in those days). The next morning, dressed in my sweatshirt and jeans from the day before, I arrived on time for the training and won the prize for the latest arrival: 3:00 a.m. My luggage arrived later that evening, but it was safe too. God cared for me as I traveled each week and taught me about being flexible and open to change. The average burnout rate in my job was fifteen months. These early years of surrender to God's grace allowed me to succeed in this job for almost ten years.

I learned a few lessons early on with Oracle. The first was that instructors helped each other; second, they did their best to answer students' questions. These two lessons were needed the first time during my second teaching on General Ledger in Houston. As the students did their introductions, I learned that some expected instruction on a specific model I was unprepared to teach. BP Oil hadn't used that model. That night after class, I sent an urgent appeal to my fellow instructors, and one of them came to my rescue. She spent two hours on the phone late into the night teaching me the concept so that I could answer my students' questions. I was so grateful and never forgot her kindness. I tried to follow her example by helping other instructors when opportunities arose.

Another lesson I learned early in my new job was how important taking an evening off for a fun, spiritual, or cultural activity was. The spiritual outcome of this lesson came one night while attending the musical *Les Misérables* at a theater in New York City. The evening became a mystical encounter when I realized the play was about a bishop forgiving a man who stole his mother's prized candlesticks. The bishop hoped his mercy would lead the man to salvation. The bishop's action inspired the main character to start his life anew. The play included all the elements: people suffering, tough decisions, harsh treatment, and, most crucial, salvation. The musical had themes of love, forgiveness, sacrifice, poverty, and justice. I felt like I was part of the play as it unfolded. The story imitated parts of my life, full of suffering, tough decisions, and God's saving mercy that gave me a second chance at life. Walking back to the hotel with a fellow instructor, I was floating on the message of compassion and forgiveness. I was filled with the Holy Spirit. I just wanted to yell at everyone approaching us: "God loves you!"

Another mystical evening I encountered on a night off was in Cleveland, where I visited the Cleveland Museum of Art. The museum was having a summer movie night, and all the visitors enjoyed the movie downstairs while I wandered alone through the floor of religious art upstairs. The floor was cool and quiet, and each piece of art spoke to me of people's devotion to God and their expression of that devotion through various mediums. One of my favorites was the Icon of the Virgin and Child from Egypt during the Byzantine period (sixth century). It was amazing that it survived all these centuries and reminded me of people's care for beautiful art representing Christ. My time felt ethereal, as though I was walking through God's sacred space. The silence was helping my soul find rest and refreshment. Teaching was very exhausting. I put all my being into my classes, so taking time for myself with God was a blessing and a lesson I tried to remember.

I often rejuvenated my spirit and energy by visiting family members and old friends living in different parts of the country where I happened to be teaching. One example was my cousin Patty, who lived in Atlanta. I got to visit her several times and provided a listening ear and caring heart after the death of her older sister. God's timing was always perfect, and these mystical glimpses helped my soul, as well as the person I visited.

Purchasing a single ticket for concerts and plays also added to this renewal. I learned to enjoy events like the Rockettes in New York City or an opera in San Francisco. Even though I was alone, I didn't feel lonely because Jesus was always with me, and He filled me with His divine love as the music warmed my heart. I learned to do Centering Prayer while I waited for breakfast to be delivered by room service. These spiritual glimpses amid the busyness of my life fueled my soul and helped me develop vital self-care—something that helped me spend many years in a demanding job without burning out. Well, at least most of the time—as you will see later in the book—I let life's events push me near the edge, and I had to return to this simple lesson in self-care to keep me from careening over into the abyss.

GOD GUIDING ME

Soon after I started with Oracle, I entrusted my schedule to God. It was constantly changing and, at first, made me a bit crazy. But, with God in charge, I just looked for the blessings. Flights were sometimes delayed or canceled—like when I was stuck in an airport for several hours with a fellow instructor. I could've given up in frustration, but instead, we talked, and he told me he was going through a divorce. He hadn't told anyone at work but needed to tell the story to help him heal. Having been divorced and trained as a spiritual director, I could listen with empathy and understanding. I saw the blessing in knowing that this encounter wouldn't have happened if our planes hadn't been delayed.

Other lessons I learned on the road were painful and a bit comical. I'm a klutz. I always joked that my mom should have named me Grace because I have often been so ungraceful. On a trip in June 1998 to our education center in Washington, DC, Kim told me to take the tram for two dollars instead of a cab for fifty dollars from Dulles Airport to my hotel. While boarding the tram, I slipped, and all 100 pounds of books and clothing rolled over my foot, breaking one bone. Ouch!

I had to teach with the broken foot for the whole week. Oracle didn't have a substitute instructor to rush to my rescue. I was on my own, but God was there. His plan was for me to rest for four weeks after the doctor put a pin in my foot, so Oracle had to cancel all my classes. I was glad God arranged some time at home. I had been teaching a lot and needed the break. I'm sure Oracle didn't appreciate my schedule change, as I was the only one in the world who taught that particular class. My classes were full, so I estimated that the fifty-dollar cab ride savings cost Oracle about $50,000 or more in revenue. To add insult to injury, my vice president put a note in my record that I never had to take a tram again. But this note meant I could always get a cab, so in a way, that insult was actually a blessing. And the four weeks at home were filled with hugs, laughter, and catching up with my family. Thank you, God!

LOST AND FOUND

I got lost a lot from 1997 through 1999 before I had a cell phone or navigation system. One night, I landed somewhere in Pennsylvania and had my Hertz paper map ready. As I left the rental car lot, I found four entrances to the freeway were closed for construction! By the time I got on the highway, I was lost. It was dark and late at night, but the moon was bright. I just kept praying, and somehow, I made it the twenty miles to my hotel! It wasn't the most direct route, but I was right to trust in God to get me there.

In 2000, as clunky cell phones came into being and the price was affordable, I was among the first to buy one to help me when I got lost. One night, I was in Los Angeles and went to a restaurant the hotel recommended some distance away. I got there just fine, but on the way back, I got turned around and found myself at the dead end of a narrow one-way street. I couldn't even turn around to head back in the right direction. Perplexed about what to do, I called my dear friend and sister in Christ Marti, who lived in Fort Worth. I told her my predicament, and we finally agreed, among our laughter at me being lost again and on another adventure, that I would have to back down the one-way street and hope no one hit me. So I did with Marti hanging on the phone, prepared to call 911 if I had an accident. Praise God! I finally returned safely to my hotel, and my adventures on the road continued.

SURGERY STRESS

A strange thing happened in August 1999 that reminded me, once again, to always trust God and His plan. I started leaving the classroom to go to the restroom many times a day. Finally, I went to the doctor on one of my infrequent weekdays at home. It seems I had a softball-sized cyst in my abdomen, causing the problem. Of course, my first thought was cancer! Just the word is scary. The fear of that possible diagnosis brought me to my knees in prayer, and I rallied my prayer order sisters and others for support. The surgery was brutal, taking over three-and-a-half hours as the cyst was wrapped around several organs. Waiting for the biopsy to come back was tough, but I trusted God had a plan.

When the report came back benign, I rejoiced at God's answer to my prayers. I was home for nine weeks, a blessing for the family and me. However, returning to the road after nine weeks, lifting luggage, standing to teach, and all that goes with traveling was too much. The students in my first class brought in a stool the second day because they feared I would pass out, and so did I. I appreciated their kindness and let go of my pride, as I called Kim and let him know I wasn't ready to be back at work. I learned several other lessons through the nine-month recovery and the reminder to always trust God and His plan and be humble. The recovery time taught me to slow down and ask others for help.

SHOWING UP FOR WORK

In my job, along with being present to my students as a teacher and mentor, management always stressed the importance of showing up for your class. Other instructors weren't waiting to step in and take over a class when the assigned instructor didn't show up or became ill. So, despite my busy schedule, I always did what I could to make it to my classes. Well, until Iowa! I was scheduled to fly to Iowa to teach a custom class in the summer of 2002. The client wanted the material for the two applications taught in a different order because one of their employees was out of the office on Wednesday. Since I could teach both applications, I agreed.

On Saturday, before I was to leave the next afternoon, George and I decided to wallpaper the bathroom, and it wasn't an easy project. Luckily, George and I got along okay—well, most of the time. The bathroom looked beautiful, and we dropped into bed, exhausted. A few hours later, I was awakened by chest pains. George drove me to the hospital, ignoring the wise decision to call an ambulance instead—a decision I'm still reminded of today by my son, who is an emergency room nurse.

When we arrived, the staff at the hospital rushed me back to an examining room and started many tests. The tests, thankfully, showed no evidence of a heart attack, so Sunday morning, I told the nurse I needed to leave to catch my plane to Iowa later that day.

She said, "No way. You must stay twenty-four hours when you come in with a possible heart attack." I pleaded with her that I could be fired. She didn't budge.

I finally called the manager on duty and told her I couldn't go to Iowa. Her exact words were, "You have to go to Iowa." Then I said, "The hospital won't let me out." Silence on the other end of the phone. Eventually, she said she would go and do part of the class and get someone else to cover the other application. I argued that I had told the client I would do it how they needed to meet their employees' schedules. She didn't listen to me. In the long run, the client was very angry, and I felt terrible for letting them down.

The hospital stay turned out to be four days. Luckily, all the doctor found was a minor heart problem that caused an anxiety attack that mimicked a heart attack. So I got a week at home with the family. And again, God timed the break perfectly, and I thanked Him. This episode began my relationship with Dr. Selim Sekili, my cardiologist and, later, George's doctor. But, unbeknownst to Dr. Sekili and us, God had a plan that involved him, a remarkable healing, and a near-death experience later in our lives. Stay tuned.

PRESENTING ON THE MAIN STAGE

For many years, I was privileged to present at various Oracle conventions, which were called Oracle Open World. In the Fall of 2002, I presented on the main stage right after Larry Ellison, founder and CEO of Oracle Corporation. Oracle University had never had the honor of presenting on the main stage, so our senior vice president of Oracle University met with my fellow instructor and me before we went on stage. I was nervous and unsure if I would succeed, so I spent many hours preparing. I also had hoped it would be my chance to meet Larry, but several large security guards surrounded him.

My fellow instructor was supposed to be a wizard and get the audience's attention with jokes and stories. Then, he would make me appear out of smoke as his assistant. Well, the longer he talked, the quieter the audience of accountants and financial specialists got. Finally, I appeared, and he flew off the stage. I introduced the topic, and then it was time for my demonstration. It worked perfectly before Larry's presentation when I set up the computer, but it only took about ten seconds to realize the connection had dropped. The fun of live software presentations! So I told the support folks, "Bring up the lights," and said to the audience, "Any questions?" while I rebooted the machine and reopened the application. The demo, after that point, went off perfectly.

After the presentation, I walked with the senior vice president and several customers to the Oracle University suite to answer more questions. Later, the senior vice president said to me, "That was fast thinking."

I confidently replied, "If you are teaching a class and the application goes down, reboot and keep talking. I have had a lot of practice." The next day, I appeared alone. The wizard had to fly off to another world.

Shortly after that Open World, Oracle University had several rounds of layoffs. The last Friday of each quarter was very stressful because the layoffs usually happened that day, and eventually, good instructors were caught in the layoffs. I was worried because, at my age, I knew finding another job as good as the one I had was difficult.

In the end, I was relieved to survive all the layoffs. Years later, I mentioned my relief to a member of management, and they reassured me the senior vice president didn't let my name be put on any layoff lists because of my outstanding performance at Open World. He credited how I handled the application crash during my presentation for saving Oracle University's reputation when the other instructor failed. Whether that was the reason or God's plan saved me for His purpose, I worked at Oracle for many more years. But I learned one more lesson—doing my job to the best of my God-given ability saved my career. And God and I continued on the road with more surprises as I stumbled through my life as an Oracle University instructor.

CHAPTER SIX

TEACHING ON THE ROAD

Continuing with Oracle Corporation

Daily Prayer

Lord, help me to live this day quietly, easily.
To lean upon Thy great strength, trustfully, restfully.
To wait for the unfolding of Thy will, patiently, serenely.
To meet others peacefully, joyously.
To face tomorrow confidently, courageously. Amen.
—St. Francis of Assisi

Years earlier, when God called me to train as a spiritual director, I thought I would give direction to directees in one-to-one sessions at my home or church. However, with a job that kept me on the road, I could never have regular directees. Instead, God gave me other road warriors like me to be my on-the-spot directees. I listened to them and often gave them whatever book God had me reading. I lost count of all the books I gave away. I especially remember reading a book on grief, and the lady next to me on the plane was on her way to bury her mother. God always knew and arranged mystical encounters with others who needed me. I just had to follow the Holy Spirit's nudging. Amazing!

OVERNIGHT IN ROME

This hectic life on the road often included spontaneous travel, like a twenty-six-hour trip to Rome to keep my platinum status on Continental Airlines. Other road warriors were racking up last-minute miles, and I was anxious to follow suit. At first, Porgie, as I called my sweet husband, said no. I agreed, but I wouldn't say I liked it. In my heart, I knew he was a godly man with the gift of discernment, and I knew I needed to listen to him and respect his feelings. He loves me; however, I liked my platinum status. "God, is that wrong?" I asked. "When you travel so much and are tired, is it wrong to want to be comfortable in first class or business class on the plane and have a decent meal? Something with vegetables and lots of water?"

George reconsidered. He gave me his blessings and loving words of advice in this letter he slipped into my suitcase:

> Hi, dear. I just wanted you to know that I love you, and may God bless you on your retreat. You seem to have a lot of anger toward your ex-husband, my ex-wife, and some anger toward my daughter. So I thought that if you are at the Vatican, you might like to lay them at the foot of the Cross; anger only hurts the one who carries it. Enjoy your trip. Love, George.

George was right about my anger, but I was actually angry at the world in general. Too much stress. Too much traveling. Our downtime at home was a thing of the past as management changed and profits became more important. I spent the day touring Rome. Seeing the Vatican with its beautiful art was inspiring. I spent some quiet time in the Sistine Chapel and prayed to be released from my unforgiveness, pent-up anger at others, and work stress. Family events in a blended family were proving difficult, but forgiveness and the Holy Spirit helped me find rest and peace.

The Colosseum was one of my favorite sites on that very short trip. Knowing that Christians were brutally killed for their faith brought tears to my eyes as I toured the ancient structure. I thought, *Man's inhumanity to man! When will we learn to love each other as Jesus taught?*

I wandered around the Forum and the streets of Rome, just taking in the sights and the joy of seeing all these ancient ruins. I bought a journal to capture my thoughts from a very flattering man. He made me feel beautiful. I ended my day by attending a beautiful Catholic church for Mass in Italian. The Mass was special because even though I didn't speak Italian, I knew the structure of the Universal Catholic Church's Mass, so I followed what was happening and said the words in my language. I was sad as I boarded the plane just twenty-six hours later to fly home. But I felt a new joy. Thanks to my husband's note and God, my time in Rome helped me forgive, rest, and refresh. Even though my time had been short, I promised to return to Italy someday, which I did many years later.

SNOW AND ICE!

The weather was always fun while I lived on the road. I kept telling Kim I lived in Houston for two reasons: snow and ice! But then, he sent me to the north during the worst winter weather and places like Phoenix in the blazing summer. God always kept me safe, like when I got the last seat on the last flight out of Buffalo, New York, as a massive snowstorm shut down the airport for four days in January 2003. Or when God answered my prayer in Denver with a record snowstorm on March 17, 2003, that kept me shut up in my hotel for two days.

On that particular trip, I didn't have enough time to prepare for a new class I was teaching. It was March, and the big, beautiful flakes quickly accumulated when it started to snow. On Tuesday, I carpooled to the education center with a fellow instructor, Paul, who had wanted to finish as much of his two-day class as possible before flying home. But by the time we left, the governor had closed the roads. I prayed and drove very slowly, and we returned to our hotel safely with a stranded student in the back seat.

I went out daily for fresh air between studying my material and swept the snow off my car. I was born and raised in Colorado, so I knew how to handle snow and ice, even if I didn't like them. Unfortunately, Paul didn't. By Thursday, his car was nowhere to be found. Paul took a cab to the airport when it reopened on Friday morning. Two weeks later Paul got a call from Hertz, as they still hadn't found his car! I had to teach one more long day to cover the essential topics on Friday, but I was prepared. Thank you, God, for giving me time to prep for my class.

Thanks to my husband and God, I survived an ice storm in Reston, Virginia, six months later. George always ensured I had a working flashlight or sometimes two in my suitcase. George worked for the local light company, so our house was full of lanterns, gas-powered lights, and flashlights. When an ice storm hit about 7:00 p.m., our hotel's electricity went out momentarily, but luckily, the backup generator came on, and we were okay all night.

Well, until twelve hours later when the backup generator also went out! I was on the eleventh floor and had to get to work, so off to the stairs I went with my little flashlight and a lot of prayers. As I climbed down the stairs, I picked up others doing the same thing; I was the only one with a flashlight. I was the leader, and by the time we got to the street level, I had a whole line of people following me. It was too funny, but we all got down safely. Thanks, Porgie! And thanks to God for the awesome view as we exited the hotel's outside door. The world was beautiful. Everything was coated with ice: trees, bushes, cars, and streetlights, reflecting the sun's morning rays, revealing God's glory. I paused momentarily to take in the grandeur, then rushed to my car. Despite the slick streets, my students and I made it to class safely. In conclusion, I learned early from my snow and ice adventures to watch the weather, so I was always prepared for anything and made wise decisions to keep me safe and warm, like staying in full-service hotels.

MORE TRAVEL WITH GOD

One of the biggest surprises was in November 2003, when God changed my schedule so I could go to Orlando to look for a convention hotel for my prayer order. In my free time, I was a meeting planner. My schedule contained a five-day teach somewhere when suddenly, on Thursday the week before, my new manager Terry called and said I needed to go to Orlando to cover a three-day class. I said, "Okay, what about the other two days?"

He said, "We don't have anything, so you get them off. Enjoy!"

So I called the convention bureau, and they arranged to pick me up after class and put me and my friend and fellow council member Jean Marani, who drove in to help, at their expense, in a beautiful hotel for the next two nights. The convention representative arranged visits to six hotels for the next two days, and then I flew home to Houston with a hotel already selected. And the trip didn't cost my prayer order anything! An incredible miracle!

Spring of 2004 found me delighting in the grandeur of Pike's Peak, with its ribbons of snow standing majestic over the foothills of the Colorado Rockies. I enjoyed visiting Colorado Springs as I grew up in Colorado and always felt at home with the mountains in view. One evening, I went to see the red rocks of the Garden of the Gods at sunset. The beauty reminded me of God's creative ability. The various rock structures, many pointing to the sky in the form of praying hands, and the stunning red color of the rocks offset by wisps of green plants, all under a multicolor sunset, made the park look like a great canvas of color. Only an awesome God could have created such breathtaking beauty. So many times when I was traveling, God took my breath away with His incredible beauty and helped make traveling more pleasant.

The next day, I had just finished teaching a four-day class and was going to the airport. I had an easy, quiet class, as many of my students were new to Oracle and didn't ask questions. It was such a nice change, giving me more time for relaxation. Airport security emptied my luggage when I checked in and then, at the gate, emptied my purse. I was irritated by all the extra security since 9/11 and felt violated by the intrusion into my things. The two security checks made me late to board, so I struggled to find a place for my laptop and had feelings of panic at maybe having to check it. Luckily, I was relieved to find an open space in the back of the plane only seconds before the tiny jet plane took off. Then, we ran into terrible storms with wind, rain, and lighting. We were bouncing around, and I was scared. I got out my special rosary I carried with me to help calm my nerves. George gave it to me when he asked me to marry him. I prayed the Rosary, then I prayed some of my favorite scriptures, including Romans 8:38–39:

> For I'm convinced that neither death, nor life, nor angels, nor principalities, nor present things, nor future things, nor powers, nor height, nor depth, nor any other creature will be able to separate us from the love of God in Christ Jesus our Lord.

Peace settled in my soul as I finished praying, and I eventually fell asleep until the unplanned landing in San Antonio woke me. We sat on the tarmac for over five hours, waiting for the Houston Airport, which closed because of the storm, to reopen. No one was allowed off the plane. Other stranded planes surrounded us. Our flight attendant tried to keep up our spirits by bringing drinks and passing out the little food she had. Luckily, I learned to always travel with some food, so I was okay. Time dragged on. I finished the book I was reading, and there was no onboard entertainment in those days. I was restless but trusted God's plan to keep me safe, so I continued to rest since sleep didn't come. One blessing was the airport employees emptying the overflowing toilet.

As the plane returned to the air, the pilot told us the flight plan would take us over the south side of Houston and then back north to Houston Intercontinental (Bush) Airport to go around the storm. As I looked out the window, what a majestic sight. There were so many little blinks around us as other planes returned to the air and flew toward Houston. The clouds had opened above us with twinkling stars. A ring of clouds still circled our world, lit by the lights of Houston reflecting off the clouds. It was another breathtaking sight and emphasized how small we are and how great God's creation is. I praised God as my plane touched down in Houston, as I always did, but I gave extra praise that night. Our pilots landed safely, and I was relieved to finally get off the plane. A two-and-a-half-hour flight took almost eight hours.

On a trip a few weeks later, my flight home from San Francisco was delayed—again! I was surprised as I checked in to see an old friend from my previous job. My friend and I arranged to sit together and enjoyed visiting before boarding, making the time go faster. Once we boarded, we laughed and shared stories, which made the flight very pleasant. We arrived well after midnight. I was worried and scared about going to my car alone in the airport garage. A flasher at the airport on another trip had followed me. A nearby gentleman scared him off. I said a prayer for God to keep me safe. After we got our luggage and headed to the garage, my friend and I agreed to watch out for each other as much as possible. Well, God had the situation in hand! Our cars were parked on the same floor, facing each other, bumper to bumper, in the seven-story garage with 7,500 parking spaces! Wow! I was amazed by how God always kept me safe.

THE GOLDEN ASPEN OF FALL

One of the most challenging assignments as an Oracle instructor was three months in Edmonton, Alberta, Canada. I arrived on August 1, 2004, and was the only Oracle employee assigned to help develop training classes for a client upgrading to a new version of Oracle software. The employees were used to working a very minimal eight-hour day. I worked sixteen hours a day, so I was often alone. Also, most of the client's employees didn't even take lunch, so I ate all my meals alone. I had no car, so I was limited on where to go. The nonstop flights to Houston were ten hours each way, so I only went home every other weekend. I worked the whole weekend when I stayed. I took a few hours off to take a cab and attended Mass at the local Roman Catholic Church. It was a wonderful respite in an otherwise dull routine.

I was surprised when one of the clients asked me to go on a weekend spiritual retreat in September with her and a group of lovely Anglican ladies. I noticed the beautiful fall colors as we left Edmonton's city limits. The closer I got to the retreat center, the rougher the road became, with rocks and deep ruts, and the fall colors became more beautiful. I was so surprised and thrilled to discover that the countryside around Edmonton was covered with aspen, and the trees were in full golden color against a blue sky. It was awesome, but it made me feel homesick for Colorado, where I grew up.

The retreat was entitled "On Holy Ground" and was led by the Reverend Maureen Crerar. Her church, St. Faith's Anglican Church in Edmonton, ministered full-time to the homeless of the city. Maureen shared with me about her life raising a Down syndrome son and what a special gift he had been in her life, as well as the challenges of being a woman priest. God had arranged a mystical time when we were alone, and I could listen to and support her with prayer.

Reverend Crerar asked each of us to bring our favorite angel. On Saturday night, we shared them. I brought Ariel, a unique angel figurine given to me by my friend, Sharon Lundgren. Ariel is holding a baby, representing my current eleven grandchildren under ten plus other children who called me Grandmother. I shared how the baby Ariel held made me think of Kendall, one of my special "adopted" grandchildren.

My son Bill's sister-in-law Kara and her husband were told four months into their pregnancy that their baby had spina bifida.[1] The doctor told them she had an inch-and-a-half gap in her spine and water on the brain and that they would be lucky if she lived three days. He said abortion was the best option, but they wanted their baby. Kara and Brent came to George and me for advice. We prayed with them, and I gave them a prayer blanket I made to put over the baby as Kara slept at night. Many prayers were said for the baby. By the time Kendall was born, the gap in her spine had almost closed—a miracle. Three days after she was born, I gave them a baby-sized prayer blanket for her during the surgery to drain the water off her brain. We all waited outside the operating room and prayed until the surgery ended. The surgery was successful, and as Kendall grew, she was obviously intelligent.

---

[1] Spina bifida is a birth defect in which an area of the spinal column doesn't form properly, leaving a section of the spinal cord and spinal nerves exposed through an opening in the back.

I have enjoyed watching Kendall grow into a beautiful, talented young lady who competed in and won many beauty pageants. She raised money for spina bifida research and competed on a platform that showed the world that people with disabilities are talented and valuable. Some of her life was difficult, however, because the effects of spina bifida continued throughout her life, but she walked and danced—a miracle, as some with spina bifida can't walk or need braces or crutches. I told my new friends I knew she would go on to do extraordinary things with the courage and fortitude God had instilled in her. She is truly a miracle!

On Sunday morning of the retreat, I put the prayer blanket (like the one I had given Kendall's parents) back in the car. I had brought it to give away, but I was sad I hadn't felt drawn to pass it on to anyone. About an hour later, one of the ladies approached me rather timidly. She shared that her niece's baby boy had just been diagnosed with spina bifida. I went and got the blanket from the car. The blanket was even blue! We prayed on the blanket, and she sent it to her niece. We all committed to pray for Wendy's little boy, who was due in February 2005, that he, too, would have the miracle of being healed by our awesome God.

After that particular weekend, I understood what mystical encounters God had planned for me when He sent me to Edmonton. First, there was a deep spiritual conversation with Reverend Crerar. Second, I was meant to provide a blanket for Wendy and her baby, plus many prayers for a miracle. On the first of November, after the first snowfall, I successfully finished the training material and conducted the training classes for their team of instructors. I was relieved and happy to return to the United States and my regular teaching schedule, where I worked fewer hours and had more human contact. I never heard from Reverend Crerar or how Wendy's baby did, but I continued to pray for both of them, trusting God's plan for the gifted priest and the special child.

GOD'S SURPRISES

I'm always amazed at how God's hand directed my life, even when I wasn't aware. I had started getting emails from the Oracle office in Houston to pray for the son of one of our salespeople, Sergio. The young man had cancer, and it was serious. I added him to my daily prayer list. A few days later, the St. Justin Women's Retreat team I served as spiritual director sent out a prayer request for my friend Diana Helm's son, Michael-Jon, who was very ill with cancer. He had a wife and baby. I added him to my daily prayer list as well. I got periodic updates on both young men. It was several weeks before I realized Sergio was Diana's husband, and I had been praying twice a day for the same young man!

I wish I could say that Michael-Jon survived cancer, but, unfortunately, he died several months later, in December 2004, leaving his wife, young daughter, and his grieving parents. I was home when the funeral was scheduled. Being both an Oracle employee and a St. Justin parishioner, I called and offered to help the Oracle sales department with the reception after the funeral at St. Justin's. Sergio's manager, Scott, thanked me personally as we set up the food. Little did I know that God again was in charge, and this wasn't a random encounter.

About four months later, after life had moved on, I did a class for a client in Houston. The client asked me to demonstrate an

Oracle product that Oracle Sales was trying to sell them, which I did. A few days later, my manager called to say she had received a complaint about me—that I had claimed I was an expert on the particular Oracle product I had demoed, and I thought it wasn't a good product.

I had trained my manager on General Ledger, and she knew I always introduced myself by saying, "I'm not an expert on Oracle, but if you have questions, I'll find the answers for you." So she knew I wouldn't say I was an expert. My manager told me the vice president of sales would call me to discuss what had happened. To my surprise, the vice president was Scott, Sergio's manager, whom I helped at the funeral of Sergio's son, Michael-Jon. When he called, I reminded him, "We met at Michael-Jon's funeral."

He quickly replied, "Don't worry about the complaint. I'll take care of it."

I was relieved and surprised.

God used my faithfulness in attending and serving at the funeral and being with my dear friend and her family in a time of terrible grief for my good. Diana was such a witness to the power of Divine Mercy[2] at the funeral. Her calm, trusting Jesus attitude spoke volumes and helped me move forward with my relationship with God. And as George always says, "You can't out-give God." I did God's work by serving at the funeral, and He took care of the work complaint. Another mystical glimpse of God's plan for my life. Thank You, Lord!

---

[2] The message of The Divine Mercy is that God loves us and wants us to trust in Him and His mercy. The message is based on the writings of Saint Faustina Kowalska.

HURRICANE RITA

Traveling for my job and being away from my family, even when it was a perk like the Oracle Open World Conference, was difficult, and forces more significant than me made it even more challenging. In September 2005, I was confronted with the possibility of losing my home and possibly family members. I was in San Francisco, presenting at another Oracle Open World. As I watched the news from my hotel room one morning, I saw a massive hurricane in the Gulf. The projections said Hurricane Rita would be a Category 5 and hit Houston directly. I saw the path was projected to go directly over my house. The news caught my attention! I began praying for the safety of my family and my city.

My family came first, so I did all I could for them before I went to the demo booth. I immediately started calling to find a safe place for my family to evacuate as my heart filled with dread and fear. I called my daughter Susan and told her to immediately take Isaiah out of school, pack food, water, clothes, cash, valuables, and family picture albums, and head for Amarillo. I had rooms there for them. Then I said to leave the rest. I knew it would be hard for her—a ten-hour drive with a child and the worry of whether they would have a home to come back to—so I lifted up more prayers.

With a heavy heart, my mind scanned through my home of thirty years, the painting of Jesus being anointed by Mary of Bethany that a Chinese dissident painted, the charcoal drawing of my husband, the Thomas Kincaid painting called "Sunrise"[3] of a

---

[3] In December 1999 Thomas Kinkade released "Sunrise" to represent the new millennium as the Millennium of Light, and he prayed his "Sunrise" painting would be symbolic of a new dawning of God's grace and love in the years ahead.

lone Cross on a hill, ink drawings from my time in Saudi Arabia, and more. My heart was sad, and I just wanted to go home and get a hug from Porgie. I called my son, Bill, and told him to get his family out of harm's way.

I attended the conference to take my turn at the Oracle University demo booth. One of the senior managers came by and asked if I needed to go home to prepare. Another instructor had already flown home to Houston to help his wife and elderly mother prepare for the hurricane. I knew what the manager wanted to know and said as much. "What you want to know is, will I teach my class next week in Los Angeles?" I was the only instructor that could teach that class, which was full. He was taken aback and admitted sheepishly that was why he had come to see me. I said I had already sent most of my family to safety and would teach the class if nothing happened to my husband or son, who were staying in Houston, but reminded him my family came first. Also, I told him Oracle must pay my weekend expenses and change my airline tickets. He was relieved. I was still worried and wished I was home.

As I did my presentations and helped with the booth for the next two days, my mind was in Houston. I talked each morning to my family members from the safety of San Francisco, but my tension grew. My son, a paramedic, and my husband, who worked for the electric company, had to stay in Houston. Then, on Thursday, came the email from my sweet George, who, in his very simple way, said: "CC [credit cards] in lock[er] at work. Combination is . . . Love George." Tears ran down my face as I felt helpless, and my heart wanted to go home, but most of my family had evacuated, and the folks trying to escape the storm had caused gridlock on the roads in Houston. Flying home was a crazy idea. The seriousness of the storm was getting too real! I knew his message meant he was staying at the house and not at work where there was a solid concrete building. We had argued about the wisdom of him staying in our home, which couldn't stand up to a Category 5 hurricane.

On Friday, I escaped to the refuge of St. Patrick's Cathedral next to my hotel in downtown San Francisco to spend time in silence and pray with God. In my mind, I knew God was in charge, and I had to trust His plan, but in my heart, I was afraid. God had kept me safe through all the years of traveling, and now He was still with me. I knew only God could quiet the storm, and I claimed that miracle for my family and Houston. I had to hold on to God and put on the armor of God.

As I prayed, I discovered what it meant in the Nicene Creed to be part of the holy Catholic Church, the universal Church. I was joined by the warm Korean congregation that met there, and they added hugs and prayers. I particularly prayed for Hurricane Rita to weaken and go east to an area with less population. *God, I need a miracle.*

When Rita made landfall early on Saturday, September 24, she had moved east to an area sparsely populated, making landfall between Sabine Pass, Texas, and Johnson Bayou, Louisiana, and had decreased to a Category 3. Sadly, many people where the storm made landfall weren't prepared. All the emphasis in the news had been on Galveston and Houston. I praised God that my home and family were spared but prayed for those impacted by Rita's fury.

Early on Sunday, I flew to Los Angeles to teach my class. I wanted to go to a church with praise music. My heart was full of thanksgiving, and I wanted to praise God. One lesson I had learned in all the years I traveled was how to find Catholic churches when I needed a spiritual boost. I found a small Catholic church where the youth choir led the worship music that evening. It was an awesome evening, with praise and thanksgiving to God for another miracle.

FOLLOWING GOD TO A NEW HOUSE

Out of the blue, my son, Bill, called me while I was on the road and said I needed to look at a new house across the street from him. I was on the road full-time, and my family relationships had suffered, so I listened to him. It would be nice to be closer and see him, his wife, and their five children more often. Being closer to his cousin would be great for Isaiah. He continued to call me until I agreed to stop by my next weekend at home. I was too exhausted to think about moving, but spending more time with my family when I was home might be worth the effort.

George was working overtime, so I went alone to look at the house. Actually, it was just a frame of a house. As I walked in, I had an overwhelming feeling I was to buy it. I walked around the inside, praying. George and I had talked about buying a new home, but the house I was standing in wasn't it! Doubt and confusion filled my mind. We wanted a one-story with a three-car garage, not a two-story with a two-car garage.

Despite my doubts, I went with the realtor to her office to see the drawings of the finished house. Then I went back to the house and had the same intense feeling to buy it. *Really, God? How am I going to move with my work schedule? And this isn't what we wanted in a new home.* I called George and told him he had to look at the house.

He asked, "Why?"

I said, "Because if you don't, I will buy it without you."

So George came straight from work to see the house and try to talk some sense into his strong-willed wife. As he walked around, he was silent. Then he turned to me and said, "We are supposed to buy it, aren't we?"

"Yes!" was all I said. I'm so blessed to be married to a man who listens to God!

While confident, I still wasn't 100 percent convinced, so I asked God for a sign. Well, He gave us several. First, Isaiah was beaten up and his bike stolen while riding in our old neighborhood. Then, someone followed Susan home from work. Her quick thinking kept her safe as she drove to a more populated destination. A few nights later, gunshots behind our house woke us. Sadly, our old neighborhood had declined in my thirty years there.

So, still struggling with God's plan, I went to do the walk-through and final inspection after the house was finished, looking for a reason not to buy the house. They had put a white enamel sink in my stainless steel kitchen! And the builder said they couldn't change it! I went home in tears and told George the only way we could buy it was to replace the sink as soon as we moved in! The following day, the builder called to say he had checked the plans, and the sink was wrong. He replaced it with a stainless steel sink, and we bought the house.

We still didn't know why God had directed us to this house, but over the years, His plan became clear as Isaiah went to the nearby Catholic high school. His life there had ups and downs, but his painting and swimming skills grew immensely. The school also had an excellent program for dyslexic students like Isaiah. Toward the end of his senior year, God gave us a new one-story house with a three-car garage, but more about that home later.

Traveling was getting more challenging, and now, with a beautiful new home close to my family, I was in tears most Sundays as I hugged George and headed to the airport. It took me months to unpack, and the house was a mess, adding to my desire to stay home. When I came home one weekend, Bill surprised me by rearranging my furniture into a better configuration. I was so grateful. I prayed but didn't know what path God wanted me to follow or where I should go.

CHAPTER SEVEN

CHANGING DIRECTIONS

Simplifying My Life

Christ, The Living Vine

To Christ the living vine, we pray:
O Lord, come to our help!
Simplify our lives.
You are the vine, and we are the branches.
May we always be one in you.
You, Father, have pruned us
and cleared away the dead parts of our lives;
May we put forth new life.
You have watered your vine with
the living water that flows from the cross;
May we grow deeper through prayer
and become one in heart and mind with you.
You have nourished and protected your vine in faithful love;
May we always bear fruit for your glory. Amen.
—Author Unknown

God knew I needed to leave the road and started putting events in motion unbeknownst to me. I loved my job as an Oracle instructor and found the challenge of keeping up with Oracle's software exciting, so I hadn't thought of leaving Oracle University. I applied for an Oracle University manager position late in 2006, as did several others. The person who got it was one of my closest friends. I was happy for her because, during the interview process, I realized I didn't want the job. I enjoyed my career as an instructor too much to give it up. My friend was soon my manager.

FROM ASHES TO JOY

In the early years, our managers cared about us. We got a week off every few weeks to reconnect with family and ourselves. Later in my career, as profits became more important than employees, the benefit of time off at home disappeared and was replaced by more work, pushing me toward exhaustion and burnout. As 2007 began, I mainly taught a five-day course on the new features of the recently released Oracle Financial products. The constant addition of new features required more prepping and extra energy because the students asked many questions I had to answer, leading to working eighty-hour weeks.

I struggled with the lack of time at home and downtime, so I read Emilie Griffin's book, *The Reflective Executive: A Spirituality of Business and Enterprise,*[1] to find some answers. In this book, she tackles the challenge of finding spirituality and seeing God's presence

---

[1] Emilie Griffin, *The Reflective Executive: A Spirituality of Business and Enterprise* (New York: The Crossroad Publishing Company, 1993).

at work. Emily taught me that praying and asking God to help me better understand my role and where God was leading me through my job was essential. I realized God was teaching me skills to teach spiritual topics as opportunities arose. The book also challenged me to daily surrender to God and let His gentle leadership guide me in conducting my business affairs and other aspects of my life, being open to each day's adventure with God.

But I was slipping and too tired to do quality teaching. Since becoming my manager, my boss gave me challenging classes without adequate preparation time, including new courses. I would get up at 4:00 a.m., prep until I had to leave for class, and then prep until 10:00 p.m. when I fell into bed. Several weeks of that schedule were exhausting.

My job had utterly burned me out, and I felt I couldn't go one step further. As Lent 2007 approached, I felt my life was in ashes, and deep depression set in, so heavy I could hardly move. Tom Conry's song "Ashes"[2] reminded me of how I have offered my failures, gifts not given, and dreams not realized to God as an offering of ashes and that my stumbling needed God's direction. I felt I was stumbling more each day in my job, and only God could help me find my way.

Then, on Valentine's Day—a week before Ash Wednesday—my hotel room was robbed. My laptop and jewelry were stolen. I had stopped by my room on the way downstairs to get a quick supper in the hotel restaurant and left my computer and jewelry in a locked suitcase. When I returned, the locks had been cut off my suitcases, and the items were gone. I had always felt safe in my hotels, so the

---

[2] "Ashes," music and lyrics by Tom Conry, released originally in 1978.

robbery shocked me. The hotel called the police and moved me to a suite. I just wanted to go home and get a hug from George. The robbery was the last straw in a tough year of events, including the move to the new house, surgery for George and me, my dad's Alzheimer's diagnosis, job pressures, and many weeks of travel in freezing weather. My only lifeline was the next two weeks off work and at home.

My boss wasn't sympathetic when I called to tell her about the robbery. She said she planned to call me because she needed to change my schedule. She informed me that I had to go to Maine the next week and, the week after that, write a class and deliver it in "Nowheresville," Texas, two hours north of Dallas. My hope of two weeks at home faded away. I asked, "How will I book travel and write a class without my laptop?" My boss said to borrow one, which wasn't a realistic possibility as I was the only Oracle instructor where I was teaching. My depression deepened. I went back to class but could barely teach. My students were kind and supportive even when the tears started flowing while teaching the class—something that had never happened before, and I found it very embarrassing. I got through the class and flew home two days later.

I had an appointment with a new doctor on Friday of that week to do a biopsy for possible cancer. I completely melted down in her office, bursting into fresh tears. I told her what was happening, and she said I needed to stay home and rest. I kept telling her that I could only stay home if I were in the hospital, and she kept telling me I just needed rest. She finally left the room. When she returned, she handed me a note putting me on indefinite medical leave. She also gave me three cards for therapists and told me I must see one immediately. I called and told my boss, and it took less than ten minutes for her to replace me on the "You Have To Go Maine and Teach" trip! I was furious! The stress of almost losing my time at home was the beginning of the end of working for her. When I got home, I called all three therapists and made an appointment with the first one who called back.

At the end of the first appointment, my therapist said she gave her patients homework, and mine was to read the book *Life of the Beloved* by Henri Nouwen. I was shocked. What kind of therapist assigns Nouwen on your first visit? Nouwen is an influential spiritual writer whose books are full of wisdom and profound teachings and whom I read often. I found his books inspiring and a blessing in my spiritual life. Only God could have directed me to a therapist perfectly fitting my needs. I still hadn't unpacked my many boxes of books from our move eight months earlier, but I knew I had that book; however, I had never read it. So I went home and started unpacking the boxes—or rather, piling books all around me. It was healing, just touching all my favorite books that had fed my spirit over the years, and sure enough, I had a copy. Well, actually, I had two copies.

A couple of days later, God directed me to pull out from that same pile a little book on *Forgiveness and Inner Healing* by Betty Tapscott and Father Degrandis, and I started reading through it. This little book helped me forgive people who hurt me many years ago. Again, God was showing me that I needed to forgive, and as I reread the Forgiveness Prayer after all those years, God surprised me with the knowledge that my meltdown was partially due to unforgiveness. Again, I realized I had pent-up anger at many people and events. Being in an abusive marriage and a people pleaser since childhood had caused me over the years to stuff anger and unforgiveness rather than deal with it. George had helped me in the past when he put the letter in my suitcase on a trip to Rome and continues to help me see when this flaw happens again. He reminds me that unforgiveness hurts the person who carries it the most. So I needed to forgive:

- My dad for having Alzheimer's and not being there for me mentally.
- My boss for pushing me too hard.
- The person who robbed my hotel room and turned my life upside down.
- God for taking over a year to sell my old house when he gave me my new home.
- Those in my prayer order who continued to attack me as a Roman Catholic.

I attended the Cenacle Retreat House for an individual silent retreat the following weekend. After meeting with my spiritual director, I walked their labyrinth around and around and around until God's healing balm began to soothe my wounded soul. I spent the day among the spring flowers in the warm Houston sunshine, journaling, praying, and resting in the Lord. A couple of weekends later, I attended an awesome St. Justin's women's retreat on "Waves of God's Love" and let the waves of His love and the love of my sisters wash over me, healing more of the layers of hurt. My joy began to return, and I felt stronger than I had in many months.

I had scheduled some vacation time before being put on medical leave, so I went ahead with the vacation. I led a retreat in Atlanta on the Path to Forgiveness. God had surely put teaching that retreat on my schedule before my breakdown. He knew what I needed even before I did. Again, I was further healed as I shared my stories and read the Forgiveness Prayer to the group. I was amazed when one of the attendees shared on Sunday morning that she had forgiven the man who had killed her daughter. WOW. Thank you, God, for helping her on her path to healing while also helping me.

By Easter, I was singing alleluia all day long. I came so far in forty days, from ashes to joy. God restored not only my joy but also the things I had lost. As a result of the robbery, I got a new computer. But better than that, my coworkers, who heard about my robbery, began returning files I had given them over the years to rebuild my library of training materials. Other people called, prayed for me, and sent flowers and small gifts, which all helped to lift my spirits. I also gained an understanding of deep depression, something I had never experienced before, making me more compassionate toward others.

Then, a few days after Easter, I returned to the doctor who had put me on medical leave and introduced the real me—a joyful, spirit-filled child of God. She was finally able to do the biopsy, and it was negative. No cancer! Praise the Lord! And I returned to the road for a few more months. The workload was even heavier. I had to teach several new versions of our software without any preparation time. I also started coaching other instructors with lower than Oracle's desired evaluation scores. One, in particular, Barbara, became a good friend, and I worked with her weekly to help her improve her evaluation scores. The stress was taking a toll on her health and mine.

SUSAN'S GROWING PAIN

In addition to the stress at work, my daughter, Susan, who had surgery six years ago, needed more surgery. Initially, she injured her back while at work. Then, she got caught in a Houston flash flood days later. Her engine stalled out, and the water around her car was rising at a dangerous rate, so she decided to walk through the water to her brother's home nearby. Unfortunately, the pressure of her walking against the water further damaged her back—to the point that walking, school, and work all stopped. Isaiah was four.

Susan couldn't get out of bed. I was on the road nonstop, as always. I felt terrible and could not help her other than praying continuously. George would prepare Isaiah cereal and put a small milk pitcher in the refrigerator before leaving for work. Isaiah would get up, make breakfast, and take his mommy the food he could reach. The doctor tried physical therapy and surgery to remove the damaged disc. Her back was better for a while, but as time passed, it became clear she needed more serious surgery, and she had more pain. I needed to be home for the surgery to care for her and Isaiah. There was no guarantee she would walk after the surgery. I told my boss, who said she would see if she could find something I could do off the road for a few weeks. Susan kept postponing the surgery and suffering more and more pain.

SURVIVING THE TAX CLASS AND MORE

Then, along came the new Tax class in July 2007. Another instructor, Wally, and I were to attend the class rollout at the San Francisco Education Center so we could eventually teach the class. It's always a treat to be in the center of San Francisco. We arrived early with the two writers who had written the course material.

The other students started to arrive, but the project manager who was supposed to teach the class didn't show up. I got drafted to teach the class. Not having even read the material, I did my best, but it was a stressful three days with many questions I couldn't answer and labs I couldn't do.

At lunch on the second day, I heard Wally talking on the phone to a manager from the group that wrote our curriculum. She had offered him a job, and he had taken it. I knew her, too, so I grabbed the phone from him and asked her when she would offer me a job. Her answer was, "How about now?" So, of course, I said I would take it. I immediately felt the job offer answered many prayers and was God's way out of a bad situation. This new job would allow me to work from home, and Susan could finally have her surgery.

Predictably, my boss didn't take my request for a transfer well. She held me up for three months, which was Oracle's policy if the person's job was essential. Susan again had to postpone her surgery twice and endure even worse pain. My boss told me if I taught a two-week class, taught the certification session at the Oracle Open World Conference, and prepared the presentation for another instructor to present at Open World, I could transfer.

In late October, my last two-week class covered six products highlighting the new features of our latest release. It was impossible to teach. The people new to Oracle needed the basics, and those experienced with Oracle complained we weren't going into enough depth on the new features. I worked extra hours to give all the students what they needed. I was so exhausted that two of my fellow instructors, Paul and Barbara, came to help me with a couple of sessions. They were worried about me. I had developed a gray coloring, which I was told was a precursor to a heart attack. My cardiologist was very concerned, as was my family.

I went home for the weekend between the two weeks of class. My St. Justin's Women's Retreat Team had a planning session on the beach in Galveston for their next retreat. I went and let them pray on me intensely. Performing healing prayers as a group was essential to our retreats and team activities. God revigorated me as they surrounded me with their love and soaked me with their prayers. The mystical healing gave me new energy and renewed my tired body and soul. I was able to finish the last week of class.

I still had to do two more chores. I enjoyed the challenge and excitement of presenting at the Oracle Open World conventions. I resented my boss demanding that I write the content for another instructor to present at Open World to be able to transfer, plus not giving me time to do the work. I felt it was a real slap in the face after almost ten years of travel and hard work, but I just wanted out so Susan could have her surgery. I did prepare the PowerPoint presentation but not to my usual standards, nor did I design the demos. I told the other instructor I always taught by doing my demos on the fly without a script, which was true. I was furious about the unfair demands.

My boss also required me to teach an intense prep session with the same instructor the Sunday before Open World began for customers taking the certification tests. We agreed to alternate chapters. I did the first chapter, and she did the second chapter. After she taught, the students approached me and asked me to teach the remaining six chapters. Then, my boss said the other instructor wasn't feeling well. So, my last day at Oracle University was very tough as

I taught seven chapters for a class I didn't usually teach. But I made it, and the students were happy. I was proud I left Oracle University with a quality ending, just as I had always tried to do. I'll always be grateful to Oracle University, the many folks who mentored me and shared the road with me along the way, and God for giving me a job at Oracle where I could earn a decent living. And even more than the job, I'm grateful to God for guiding my stumbling steps along His path as He traveled the road with me and kept me safe.

My boss reneged on her invitation to dinner after the sessions; honestly, I didn't want to spend any more time with her. I had a quiet dinner at my hotel in tears; all the hurt I felt came pouring out with the relief that she was no longer my manager. Our friendship was done. I walked away, and as it says in Matthew 10:14: "Whoever will not receive you or listen to your words . . . shake the dust from your feet." And even though it was tough, I eventually forgave my boss for her harsh treatment, just as God required. I was excited about my new job and praised God for implementing His plan to provide rest for me and time at home so Susan could have her surgery.

A NEW BEGINNING

The next day, Monday, November 5, 2007, I met my new manager, Julianna, and worked for her for fourteen years. She was an excellent manager, and leaving Julianna would become the saddest part of retiring from Oracle. God helped me survive and escape a bad situation through this fortuitous transfer. My good friend Barbara also joined her team with Wally from the Tax class. And yes, Susan finally had her surgery, which was successful.

One of the sad things I found out later was that a group at Oracle University needed a person for six months in a work-at-home position. My boss never told them that I needed a work-at-home job. But in hindsight, the transfer was better for me in the long run. As Genesis 50:20 says: "Even though you meant harm to me, God meant it for good, to achieve this present end."

In our new jobs in the writers' group at Oracle, Wally, Barbara, and I started documenting the new Oracle applications, and sometime later, the Oracle curriculum for Oracle University (OU) was added to our workload. Our experience at OU helped us move into lead positions in the writers' group. We created two courses that combined all the financial applications for the newest product. The three of us taught the two courses over two weeks to the Oracle University instructors who needed to learn the new material. The project managers for each application attended to answer questions. When I taught the Assets section, the project manager turned to Julianna and asked, "Where did she come from?" It seems he was quite impressed with my teaching skills. OU trained me well and gave me lots of practice. God had plans for those skills as my life continued, not only in the writers' group at Oracle but later in teaching retreats and quiet days and leading programs on many spiritual topics.

GEORGE'S CLOSE CALL

I worked from home for many years, which helped when emergencies arose, like when my sweet husband, George, had a close call in November 2009. I had been away on one of my retreats. When I returned home late Sunday afternoon, he was in bed—unlike

George. He said he had been sick since Thursday but didn't tell me because he didn't want to ruin my retreat. He had gone to the doctor on Friday, but the doctor couldn't find anything wrong, so he didn't do any lab work. George's stomach was now extremely swollen, and he had a cough. I asked him what he had eaten. He said nothing since Thursday.

Monday morning, we went back to his doctor, and again, he couldn't find anything wrong, so the doctor didn't do lab work or tests. He just told George to rest. On Tuesday morning, as I walked out the door to escort Isaiah to the school bus, George said, "My urine was more blood than water this morning." I didn't know what to do. I started praying for guidance, and God said, "**Your mother went to the hospital on Tuesday and was dead on Saturday.**" I took that message to mean it was serious and we needed to go to the hospital. So we went to the emergency room after Isaiah was on the bus.

The following nine days were full of ups and downs, worry and prayers, support and hugs from family and friends, and God's miracles. As I waited in the emergency room, I started sending out texts and emails for prayer support, telling everyone that George had been breathing funny for a few days and was very sick. After many tests, the doctor said George was in renal failure, and his kidneys had shut down due to a severe urinary tract infection.

By that afternoon, we were in the intensive care unit (ICU). The doctors added sepsis to his diagnostics—blood poisoning from the terrible urinary tract infection. They finally put him on IV antibiotics and a catheter. They told me we would be there for a while. I couldn't use my cell phone, so email messages from my laptop to family and friends kept me calm. A friend from our church brought me a late lunch. When she heard it was sepsis, she shared with me that only 50 percent of people survive. WOW. We needed a miracle! My friend called our new priest as we needed all the help we could get. Father Kulma rushed over and gave George the anointing of the sick.[3] What a blessing. As the evening wore on, George was more and more delirious. They made me go home at 10:00 p.m., which was probably a blessing as I got some sleep in my bed and some healthy food to eat.

On day two, I was back early. George was now running a high fever. I continued to beg everyone to pray. George's son and daughter arrived and spent much of the day with me, which was comforting. They were also sending out prayer requests. We all were storming the gates of heaven. The following two days had ups and downs, and we sent out more prayer requests. Six doctors from different specialties were doing consults. I was very worried.

On day four, George started improving, and we were all relieved. His daughter, Crystal, shared that on the way home one night, she was listening to "Amazing Love"[4] by the Newsboys. She started to cry, thinking about God's amazing love for her dad by letting him live.

Day five started with a setback. George's breathing had worsened, and his stomach was swelling again. He also had a fever

---

[3] In the Sacrament of Anointing of the Sick, through the priest's ministry, Jesus touches the sick to heal them from sin and sometimes even physical ailments. The primary effect of the Sacrament is spiritual healing by which the sick person receives the Holy Spirit's gift of peace and courage to deal with the difficulties that accompany serious illness or the frailty of old age. There is no need to wait until a person reaches death to receive the Sacrament.
[4] "Amazing Love," written by Billy James Foote and performed by the Newsboys.

again, so more prayer requests were sent. I didn't want to go home that night because he always did better when I was there to run interference and hold his hand, but the hospital insisted. Day six was Sunday. I slept a bit later that morning, 7:40 a.m. instead of 7:00 a.m.! Susan said that wasn't sleeping in. George was a bit better that morning. They doubled the antibiotics as his white count was still too high, and his liver function was still off. Our church brought us the Precious Body that day. Such a blessing! And prayers around the world continued for George. Two doctors said he could go home, but the primary doctor said no. He still had an infection, and the source was unknown. When I took a break, I ran into my gastrologist in the hall and practically dragged him in to see George. God had been telling me there was a problem with his stomach. So my gastrologist finally agreed to do an endoscope on George's stomach.

On day seven, I was so tired, so while my gastrologist did the endoscopy on his stomach, I fell asleep in the lounge chair in the waiting room. My gastrologist was kneeling beside me as I woke. He apologized for not believing me. The endoscope showed a lot of damage to the stomach and the esophagus and a massive bleeding ulcer, so now George had new meds. He still had a fever. George was crying when I left him that night. He didn't want to be in the hospital anymore, which made me cry too. We were both giving in to the stress.

Days eight and nine found us both very tired of the routine, and I was running on empty. It was tough to get up and go to the hospital. I was grateful for the continuing prayers. We finally got our miracle thanks to the incredible prayer support and God's grace and mercy, and George got to go home late on day nine. What a relief. We were both joyful at being at home again.

Little did I know on the first day that my "home and office" would be a hospital room for nine days. I was grateful for an excellent hospital staff that helped me feel at home. Thanks to their generosity, I could be near George and communicate with the outside world. Not only did it help me keep working, but it also sidetracked me from worrying.

A few days after being discharged, his new doctor told us that a kidney stone caused all the drama. George had a procedure the month before to break up the stone. One of the pieces got stuck in his urethra, unbeknownst to George. The doctor who did the original procedure never checked on George or returned my phone calls. I was very angry but was glad George had a new doctor. The ulcer resulted from George taking too much pain medicine due to the pain of the stone. I was thankful for all the prayer support and answers to prayers. He had to have a few more procedures but recovered in a few weeks. Praise God for all the miracles!

THE LIGHTS WERE GETTING DIM

In early 2014, George and I saw Dr. Sekili, our longtime cardiologist. George and the doctor chatted, and I heard Dr. Sekili say, "Maybe you should have a heart catheterization[5] since it has been over ten years since the last one."

I chimed in and said, "Yes!"

So, a few weeks later, as I sat in the waiting room, I was praying, but the procedure seemed to be taking longer than it should. Finally,

---

[5] Cardiac catheterization is a diagnostic procedure that assesses how well a patient's heart is functioning. The procedure involves inserting a tube and pushing a small camera through an artery into the heart to see what is going on inside the heart.

Dr. Sekili appeared. He said, "Everything is fine." One look at his face told me that wasn't true. He was white as a sheet. He quickly ushered me into the private room off the waiting area. Then, Dr. Sekili said George's heart stopped during the procedure, but they got him back quickly. He said it was only the second time in all his hundreds of heart catheterizations he had done that he had a patient's heart stop. I could tell Dr. Sekili was visibly shaken, and so was I. I started asking many questions, the first being, "When can I see George?"

Dr. Sekili explained that four wires carry the electrical impulse to the ventricles. George only had one; the other three were gone. Dr. Sekili thought it was a side effect of George's swine flu as a child. The tiny camera used in the heart catheterization touched the remaining wire and stopped his heart. As George tells it:

> I was watching the monitor and saw my heart stop.
> I remained calm while Dr. Sekili and the staff ran
> around like squirrels and told me to cough, keep
> coughing, and cough harder!

Then he always adds as a joke: "I kept coughing, but the lights were getting a little dim." Luckily, he never lost consciousness.

Dr. Sekili called his friend, the doctor specializing in heart defibrillators, to come over during his lunch hour. The doctors decided that they would put in some form of pacemaker depending on the damage they found the following week. George was given the Cadillac of defibrillators that performed all the heart functions possible. George's heart function was only 25 percent before the defibrillator, and it was now almost 60 percent. The timing and the results were indeed a miracle, as the last wire could have stopped at any time, and he would have died immediately.

RETIREMENT

The best way I simplified my life was by retiring in November 2021. My twenty-four years at Oracle were like a pond you toss a rock in—ripples going out further and further. Some folks are in the inner circles and remain close, others come for a while and then flow out, and still others reappear and cross into your life again. Leaving my friends was one of the saddest parts of retirement.

My time at Oracle parallels another story that began in 1980 and ran through my whole life. I encountered persecution, credit card fraud, power struggles, and more. The encounters of mystical significance unfolded without me knowing where God was leading me. I continued to stumble through His plan and hoped if I trusted Him, He would lead me on the right path. Years later, I can now see God's plan clearly, and I'm in awe of how far He took me and my prayer order. God surprised me by teaching me many lessons and providing an unexpected miracle. I came to believe what Thomas Merton's prayer in *Thoughts in Solitude* says: "And I know that if I do this, you will lead me by the right road, though I may know nothing about it. Therefore I will trust you always . . . I will not fear, for you are ever with me."[6] Amen.

---

[6] Thomas Merton, *Thoughts in Solitude* (New York: Farrar, Straus and Giroux, 1958, 1999), 80.

CHAPTER EIGHT

HANNAH MEANS GRACE

Growing in The Order of the Daughters of the King

To fall in love with God is the greatest of all romances;
To seek Him the greatest adventure;
To find Him, the greatest human achievement.
—St. Augustine of Hippo

Nothing is more practical than finding God,
That is, than falling in Love in a quite absolute, final way.
What you are in love with,
what seizes your imagination, will affect everything.
It will decide what will get you out of bed in the morning,
what you do with your evenings,
how you spend your weekends,
what you read, whom you know,
what breaks your heart,
and what amazes you with joy and gratitude.
Fall in Love, stay in love,
and it will decide everything.
— Fr. Joseph P. Whelan, SJ[1]

---

[1] Jesuits.org shares the following quotation by Fr. Joseph P. Whelan, SJ (and often attributed to Fr. Pedro Arrupe, SJ) to celebrate Valentine's Day.

Step back with me to 1980 when my first husband and I helped start Christ the King Episcopal Church, a small mission church. After two years, the rector encouraged the church women to start a Daughters of the King[2] chapter. I went to the meeting knowing very little about the DOK. There, I learned that the Daughters took a lifelong vow to pray daily, serve God, and evangelize women and girls, and it was simple to become a Daughter. All we needed to do was attend three meetings. After that, we could become Daughters and receive our silver crosses—symbolizing our lifetime vow and membership.

At that initial meeting, I had no clue why I was there and didn't feel called to become a Daughter. I was going along with the crowd and our priest's wishes, but something in my heart told me that a habit of daily prayer and participation in a community of women who prayed would be helpful in my life. I was often lonely and isolated from my family and others. The abuse in my marriage had dried up my faith and caused me to stuff my feelings inside a shell throughout that time in my life. The introduction of DOK in my life relit a tiny spark of faith almost immediately. It was as though God rekindled a flame I still had deep in my heart, and I began to grow in the DOK.

I attended my three meetings and got my cross in August 1982. I started praying daily, watching for opportunities to serve others, and evangelizing as occasions arose. Wearing my silver cross each day helped me have open conversations with others. It felt good

---

[2] The Order of the Daughters of the King, Inc® (DOK) is a women's prayer order started in 1885 in the Episcopal Church. A Daughter pledges herself to a lifelong program of prayer, service, and evangelism.

to have Christian friends to share and pray with and help fill the gap of meaningful relationships I had experienced since moving to Houston in 1978. As I reflected on that special day, I thought, *I'm amazed at how God had started the plan for my life. The Daughters would become my dear friends and spiritual mothers, and their prayers would eventually save and restore my life.*

In 1986, as things at home got worse, I planned to run away from my abusive husband with the help of my company and Scott,[3] a business friend who lived in New York. The first step in my plan was to travel to New York City—under the guise of a fake business trip—so I could find a job and a place to live. I had grown through DOK to be more confident in my decisions and was realizing that the abuse had to stop. Several of my sisters in DOK and coworkers supported my plan. I was afraid to stay any longer. Tom, my abusive first husband, had tried to commit suicide a few days before I was to leave by taking an overdose of pills. After he passed out, I took him to the hospital.

At church the following day, I was exhausted and turned my life over to God. I prayed all through the service for His guidance. I truly surrendered my life to Him. My sisters in DOK surrounded me and embraced me with hugs and kind words. But questions kept going through my mind as my favorite song, "I Am the Bread of Life," played during Holy Communion. *Could I run away and leave Tom in the hospital? Was New York City where I should go?* As I stood up to leave church, I heard a mighty voice say, **"Everything will be okay with Scott."** I felt like a ton of bricks had been dropped on me. I had to sit back down. The voice was so strong; I knew God was

---

[3] Name changed.

speaking to me, reassuring me that the business trip to New York was the correct decision.

After I returned from a successful trip to New York City, doubts started again, so I went to see my priest for one more confirmation that I should run away and I was indeed following God's plan for my life. I still had the fear I couldn't make it on my own. While listening to her, God spoke over my priest's voice and said, **"You have done everything I told you to do."** God's second mystical message in less than two weeks gave me the peace and courage to go on. A serenity enveloped me, and a few weeks later, I ran away with my daughter Susan, leaving my son Bill, who was a senior in high school, with one of his teachers.

MOVING TO MY SECOND DAUGHTER CHAPTER

I did follow my plan with God's help and the help of many others in September 1986. I had been attending Al-Anon secretly in Houston, so I continued in Connecticut, where God arranged for me to live and work. After I ran away, my husband joined AA and stopped drinking. He was attending therapy and seemed to be making progress. After much prayer and discussion, we reconciled in January 1987, and Susan and I came home to Houston. My husband decided to move us back to Ascension Episcopal Church, where we attended before helping to start Christ the King. I knew he was trying to stop me from attending DOK because he blamed my sisters for my running away. He didn't understand God's hand in my decision. I was changing and growing in Christ, but he wanted to assert control over me again. Ascension didn't have a DOK chapter, so I talked to the priest about starting one. He said he would pray about it.

In 1988, Sharon Lundgren and her family came to Ascension. I saw Sharon's DOK cross and welcomed her. There were other Daughters at Ascension also. In a few months, Sharon presented our priest with a folder with all the essential information about The Order of the Daughters of the King, and he agreed that she could start a chapter. I was so excited that there would be a DOK chapter at Ascension as my heart missed my sisters from Christ the King. The Ascension Chapter was instituted in 1989, and I was one of its members. My husband's plan of moving me to Ascension didn't save our marriage. On September 28, 1989, the court finalized my divorce.[4] I felt free, and with therapy and time to recover, I overcame my fear and eventually felt safe. After my divorce, I sat in DOK meetings, listening to my sisters, and grew closer to God. I didn't say much; instead, I cried through the meetings. Recovery brought up many mixed feelings, and I found single parenting challenging. My sisters prayed for my children and me, and God gave me many opportunities to grow and heal.

THE HOLY SPIRIT MOVES

As my new life went on, God made a historical change in the DOK that would eventually open the door for me to repay The Order for saving my life from my abusive marriage. God put a set of events into motion that started in 1971 before I was even a Daughter. Yet, no one—not even Ethel Ripley, past national president of The Order of the Daughters of the King—was aware of the ecumenical journey God was taking her on or that her openness would lead many years

---

[4] The full story is found in my book, *Whole, Single, Free, Me! An Escape from Domestic Abuse.*

later to the spread of The Order of the Daughters of the King to the Roman Catholic Church and beyond. Here is the story Ethel told me:

> In November 1971, I was asked to represent the Daughters of the King at an Episcopal Evangelism Conference. I was the only woman and was very nervous about speaking in a room full of priests. I asked God to arrange it so I wouldn't have to speak from the pulpit. The night before, a priest sensed I was nervous about speaking the next day and asked if he could pray with me. After we prayed, he told me to look at the audience and find someone who had Jesus' presence shining in them.
>
> I awoke the following day and had a wonderful sense of peace. The session had been moved from the sanctuary to the parish hall. When I scanned the room, I was amazed to see every person in the room had the light of Christ resting on their shoulders. Miraculously, all my prayers had been answered.
>
> I prayed many times for God to help me find the priest who had prayed with me that night so I could thank him. God answered my prayers in 1985 at a Province IV [Regional] Assembly. The Daughters chapter from Calvary Episcopal Church asked me to sit with them at dinner. As I sat down, a quiet nudging said, "Ask the priest with them if he was

the priest that prayed for you." So I did, and Father Jack said, "Yes."

As we enjoyed dinner, Father Jack shared a dilemma. The Episcopal and Roman Catholic Churches shared facilities over the years because each had a fire. The Holy Family Catholic Church priest noticed women from Calvary Episcopal Church wearing small crosses. He said he had observed these women visiting the sick and taking active roles in many ministries. Then, Father Jack told him about The Order. After learning that the Roman Catholic Church had no similar organization, the priest asked his bishop for permission to start a chapter.

I was the national president of The Order, so Father Jack asked me what he should do next. He had already spoken with his Episcopal Bishop and had his permission to proceed. I asked two mentors from the Calvary Chapter to meet with the Holy Family women and guide them through the training program. With the guidance of the Holy Spirit, the historical moment arrived with the admission of twelve members to the first chapter of the Roman Catholic Daughters of the King on Saturday, December 13th, 1986. Then, the 1988 Triennial Convention[5] mem-

---

[5] Every three years, The Order holds a convention called the Triennial to vote on bylaws, elect the National Council members, receive updates on the international growth, benefit from many spiritual teachings and workshops, and celebrate as a sisterhood.

bership approved the change in the bylaws admit-
ting Roman Catholic members.

Establishing the Holy Family Roman Catholic Chapter in
Ashland, Kentucky, was indeed a movement of the Holy Spirit.
Finally, after 100 years, The Order opened to women who were
communicants of another church that was not in the Anglican
Communion. And the mystical way the historical event happened,
with the Roman Catholics being admitted before the bylaws were
changed or anyone ever thought to have Roman Catholic members,
could have only been planned and orchestrated by an awesome God.

Many years later, the historical change in the bylaws and God's
plans opened the door to the first Lutheran chapter of The Order of
the Daughters of the King, which was instituted at Zion Lutheran
Church (ELCA) on February 4, 2001.

The Roman Catholics becoming part of The Order also greatly
affected my life. During my journey of recovery that began with
my divorce in 1989, God started calling me to the Roman Catholic
Church. I attended many Roman Catholic events designed to help
divorced and widowed people heal because the Episcopal Church
at the time only had a few support groups. My DOK membership
was essential to me, so I ignored God's call to the Roman Catholic
Church at first. At a DOK meeting, I shared that I felt God was
calling me to the Roman Catholic Church. Some of my DOK sisters
started bringing me articles on the new Roman Catholic chapters
in The Order from *The Royal Cross,* the quarterly publication of The
Order of the Daughters of the King and assured me I could still
attend meetings at Ascension Chapter.

Finally, I realized I was attending the Roman Catholic Church more than the Episcopal Church, but I couldn't take Holy Communion. Not taking Holy Communion made me feel like an outsider, and I wanted to belong. I made many new friends at the various programs and events I attended. So I gave in to God's call with some fear. As I attended RCIA[6] classes, I still had my doubts about some of the teachings of the Roman Catholic Church. My fiancée, George, assured me I would understand them over time, and he was right. So, at Easter in 1994, just six months before my wedding to George and after I received my annulment,[7] I converted to the Roman Catholic Church. My confirmation was so special, with George as my sponsor. I had taken his mother's name, Theresa, for my confirmation name, but I wanted to surprise him, so I hadn't told him. It brought tears to his eyes. His mother had died just a few months earlier. My confirmation name was also in honor of Saint Therese the Little Flower. I love flowers, and George has always brought me lovely bouquets. Our wedding was a beautiful Catholic Mass with praise music and spiritual readings that meant something to us. Some of my DOK sisters attended and celebrated my new life with us. Many of them were my spiritual mothers along my journey to become a whole person, so it was only fitting they shared our joy.

---

[6] The Rite of Christian Initiation of Adults (RCIA) is a process developed by the Catholic Church for prospective converts to Catholicism to gradually introduce them to aspects of Catholic beliefs and practices.

[7] An annulment is a declaration by a Church tribunal (a Catholic church court) that a marriage thought to be valid according to Church law fell short of at least one of the essential elements required for a binding union within the church. An annulment has no effect on the legitimacy of children.

GOD LEADING ME TO OBEDIENCE

After converting to the Roman Catholic Church, I struggled as the lone Roman Catholic when attending Episcopal DOK Eucharistic celebrations. I was constantly challenged to walk in love with my DOK sisters, who thought I should unite with them by taking Holy Communion—since the Episcopal Church had open Communion for all baptized Christians.

God finally hit me between the eyes when I attended a DOK Assembly at Camp Allen in the fall of 1996. During one particular service, as we prepared for Holy Communion, I found myself debating, again, whether I should or shouldn't take Communion. I went back and forth in my mind. *God, is it right or wrong? My Catholic Church said it was wrong, but I took Holy Communion in the Episcopal Church, where I belonged for thirty years before I converted to the Roman Catholic Church. Was that wrong? God, what do you want me to do? Please give me an answer.*

As I stood up to walk down the aisle, the question still in my mind, I heard God's voice say: **"People have died over this question."** At the same time, I saw a vision in front of me. Murdered priests in white garments lying around a raised altar with beautiful gold vessels spilled on the top of the altar, blood and wine flowing everywhere. I stopped, feeling even more confused by what God was trying to tell me in this mystical encounter. I slowly walked forward and was blessed by the priest. I returned to my seat, thinking about those who died fighting for their faith. *Do I have the courage to die for Jesus? To fight for what I believe?* Tears started flowing down my cheeks. The vision's picture remained etched in my consciousness for the rest of my life, humbling and bringing me into obedience to my chosen church.

God also gave me another mystical encounter while serving as a Eucharistic minister many years later, in 2007. I was giving the cup when I noticed a strange area above the wine after the first person had taken the cup. It looked like blood—dark red and sticky. I continued giving the cup, but the spot didn't move or dissolve into the wine. It was like it was too thick to slip into the wine. After all the parishioners took the cup, I drank the rest, as is the tradition in the Catholic Church. The spot was gone when I put the cup down on the tray. I have always believed in Transubstantiation,[8] but the drop of blood just confirmed my conviction that I was to be obedient and only take Holy Communion in the Roman Catholic Church.

When I attend Holy Communion with my Episcopalian or Anglican sisters, I go up and am blessed by the priest. I do this out of love. Although I don't take the bread and wine, I'm there in full communion with my sisters, receiving their peace and love and loving them in return while respecting them, their beliefs, and their clergy, as well as my own.

Then, God unexpectedly gave me more understanding of the vision in a faraway place in the spring of 2019. I felt strange when I walked into the Cathedral of Glasgow, part of the Church of Scotland. As I walked, I saw the vision again of the priests dying around the altar—another mystical encounter so many years later. *Is*

---

[8] Paragraph 1431 of the Catholic Catechism states: By the consecration, the transubstantiation of the bread and wine into the Body and Blood of Christ is brought about. Under the consecrated species of bread and wine, Christ himself, living and glorious, is present in a true, real, and substantial manner: his Body and his Blood, with his soul and his divinity (cf. Council of Trent: DS 1640; 1651).

this where the massacre took place, or is it just a reminder of the struggle that took place in many churches during the battles between Protestants and Catholics? The church felt cold to me, like an empty tomb. Most of the church was a museum filled with plaques and other memorabilia honoring scientists, military heroes, and other citizens who added to humankind's history. In the center was a small worship space buried inside the cold, dark walls. I felt God's sadness over His children fighting in His holy places. My tears flowed as I continued to walk through the cathedral. I realized that the constant strife between God's beloved children broke His heart. What I learned was that we have more in common, Protestants and Catholics, than we do apart. Salvation through faith in Jesus Christ matters most. We have a greater enemy in the world who wants us to fight each other rather than grow together in respect, mutual love, and understanding that would go far to bring peace to the world.

STARTING HANNAH CHAPTER

In 1996, my sisters from the Ascension Chapter encouraged me to start a Roman Catholic Daughters of the King chapter. My sisters were always loving to me, but a part of me wanted Roman Catholic sisters. I prayed for God's will, and one day, I heard a phrase on the local Christian radio station: "Hannah means grace." Hmm . . . I began reading the story of Hannah in the first and second chapters of 1 Samuel every Saturday night at Mass. Hannah had incredible faith and was a prayer warrior. I found God's answer in her story and started the Hannah Chapter on January 26, 1997, at my new church, St. Justin Martyr Catholic Church, with the help of my Episcopalian sisters. The chapter's name reminded me of God's grace in saving and restoring my life. Many attended our installation and celebrated the first chapter in the Roman Catholic Archdiocese of Galveston-Houston. I was joyful, as I now had sisters in my church. Little did I know then that my movement to the Roman Catholic Church and starting Hannah Chapter was just one more step in God's plan for my life as a Daughter of the King.

GRACE JUNIOR DOK CHAPTER

The institution of Grace Junior Chapter[9] fulfilled a goal God had put on my heart since starting the Hannah Chapter for the Senior DOK. Following Hannah's name, which means *grace*, it seemed only right that the junior chapter's name had to be Grace, and the first members agreed.

Many Daughters from all levels of The Order attended this historic institution (the first in the Roman Catholic Church), and the National Junior Daughters Chair presented the charter to Father Tom Rafferty on April 29, 2001. My heart was full of thanksgiving and joy as I watched the ceremony. I prayed, "God, please help all these young girls grow closer to you through Junior DOK."

I had felt God called me to be the directress, but because of my job and other activities, I found the mother of one of the Juniors to be the directress. She did a good job, but her daughter lost interest, so she resigned. Another Senior DOK stepped forward in answer to my prayers and the nudging of the Holy Spirit. She was younger and energetic. The girls loved her and thoroughly enjoyed the activities

---

[9] Junior DOK is open to girls seven to twenty-one who make a promise to pray daily and serve others. Junior chapters are under the direction of a directress from the Senior DOK chapter at their parish.

she planned. I breathed a deep sigh of relief and went on with my traveling.

In 2003, I got a call about an incident at one of the meetings. I sat in on the Junior Daughters meeting on my next trip home. All was going well until, suddenly, the directress' behavior changed. After prayer and discussion with Father Tom, I asked her to step aside temporarily while we sorted things out, and I became the temporary directress. The directress went to the doctor and discovered she had a brain tumor that was causing the personality changes and other health issues. The Juniors made her get well cards and prayed for her at every meeting, as did the Senior DOK. God did answer our prayers, eventually, when she recovered from the cancer. Unfortunately, she wasn't strong enough to return as the directress.

Since I thought my time was temporary, I refused to be called directress and kept looking for someone else. I had no luck, but after many months of ignoring the call, I realized God wanted me to be the directress. Still worried I couldn't do the job adequately, I gave in to God's plan. The Juniors taught me to love God in the simple faith of a child. Their sweet acceptance of all, their search for a relationship with God, their hunger for more prayers, and their pure love of life spoke volumes. I grew by leaps and bounds as their directress. I was blessed and challenged by developing service projects and trying various prayers to keep the Juniors invested and growing. Thank you, God—you knew best!

SHARING THE DIVINE MERCY CHAPLET

In December 2006, I invited my Junior Daughters to a slumber party. We had so much fun. My daughter, Susan, helped the girls make and wrap fragrant bath salts as Christmas gifts for their moms. We enjoyed pizza and other goodies, followed by games. After getting ready for bed, I wanted to close the evening with prayer before we all climbed into our sleeping bags. So I introduced the girls to the Chaplet of Divine Mercy[10] musical version, a prayer I had grown to love.

The girls were giggling and moving around as young girls do when in a group. I put in the CD, and we started to pray. At first, the girls said the opening prayers but didn't fully participate. I continued to pray and embraced the spirit of the Chaplet, and as the beautiful refrain, "For the Sake of His Sorrowful Passion," was repeated over and over, gradually, one by one, the girls were on their knees, singing at the top of their lungs. The singing was so beautiful, full of voices—many more than just my girls singing. The Holy Spirit filled the room.

After the Chaplet finished, the girls were reticent. Finally, one of them said, "Miss Kathy, did you hear the angels singing with us?"

"Yes," I said, "I heard the angels singing with you, making the most beautiful music for our Lord Jesus."

All the girls quietly shared their experience of the angels coming to sing with them and how the Holy Spirit filled the room. An extraordinary mystical encounter and memorable time with God and my beloved girls that deepened all our faith. I learned that if I provided meaningful prayer time, the Holy Spirit would enfold my sweet girls in God's divine love and accomplish much more teaching than I could ever do with words. I also learned I didn't have to do

---

[10] The Chaplet of Divine Mercy is a powerful prayer that asks for God's mercy and is prayed on a rosary. To learn how to pray the Chaplet: https://www.thedivinemercy.org/message/devotions/pray-the-Chaplet.

everything for the girls. God filled the gaps and took the girls and me further than I hoped for or imagined.

LITTLE DAUGHTERS OF THE GOOD SHEPHERD CHAPTER

My Juniors traveled to Down Home Ranch[11] in Elgin, Texas, twice in 2004 and 2005. The girls loved the ranch and all the activities. On the second visit, we had a slumber party in one of the bunkhouses with the Down Home special needs young adults studying to be Junior Daughters. Their disabilities made it too difficult for them to do the Senior DOK study, so Sharon Lundgren, a house mother and national president of The Order, created a modified study.

The girls spent the day doing crafts, playing games, and enjoying each other's company. Then, after getting into their pajamas, I read them children's stories until they started falling asleep. It was a mystical encounter with my girls and the Down Home young women bonding as sisters with the Holy Spirit filling all our hearts. I saw my girls soften and be gentle and considerate as they helped the young women at Down Home. All of them shared laughter and simple joy at being outside in God's creation that filled my heart with thanksgiving for the marvelous place my friend Judy and her husband built at God's direction.

---

[11] Down Home Ranch is a working farm and ranch, founded in 1989 by my friend, Judy, a Daughter of the King and her husband for their young daughter born with Down syndrome in Elgin, Texas. The Ranch is inspired by the writings and work with adults with intellectual disabilities of Henri Nouwen and Rudolf Steiner and driven by the lack of resources available to these special children and adults.

One Saturday in 2005, the Down Home Juniors joined my Juniors at St. Justin Martyr for a day of making crafts, eating, and learning. I enjoyed watching my girls gently help the Down Home Juniors with the crafts, laughing and talking as girls do. I taught all the Juniors about the Trinity. I prayed for several weeks about introducing the concept, and God gave me this analogy: Ice, Water, Steam: Father God, Son Jesus, the Holy Spirit. The first three are forms of water, and the second three are "the Godhead, [which]. . . is one, their glory equal, and their majesty coeternal."[12] It was simple, but all the Juniors grasped the Trinity concept: Three persons united in One God.

Later, on August 13, 2005, the institution of the Little Daughters of the Good Shepherd Chapter took place at St. Justin Martyr with Sharon Lundgren as directress and Father Tom officiating. It was a glorious and historic event, the first chapter of Junior Daughters with Disabilities and the second junior chapter in the Roman Catholic Church. And it was beautiful to watch the lessons my girls learned with these precious young ladies. My girls became kinder, more tolerant of others, and grateful for the small blessings in their lives. My prayers were for my girls to carry these experiences with their sisters in Christ throughout their lives. Thank you, God, for the Little Daughters of the Good Shepherd.

THE CINDY OLSEN CHAPTER

In early 2007, my Senior and Junior chapters struggled after Father Tom left our church. The Seniors started fading away because a

---

[12] Catechism, paragraph 266.

Catholic women's group began at the church and attracted members by stressing the Episcopalian roots of The Order versus the Catholic roots of their group. Then suddenly, I received a letter telling me the Juniors couldn't meet at St. Justin's facilities anymore. St. Justin's was my girls and their families' church home. Several of my parents were upset that the girls couldn't meet in their home church and complained to the Archbishop's office even after I asked them not to, which made the problem worse. I no longer felt welcome at St. Justin's. George said, "Let's dust off our feet and go to St. Edith Stein." We had moved several months earlier but continued to drive a long way to St. Justin Martyr instead of going to St. Edith Stein Catholic Church[13], a mile from our new home. I was heartbroken to leave St. Justin's, where we had many close friends. The change turned out to be God's plan to bless us with new friends and new ministries. I met with the Juniors temporarily at one of the Junior's homes to keep the peace.

I started praying for a new meeting place for my precious girls where we would have more space for crafts and service projects. In 2008, God led me back to Christ the King Episcopal Church, not far from St. Justin. I said "back" because I helped start the church and the Daughters chapter in the 1980s when I was still an Episcopalian. The Daughters there supported and prayed for me while I was in my abusive marriage. It was in that church that God first spoke and encouraged me to leave that marriage. And here I was twenty-six years later, meeting with the priest and some of the same sisters and

---

[13] St. Edith Stein: Saint Teresa Benedicta of the Cross was a Roman Catholic convert from Judaism, Carmelite nun, philosopher, and spiritual writer who was executed by the Nazis at Auschwitz concentration camp because of her Jewish ancestry and who is regarded as a modern martyr.

pleading for a place for my girls. In exchange for a place to meet, I promised I would help them start a junior chapter.

So, we began. I had three new Roman Catholic girls who needed training, and they had four interested in Junior DOK. My older girls helped me with the training, which made me proud of how well they had learned their lessons. They were beautiful examples of what it meant to be Junior DOK. To my surprise, God's miracle provided the place, and Ruth, an assistant directress for my chapter, and Veronica, from Christ the King, to train as their directress. I was so relieved that I had help and support. I told the girls to pray about the name of the new Christ the King chapter, but nothing was agreed on. We continued to study, and as it got closer to submitting the charter of the new chapter, I again asked them to come up with a name. The girls suggested several names, and then the name Cyndy Olsen came out of the air. Cyndy was my friend and DOK sister in Christ when I attended the church in the 1980s. Between the first meeting, where I asked for a place to meet, and two months later, Cyndy died from a blood clot after surgery. I was so sad when she died, but her funeral was a celebration of the beautiful person she was. Her Senior DOK chapter did the special service DOK has for our members who have died. Several Juniors attended and were touched to see the DOK sisterhood in action. We all immediately knew the name was a spiritual inspiration from God. I was overjoyed that the girls wanted to remember her by naming the chapter after her.

The Cynthia Olsen Episcopal Chapter at Christ the King Episcopal Church was instituted on October 5, 2008. All my Juniors in both chapters met, played, served, and grew together. It was heartwarming to see them growing together. Eventually, the lines between Episcopal and Roman Catholic Juniors blurred, and they became sisters in Christ. It is a beautiful testimony to the girls' love and respect for each other. It taught me that it is possible to cross denominational lines with respect, love, and understanding.

A year prior, this ecumenism wasn't as clear to me. One evening in 2007, while driving my granddaughter, Courtney, home after the party, she asked me when she could become a Senior Daughter. Her comment made me think, *Will there be a place for her and the other non-Episcopal girls? Will this excitement for being a Junior DOK continue when they become Senior Daughters?* My oldest Junior DOK was a Methodist. She had been a faithful Junior for eight years and had just turned sixteen. She was one of many examples of why I continued to pray for God to open the doors of The Order and remove the prejudice on all sides.

Jesus, like our sweet Juniors, saw no divisions other than those willing to give up their lives and follow Him. My prayer continues for all the members of The Order of the Daughters of the King to walk in the procession in heaven and sing: *Lift high the cross, the love of Christ proclaim, Till all the world adore His sacred name*[14]—Junior and Senior, black and white, rich and poor, Episcopalian, Roman Catholic, Lutheran, and Anglican, and more, in a sisterhood where all members are equal and secure in unconditional love for each other and our Lord.

ADVENTURES WITH THE JUNIORS

God's plan for me as a directress also involved taking my Juniors from 2006 to 2012 to three triennials and several Province VII and

---

[14] Lift High the Cross is the hymn of The Order. Words by George W. Kitchin and Michal R. Newbolt and music by Sydney H. Nicholson.

Diocese of Texas Junior DOK retreats. Watching the girls bond and mature in their walk with Christ on these outings was inspiring. Those who could go would go back to our chapter meetings and share with those who couldn't go with us. I learned that making these outings possible was essential for the girls' bonding and spiritual growth, so I started reaching out for scholarships and funds from other sources. Amazingly, God always provided enough.

Ruth, Veronica, and I helped my dear friend Patsy Thompson, Junior Director for the Diocese of Texas, with retreats held at Camp Allen. She was a gifted leader. She taught the girls about giving to others when we made dolls to send to our Junior Chapters in Central America and pocket prayer bears to send with the troops going to Afghanistan and other overseas assignments. Mystical glimpses filled the retreats as the Holy Spirit touched the girls in various ways. One of my girls had a beautiful servant's heart and was always in the kitchen helping with the dishes and other tasks. Others sought out new girls or girls alone from their chapters to befriend.

My oldest granddaughter, Courtney, one of the few who could sew, spent hours at an old antique sewing machine with me and another Senior DOK sewing the finished dolls together for the others. To this day, she still talks about the beautiful experience she had serving the other Juniors. My granddaughters both went to one retreat. The youngest, Erin, bonded with Patsy and had several conversations with her. I was thankful, as Erin wasn't a Junior Daughter but now felt included. Everyone loved Patsy. The girls responded one year by bringing books to recreate Patsy's spiritual library, which was lost along with her home and all her possessions in Hurricane Ike. Patsy's giving spirit inspired them to share.

One of the most mystical encounters was when Patsy wanted to try healing prayer with the girls. She feared none would come up and let us pray on them, so I asked a couple of my older girls to go first. Well, that didn't work. As soon as Patsy announced what we were doing, all the girls raced to sit in the chair and be prayed on first. So much healing and tears happened with the Holy Spirit filling the room and all our hearts. For some girls, it was the first time anyone had prayed on them, and the Holy Spirit especially touched those girls with God's divine love. The most touching part of the service for me was when the girls all surrounded Patsy, who suffered from leukemia and prayed for her. Later, I was excited to see some girls return to their churches and triennials, where they volunteered for the healing prayer ministry.

MY GIRLS MOVE ON

At the 2012 Triennial, most of my Junior Daughters — Episcopal and Roman Catholic — transitioned to Senior Daughters into a new senior chapter called Mary of Magdala, all but my sweet Methodist Junior. As a Methodist, The Order still hadn't opened enough for her to become a Senior DOK. I was heartbroken.

The girls wanted to stay together in one chapter. Grace's chapter was disbanded, and Cynthia Olsen went on with younger girls. The new senior chapter met for the first time at my home on June 29, immediately after the Triennial, to elect officers and make plans for continuing meetings. Unfortunately, many girls were off to college in the fall, so the chapter eventually faded away. Some Cynthia Olsen girls entered the senior chapter at Christ the King Episcopal Church and helped with the continuing junior chapter as assistant directresses. I was sad to end a significant and growing time in my life. The Juniors taught me so much about acceptance of others, enthusiasm at serving, an exuberant thirst to grow deeply in their faith, and joy at spiritual experiences. And even when they kept me up all night, asked me hard questions, or let their energy run well beyond mine, I loved my girls. I continue to pray for them and keep in touch with as many of them as possible. I have watched their social media as they graduate from college, start new jobs, experience life challenges, marry, and have beautiful children. I will be eternally grateful to God for including these beautiful years together in His plan for my life and each of theirs.

Before my joyful time starting Hannah Chapter and leading my sweet Juniors, God had started planting seeds for another part of His plan—a plan that would take me further than I ever dreamed or thought possible in The Order but accompanied by suffering and prejudice.

CHAPTER NINE

MOVING FROM BACKGROUND TO CENTER STAGE

Serving at the DOK National Level

Holy Women

Guide us by Your love, Jesus.
Our feet to follow Your way, as the women who traveled with You.
Our hands to offer kindness, as the woman who anointed You with oil.
Our hearts to stay despite fear, as the women at the foot of the Cross.
Our eyes to the empty tomb as the women who came on the third day.
Our ears to hear and know You, as Mary's when You spoke her name.
Our mouths to tell of You to all, as the women who told You had risen.
May all we take in, and all we give be guided by love in You, Jesus.
Amen.[1]

---

[1] Used by permission of Rev. Wendy K. Abrahamson, in *Echoes of the Spirit: Women's Prayers and Meditations*, Margaret Graham Beers, editor (Cincinnati: Forward Movement Publications, 2000), 5–6.

TRIENNIAL 1997: PHILADELPHIA

A few years after my conversion to the Catholic Church, I attended the National DOK Triennial retreat in Philadelphia in June 1997. This was my first experience with DOK at the national level. During that adventure, Joan Dalrymple from my Episcopal chapter at Ascension surprised me by meeting me at the airport. She took me to the hotel and guided me through the events. I was so grateful for her company and guidance.

At that Triennial, the business meeting discussion about full membership for the Roman Catholics got quite ugly and was tough to sit through for Roman Catholics present. Even though the National Council ratified the change to allow Roman Catholic members, not all the Daughters accepted the change. The angry and prejudiced comments against my church hurt me. I stayed through all the discussions, but tears flowed with my disappointment and sadness when I returned to my room. I questioned my future in The Order. Then I remembered that our founder "Margaret Franklin and our first sisters were not interested in making Episcopalians out of others; they were interested in introducing them to the living God, and His name is Jesus, the Christ."[2]

In my heart, I felt the Roman Catholic members belonged, and so I remained faithful to The Order. Other Roman Catholic chapters began to be born, slowly giving me more sisters and much joy. The three Houston chapters became the first Roman Catholic Archdiocesan Assembly in The Order on June 17, 2000. As I was installed as archdiocesan president, joy and gratitude to God filled

---

[2] Sharon Lundgren, *Revive Us Again: A Daughter's Spiritual Journey* (Self-Published, Sharon Lundgren, 2015), 42.

my soul. I never dreamed I would be a diocesan president. I was so thankful for the presence of many Episcopal and Roman Catholic sisters and leadership from all levels of The Daughters of the King. Father Tom became the first archdiocesan chaplain. Amazing! When I hesitated to convert to the Roman Catholic Church because of my DOK membership, I never dreamed that there would eventually be three Roman Catholic chapters and now a Roman Catholic archdiocese assembly with me as president. I watched God's plan unfold in awe of how far He had taken me in the DOK. I thought, *You continue to surprise me. Is there more to come, Lord?*

TRIENNIAL 2000: DENVER

Little did I know how God would change my life and challenge me in ways I never dreamed of at The Order of the Daughters of the King Triennial Retreat in Denver in June 2000. To everyone's surprise, the current Roman Catholic affiliate representative on the National DOK Council, who had been on the board for the last three years, had decided to step down.

I was suddenly called into the National Council meeting with the newly elected president, Joan Millard. I didn't know her personally, but Sharon Lundgren had given her my name. In shock, I was appointed the Roman Catholic representative for the next three years. It was obvious that God's hand was in this appointment as the newly elected first vice president of The Order was Sharon Lundgren, who belonged to my former chapter at Ascension. Usually, two people from the same chapter don't serve simultaneously at the national level of The Order. God called me to the Roman Catholic Church and nudged me into starting a Roman Catholic chapter, which solved the conflict and opened the door for me to serve nationally. God put His plan into motion even before I knew where He was leading me. I thought about serving at the national level after attending my first Triennial in 1997 but didn't expect it to become a reality. Amazing!

Since the first Roman Catholic chapter was established in 1986, all the triennials have discussed Roman Catholic membership. As I joined the National Council, I didn't realize that a time of persecution was beginning or that God had particular work for me to do. As I took possession of the National Roman Catholic Banner, I assumed my time on the National Council would be quiet. I planned to sit in the background, installing new Roman Catholic chapters and reporting on Roman Catholic events.

FRAUD AND GOD'S SAVING GRACE

Well, sitting in the background was short-lived. Two months after the Triennial, I got a call from the national treasurer, Grace Peyton. She asked if I was a CPA, and I said yes. She said she needed me to look at the financials because she thought The Order was in trouble. Well, she was right. We had a deficit balance of over $110,000. A dues increase should have been submitted and passed at the 2000 Triennial. The shortfall was being hidden by asking DOK members to pay their dues earlier than our September 1 due date. That wasn't all.

A few weeks later, I got a call from a good friend who was the membership chairman for the Diocese of Texas. She said she thought the Diocese of Texas was short-paid on the diocese's share of the dues collected and distributed by the national office. My inexperienced and trusting mind thought there must be a logical explanation. I told her I was going to the national office and would check it out so I could explain the numbers to her when I returned to Texas.

What a trip that was! First was the historical dedication and blessing on Saturday, October 21, 2000, of the Margaret J. Franklin[3] Center in Woodstock, Georgia, the new home of our national office, archives, and chapel. It was a beautiful celebration and time of praising God for His goodness in giving us a permanent office.

Then, back to business. I looked at the dues payment records. I was shocked to find several southern dioceses and provinces, not just the Diocese of Texas, had been short-paid their dues amounts collected by the national office. My friend was right! And I was worried. The problem was that The Order didn't have the money to pay them. So the council quietly asked the dioceses and provinces to forgo the payments, and luckily, only one diocese insisted on payment.

Then, this appointed Roman Catholic representative, who wasn't an elected member of the council, had to meet with the national executive board and Bishop Steve Jecko, The Order's Chaplain, to explain what I had found. I had never met him and was very nervous. I sat across the table from him and slowly read email after email where the national office administrator had lied about the province and diocesan dues payments. Bishop Jecko's eyes got wider and wider, but he never said a word. Finally, when I was done, he turned to the National President Joan Millard and said, "You have a problem."

Eventually, a local, retired CPA volunteered to do an audit, straighten out the books, and help us set up proper accounting procedures. Sadly, he found more fraud. The office administrator

---

[3] Margaret J. Franklin founded The Order. Her greatest characteristic was her gift of hospitality. Her words in the 1892 issue of *The Royal Cross* ring out today: "Let us remember our first work is the salvation of souls."

was allowed to quietly resign if she returned the personal items she bought with The Order's funds. The items appeared at the office, so no charges were filed. Her resignation caused more stress. We had to find a new office administrator.

A few people came for interviews, but we all felt God's choice was one particular candidate. The day she interviewed, her mother was quite sick. We formed a prayer circle to pray for her. I was next to her, holding her hand. As we prayed, I started crying and couldn't stop the intense tears of grief. I didn't understand why. Our chosen candidate seemed to find peace as we prayed. We learned later that her mother had passed as we were praying. Joan Millard explained the mysterious event to me. She said, "A person will take on another person's grief, freeing them and giving them peace." That was what I had done. Understanding the mystical experience helped me let go of the grief. We were all relieved we found a new office administrator and felt she was God's choice.

In hindsight, buying the national office building was a good decision. The national office had operated out of the office administrator's basement. With her unexpected resignation, the new office saved The Order from being homeless in the short term. However, how the new office space was financed wasn't a financially sound decision. The Order was left in a precarious position when the council used restricted funds to pay for the building rather than soliciting donations from the membership. The new National Council managed to shore up the finances by asking quietly and positively for assistance in every issue of *The Royal Cross*. Many council members also contacted members who could give more significant contributions. The National Council members didn't take reimbursements for their expenses, gifting The Order over $50,000 during the three years of their terms. God did his part by putting on members' hearts to give. This story appeared in the Spring 2002 issue of *The Royal Cross*:

> When I got my *Royal Cross* and read about the shortage of the general operating fund, I realized that this was my answer to God's request. I know $10.00 isn't a lot, but that's what God told me to give.[4]

God taught me many things through these financial challenges. I grew to understand The Order's finances, how the dues payments affected the cash flow, and the importance of letting the membership know when a dues increase was needed. I also learned that God answered our prayers and led us to be good stewards of The Order's money if we prayed and trusted Him. At times, I still felt unsure when I tried to help because of the ongoing lack of respect. Some were continually reminding me of my position as an appointed Roman Catholic. But I forged ahead as I felt God was directing me and helped the national treasurer, who was also under attack for trying to tighten the budget and get us through a lean time. When asked, I gave her moral support and sound financial advice and helped prepare the budgets. The most important lesson I learned was how important it is to be fiduciarily[5] responsible. The Order's funds are for the benefit of The Order, and I learned the importance

---

[4] Grace Peyton, "Notes from the Treasurer," *Royal Cross* 70, no. 2 (Spring 2002): 7.

[5] A fiduciary duty is the legal responsibility to act solely in the best interest of another party. "Fiduciary" means trust, and a person with a fiduciary duty has a legal obligation to maintain that trust.

of the National Council praying and voting on expenditures with that in mind.

ONE MORE JOB!

As if helping with the finances didn't add enough work to someone who planned to sit on the sidelines, I became site chairman for the Triennial National Convention. How did that happen? I traveled 100 percent for business, living in hotels throughout the country and in Canada. I told our first vice president and Triennial chairman, Sharon Lundgren, that I could check out hotels in Minneapolis, the site of our next Triennial, on an upcoming business trip. When I got home, I called her and told her I had brochures and other information for the various hotels. She surprised me by saying, "Keep them. You are the site chair." In shock, I just said okay as I hung up the phone. Then, I turned to my husband and told him what had happened. I said something about Sharon being a strong personality. He said in his simple way, "Then she has met her match in you." His remark gave me the strength and courage to proceed with the job and many other challenges God put in my life.

Still, I questioned God's plan for my life. I worked very long hours at my job and thought being on the council would be a minimal job. Now I was helping with the finances and acting as site chair for the next Triennial. Many thoughts ran through my mind. I questioned God and whether this was what He had in mind when He appointed me to the council. I know He helped me return to school and get my accounting degree and CPA license so I could help The Order with their finances in their time of need, but site chair too? But then again, He allowed me to get the training to do the site chair when He opened the door for me at my public accounting firm as a new staff accountant at forty-two. My hiring was a miracle in the world of Big Six accounting. I was assigned to the Annual Oil and Gas Symposium as the site chairperson. I did two events for over 400 people from around the world. Perfect training for the site chair of The Order. God had equipped me long before I was appointed to the council, just as it says in 1 Thess. 5:24: "The one who calls you is faithful, and he will also accomplish it." *God, Your faith in me is humbling.*

SURVIVING FINANCIAL SHORTAGES

Due to the financial shortages, we met as a National Council in Houston in October 2001. Ascension Episcopal Chapter and Hannah Catholic Chapter were the hostesses, providing meals and meeting space to keep costs down. The Roman Catholic Daughters gave the members of the National Council a set of Brass Stations of the Cross[6] for the National Office Chapel and *The Way of the Cross* prayer books[7] for employees and visitors to pray the Stations of the Cross meditation. In addition, they presented each member with a blessed prayer blanket the chapter had made.

Hannah Chapter started making prayer blankets a few years earlier after one member was very ill with cancer. Our priest brought a prayer blanket from another Catholic church, and several members

---

[6] Stations of the Crosses: Also called Way of the Cross, a series of fourteen pictures or carvings portraying events in the Passion of Christ, from his condemnation by Pontius Pilate to his entombment.

[7] *The Way of the Cross with Text from the Scriptures* (Baltimore: Barton-Cotton, Inc., 1965).

took the blanket to the hospital to pray for her. After praying, the blanket was placed over her, and she fell asleep. The blanket was still in place the following morning when she woke, but our sister in Christ was completely healed. Her new images showed only scar tissue where the cancer had been. A miracle that even surprised the doctors. We knew God healed her, but the prayer blanket gave her hope and comfort.

Our chapter began having sewing sessions on Saturday, where all members helped cut, iron, and sew the blankets. My husband, George, supported us by washing and cutting the material before our sessions. And I also took blankets home to sew. We left all the finished blankets under the altar during a Mass, and our priest blessed them. I often took blankets to people in need and with me on the road for people I met. God healed many in different ways, and their stories built my faith and helped me believe even more in miracles. The prayer blanket ministry strengthened our chapter's sisterhood and reminded those who got the blankets of God's divine love and healing.

In December 2001, my husband, George, accompanied me to the national office for the first national day of spiritual reflection and the chapel's dedication. He hung the Stations of the Cross in the chapel with the help of another husband. Hannah's chapter had presented the Stations to the National Council when we hosted their meeting earlier in the year. I was filled with joy as I saw our gift of the Stations adorning the chapel. I felt excited that the Roman Catholics had such a special gift and looked forward to the future.

Genuine Southern hospitality was provided by Past President and Adviser Ethel Ripley when the National Council met at her beach home on Pawleys Island in November 2002. Again, the location was part of our cost-cutting plans. She was assisted by some of the Daughters' chapters in the coastal South Carolina area. Her home was historic and beautiful. Marti, my best friend on the council, and I shared a double bed and got scolded by "Mother" Ethel for giggling too much. You would have thought we were teenagers, not grown women, but it is one of my fondest memories of Ethel. She was another of the spiritual mothers that God used to help me grow closer to Him. One of the things Marti and I talked about that night was my writing a book about my abusive marriage and recovery. (It only took me many nudges from God and eighteen years, but I finished that book!)

During the council meeting, we discussed the bylaws and the possibility of giving the Roman Catholics, Lutherans, and Anglicans the right to vote and run for office. I'll never forget that someone in the back row hollered, "That means we could have a Roman Catholic president, and the Pope would take over The Order!" I laughed out loud at the ridiculousness of that statement. Laughter was how I learned to cope with many prejudiced comments, which often helped me survive my time on the National Council.

TRIENNIAL 2003: MINNEAPOLIS

The Order miraculously made it through the three years with our members' generosity and the National Council's frugal planning. And thankfully, the dues were raised at the 2003 Triennial, which solved the financial problems. Father Tom accompanied us to the Triennial, and we had Catholic Rosaries and Masses. He inspired all who attended the Triennial. Episcopalian Bishop Bill Skilton, International Chaplain of The Order, came to one Mass and had

Father Rafferty bless him during Holy Communion. I had tears in my eyes to see this beautiful, interdenominational gesture. Father Tom was also vital to the healing service and the prayer team activity. He was a compassionate and caring minister of Christ's love to all the attendees, and I was blessed to have him as my chaplain and adviser. God couldn't have planned for a better priest to introduce the members of The Order to what it meant to be ecumenical. Father Tom won over all the Daughters with his perfect testimony of divine love.

At the business meeting, the decision was made to send the question of opening The Order's membership to other denominations to a committee. God's mysterious movement continued to change The Order. Sharon Lundgren was elected our new national president and I was appointed the national Roman Catholic representative for the next three years. She and I led the closing procession carrying the National Episcopal and National Catholic Banners. I felt on top of the world. I never dreamed that a simple Catholic would be co-leading the Triennial Procession! Wow! Truly a miracle that I had come this far with God's nudging. And I wondered, *What will these next three years on the National Council bring, Lord?*

CHAPTER TEN

ENJOYING THE CALM BEFORE THE STORM

Working on the DOK National Council

Father in heaven, form us in the likeness of
Your Son and deepen His life within us.
Send us as witnesses of gospel joy into a world
of fragile peace and broken promises.
Touch the hearts of all people with Your love so
that they, in turn, may love one another.
Make us feel more urgently the call to work for the salvation of all,
until You have made us all one people [one Order].
Inspire the hearts of all Your people to continue
the saving work of Christ everywhere
until the end of the world.
Grant this through Christ our Lord. Amen.[1]

---

[1] Benet A. Fonck, *Called to Build a More Fraternal and Evangelical World: A Concordance to the SFO Rule* (Quincy: Franciscan Press, 2002), 42, 96.

As I continued as the national Roman Catholic representative, my workload increased as I helped in many areas—including transportation during council meetings and logistics. Despite the busyness, I was enjoying my service and relieved to no longer be involved in the finances of The Order, with the election of a new treasurer and the dues increase. Sharon Lundgren was a good president, keeping things moving and organized. The council was amiable, and I had many friends from my previous term.

Early in 2004, I learned that three new chapters in Oklahoma were beginning to form, one in the Roman Catholic Church and two in the Anglican tradition. I believed the Holy Spirit spurred on the changes to make room for all DOK leaving the Episcopal Church due to changes voted on at the 2003 Episcopal General Convention.[2] I could only hold on and see where God's plan led. Again, there were other tasks that God wanted me to do, including being site chairman of the upcoming 2006 Triennial in Orlando.

A TRAIN WRECK

I was in Edmond, Oklahoma, in the spring of 2004 with the Province VII president to present the charter to a new Anglian chapter. While I was showering Sunday morning, God gave me a vision. I didn't think showers were where you get messages from God, but that was what happened. In the vision, Jesus was the

---

[2] See the Archives of the Episcopal Church for a list of changes at: https://www.episcopalarchives.org/cgi-bin/acts/acts_resolution-complete.pl?resolution=2003-C051. The changes were the trigger for churches to start leaving the Episcopal Church.

engineer, his hair flying in the wind and a look of excitement on His face as He steered a speeding freight train. The Daughters behind Him held on for dear life as the train sped down the track. They had mixed feelings of joy and excitement. Others waved from the side of the tracks, afraid to get on the train with Jesus. Ahead, we could see other Daughters building a barricade of lumber. The train was headed for them, and beyond was a vast open valley of unlimited growth. Those on the train knew prayer, unity, and His divine love would save The Order. The only way through the barricade was with Jesus at the controls.

As I watched the scene, I asked, "What if we derail?" Then Jesus showed me the train wrecked, off the track and on its side. Daughters from the train were walking away with Jesus, around the barricade, into the valley where The Order would grow exponentially. I journaled about the vision later in the week, and God consoled me with these words:

> *I will be with you on the train. Even if the crash blocks the track, you can walk toward the front and around the roadblock and abandon the wreckage for a new course, a new path, a new order, leading others with you . . . I am your strength and have empowered you for this time. Love, God.*

The vision scared me, and His words left me pleading with Him to help me surrender to His will. His call to guide me through each step—until The Order reached that new vista He showed me—left me hopeful that The Order would eventually be open to all women.

It was an incredible vision, although I pondered the truth behind the analogy. *How would God accomplish the opening of The Order, and would it be a train wreck on the way?*

SOLVING PROBLEMS

By our second council meeting in November 2003 at our national office in Woodstock, GA, the new National Council had quickly become aware of my reputation as a problem-solver. One example happened at that meeting. I flew in later than others because of my work schedule. As I turned on my cell phone, I received a message from one of the council members, Dr. Doris Bradley.[3] Her plane arrived late, and in her hurry to meet her ride to the office, she accidentally picked up the wrong suitcase. She did not discover her mistake until several hours later. The national office is forty-two miles from the airport through Atlanta traffic, so she wanted me to get her suitcase.

I drove to the national office with her bag and my luggage. I found the owner's phone number in the suitcase she had erroneously taken. After talking to his wife, we called him and learned he needed the bag as soon as possible because he was singing the national anthem the next morning at an event. Doris and I set off to return the suitcase, not realizing the special encounter God had planned for us. It was now 10:00 p.m.

The man was so relieved when we got to the hotel he immediately came down to thank us. Well, he introduced himself as a doctor, and soon, he and Doris were chattering away about his practice

---

[3] Dr. Doris Bradley, Professor Emerita of Speech and Healing Sciences, University of Southern Mississippi, Hattiesburg, MS.

as a plastic surgeon specializing in cleft lip and cleft palate and her work helping children who had cleft lip and cleft palate speech impairment. He was familiar with Dr. Bradley's work and was excited to meet her. Wow! A God incident planned by our awesome God to show us what a small world we live in. We returned to our hotel at 1:00 a.m.

A UNIFIED NATIONAL COUNCIL

With love and cooperation, the National Council grew as a sisterhood by our third council meeting in November 2004. What a blessing! The previous council had turmoil at many meetings, partly because of the financial challenges, lack of organization, and struggles among some members. I learned from the new council that the meetings could be run well to accomplish business, and the members could be kind and respectful to each other. The council, listening to God's nudging, started slowly to determine the best way to open the membership and fulfill God's will for The Order.

Membership had remained an issue at each Triennial Convention and kept each council busy since 1986. The new council started with a survey asking the membership if they wanted to open The Order to all women in all denominations or expand the membership rights, allowing the current affiliates, Roman Catholics, Anglicans, and Lutherans, to elect voting delegates to Triennial. The responses were low, and the results split. So the council, after prayer and discussion, believed that the work God was calling them to do was to examine the question of full membership for the affiliate members.

Considering full rights for the affiliate members was a surprise and changed from the previous councils. I was thankful that others' hearts were moving toward giving all members full membership. As a Roman Catholic, I was tired of the constant conflict and discussion, so the new mindset on the National Council was a welcome development. I genuinely love The Order, and I planned to stay.

The National Council, including me, worked hard to maintain that unity. After twenty-four hours of prayer and discussion at the November 2005 meeting, the council made a surprising decision and voted to allow all members, including affiliates, to have delegates and voting rights for the first time in The Order's history at the next Triennial. This decision included me. I was thrilled.

I considered the decision a miracle that only God could have brought into being with the groundwork He had already accomplished for many years. His plan was coming to fruition, and I was grateful to be a small part of the plan. It was humbling to see all that was happening.

STANDING FOR THE NATIONAL COUNCIL

After the decision, God started to put it in my heart that I should stand as a nominee for election to the National Council. There had never been a non-Episcopal sister elected to the National Council, but I believed I met all the qualifications and had the right to stand for council. As I reread the current bylaws, I could find no reason for me not to stand. I more than met all the qualifications. My dues were paid, and I had been president of our archdiocese assembly and a member of The Order for twenty-three years. The more I prayed, the clearer the message got from God for me to stand. When I suggested my standing for council to my Archdiocese of Galveston-Houston Assembly, the Daughters were excited and nominated me.

The current president, Bati Bickerstaff, sent in my nomination form in the first part of January 2006. When Sharon Lundgren found out, she and I exchanged several emails and letters in which she informed me that she had removed my name from the list of candidates. She felt my standing would cause a problem on the Triennial floor as some opposed having Roman Catholic members in The Order.

I was crushed, and I prayed to God and asked Him, "Am I wrong, Lord? What do you want me to do? I want to follow You. I'm so tired of fighting—of being a crusader." I realized that God gave me the strength to do this—to fight for the underdog in The Order and other times in my life. I also had the support of several council members, for which I was grateful. I knew Sharon was in a tough place, and I wasn't trying to make Sharon's life harder. My standing for election, in my opinion, was vital to give full membership rights to the Anglican, Roman Catholic, and Lutheran members. I felt God was calling me to accomplish this precedent. I hoped I could make Sharon see this and change her mind. I continued to pray until God gave me a clear direction: to stand or not.

Many council members encouraged me to stand, but I was conflicted by the messages I received from God and the desire to be obedient to the national president, who was also my longtime friend. So I went to see Father Mike Gemignani, who had been one of my instructors in spiritual direction school and a longtime chaplain for various levels of The Order. I hoped he would help me sort out what I believed, what God was calling me to do, and what Sharon told me to do.

Well, let's say I didn't expect his reaction. He surprised me when he said he would be the parliamentarian at the Triennial business meeting and had already discussed many scenarios with Sharon. He convinced Sharon to let me stand for the National Council from the Roman Catholic Archdiocese of Galveston-Houston—a historic event. I was relieved by the turn of events and hoped Sharon wasn't angry with me. I still felt that God wanted me to stand. I didn't think I would win, but I felt honored to be nominated and set a precedent for those who would come later.

TRIENNIAL 2006: ORLANDO

Twenty-five sisters stood for election to the National Council. The results were read in alphabetical order by last name. I was counting, and fourteen of the fifteen council positions had been chosen, but there were many good candidates before my name, which was last on the list because it started with W, so I figured I had lost. Even though I had been site chairman on two triennials and was well known, having written many articles for *The Royal Cross* as the national Roman Catholic representative and been instrumental in helping restore the finances of The Order, I was still a long shot. I stood to set the precedence for those who came after me. But then they skipped all the names in between and called my name. Wow! God did have a plan for me and The Order. Also elected was my co-council member and friend Jacque Crosby, who stood as an Anglican candidate.

Then, I was elected national treasurer in the closed-door council meeting. As I stood alone—where only moments earlier, there existed a circle of qualified candidates for national treasurer—and realized that I had been elected unanimously by my fellow council members, I broke into tears. What an awesome God we serve! If anyone had asked me a year earlier if, on the twentieth anniversary of the Roman Catholics joining The Order, a Roman Catholic would be elected to the National Council and the executive board, I would have laughed. Too many barriers existed for that miracle, yet I stood there in disbelief and praised God's awesome plan.

In hindsight, my election gave me a new confidence in my ability to lead within The Order and other arenas with God's help. I was touched that many sisters loved me and supported me with their prayers. There were others who didn't respect my leadership, which caused me three tough years. My courage and faith in God grew exponentially because I relied on Him for guidance and listened to Him rather than my detractors. I learned to keep emails short and to the point and always think before I respond. The email was gone once I hit the send button; sometimes, its message had unintended results. I learned to speak the truth clearly and stand up for what was right while listening to others' concerns and wise advice.

God's mysterious ways continued to amaze me. As the new national treasurer, I thanked those wise leaders who brought The Order to this time, a time of unity, equality, and bridging the gap among Christians. It was a time when affiliate members had full rights to vote, stand for the National Council, and serve as God called them. Opening The Order to other denominations had been a long journey. It continued with each new council listening to Christ as their guide to lead The Order to become an international, ecumenical Christian order of women united in prayer, service, and evangelism.

During the next triennium, I pledged to continue encouraging and supporting those called to new churches. Daughters are a community. My personal road was made so much easier because of the love and support of my Episcopal sisters at the chapter, diocese, province, and national levels. We all follow our Lord Jesus Christ! I pray that God's graces of forgiveness and love will fill all DOK with respect for each other, our different traditions, and our clergy. The National Council clarified the ruling in the Summer–Fall 2006 issue of *The Royal Cross*:

> The National Council did not change the bylaws; what they did was interpret the bylaws strictly, according to what they actually say, not according to past practice or the narrative description of affiliates in the front section of the Handbook.[4]

Even if some didn't understand or support the change, I firmly believed God was pushing The Order toward equal rights for all members by Jacque and my elections. And Sharon was right—some in The Order didn't accept or support my election to the National Council or the executive board. As a result, the next three years were full of persecution, requests for my resignation, and personal attacks, but God had a surprising ending to the story of my nine years on the National Council.

---

[4] "Q&A: A Primer for Puzzled Daughters," *Royal Cross* 74, nos. 2-3 (Summer–Fall 2006): 12.

CHAPTER ELEVEN

SURVIVING PERSECUTION AND GOD'S PLAN

Experiencing the DOK Executive Board

Learning Christ

Teach me, my Lord, to be sweet and gentle in all the events of life;
In disappointments, in the thoughtlessness of others,
in the insincerity of those I trusted,
in the unfaithfulness of those on whom I relied.
Let me put myself aside to think of the happiness of others,
to hide my little pains and heartaches,
so that I may be the only one to suffer from them.
Teach me to profit by the suffering that comes across my path.
Let me so use it that it may mellow me, not harden or embitter me;
that it may make me patient, not irritable
that it may make me broad in my forgiveness,
not narrow, haughty, or overbearing.
May no one be less good for having come within my influence.
No one less pure, less true, less kind, less noble
for having been a fellow-traveler in our journey toward eternal life.[1]

---

[1] Saint John Henry Newman, "Learning Christ," in *The Father Gilbert Prayer Book*, Father Gilbert Hay, M.S.SS.T. (Silver Springs, MD: Trinity Ministries, 1965), 5–6.

After I was elected national treasurer, my first order of business was to order an audit after The Order's books closed on August 31, 2006. Unfortunately, the auditor called me from his driveway at 5:00 p.m. on the last day of the audit, having discovered a spa charge on The Order's credit card. When he questioned our director of operations, she said she had used the wrong credit card. He asked to see the check where she had paid The Order back. During the search for the check and with further questioning from the auditor, she admitted that she had been using The Order's credit card for personal expenses for some time but was trying to pay back the money.

A busy and upsetting few days followed. National President Joan Dalrymple and I talked to her through the weekend amid tears. Joan asked for and received her resignation and confession. The National Council and office staff were notified. The Order's assets were further secured. Finally, a more in-depth audit of the previous three-year period was performed. I was exhausted from dealing with many questions, discussions with the previous national treasurer, and arranging immediate travel to the national office. Years earlier, I had helped hire our director of operations, so I was disappointed and downhearted.

It was a miracle that the auditor found the spa charge that started unraveling the theft because it had been going on since November 2004 after our volunteer CPA retired. We added a financial clerk whom he trained, and we felt we were in good hands. Unfortunately, the financial clerk gave the unopened fraudulent credit card statements to the director of operations, for her to pay. So our checks and balances didn't work. As the shock wore off and I learned more, I was devastated. She was my friend.

Next, I spent many hours preparing and filing a loss claim with our bonding company with the results from the audit and a detailed investigation on my part. Then, Joan and I filed charges with Woodstock, Georgia's Police Department, for credit card theft, as required by the bonding company. Unfortunately, the audit didn't find proof of debt repayment. Evidence of charges, late fees, interest, and employee advances totaled $62,068.89. I was shaken and felt betrayed, especially when she returned a special gift I had given her while staying at her home during a visit to the national office.

Thanks to this ordeal, new office procedures were written and implemented. While the police and the bonding company's investigations were ongoing, I couldn't disclose the details. As a result, I was accused of many things, including not forgiving our director of operations by pursuing the legal case, hiding the truth, and more accusations. Basically, as a Roman Catholic, I wasn't trusted by some people. It was a painful time, and the lack of trust continued for my entire term as national treasurer, even after settling the theft case. I didn't know how to change the few but vocal people's perspectives, so I followed God's lead and did the best job I knew how to do.

The Order's bond covered the entire two-and-a-half-year period of the theft. We received $52,068.89 from the bonding company, which was our loss repayment minus our $10,000 deductible. Over a year later, the police case was settled in December 2007, and our employee repaid the entire amount with help from a friend. I requested that she get probation and community service rather than jail time since she had pleaded guilty, paid back the amount stolen, and was well-loved by all of us in The Order, including me. And yes, I had forgiven her as I have learned to do throughout my life when people have caused me pain or disappointment. The Lord's Prayer has been my guide, and when I pray, I think about Matthew 6:12: "And forgive us our debts, as we forgive our debtors." I want to be forgiven, so I can't do less for others.

HIRING GOODMAN FINANCIAL CORPORATION

In January 2007, a call came from someone at the institution who oversaw our endowment fund. I was told to move the money as soon as possible. The person said there were discussions by the trustees that they needed to take the funds from the ministries under their oversight. The money would help them meet the shortfalls from the church property lawsuits and other consequences of the Anglican realignment.[2] The call surprised and worried me.

When I was elected national treasurer, I knew little about investments, so being responsible for The Order's growing funds was stressful. I prayed about the information the caller gave. I again felt God's intervention and protection in The Order's finances when He put on my heart to contact Steve Goodman of Goodman Financial Corporation and asked him to help. I knew him slightly as he was president of the Texas Society of CPAs, which I had belonged to since earning my CPA license. I was very relieved when he said yes. I checked several references and felt comfortable that Steve was the right person to help me. With the approval of the executive board and finance committee, I began setting up the investment account with Goodman Financial Corporation. I was still worried about the call. I thought, *Was it true?* I hoped not.

---

[2] The Anglican realignment is a movement among some Anglicans to align themselves under new or alternative oversight within or outside the Anglican Communion.

A second call came from the same person a couple of weeks later. The person said, "I told you to move the money. You must do it today. Your money is in danger." At first, I hesitated as The Order's money had been at this institution for many years. After a few minutes of prayer, God said, "**Be diligent and take care of the money I have entrusted to you.**" I then felt empowered to make the decision and called Steve. We arranged to transfer The Order's Funds to TD Ameritrade, a stable investment company headquartered in California that Steve felt was a good choice. I took a lot of criticism but didn't feel comfortable revealing my source or jeopardizing their position. Some Daughters attacked me and said I transferred the money to Texas, where some banks failed with the economic downturn in 2007. I had to laugh because it wasn't true. But I was sad that I still wasn't trusted or respected.

To make a long story short, Goodman Financial Corporation has continued as The Order's financial adviser since then and has successfully carried The Order through the downturns and other swings in the market. Goodman generously gave part of their fees back to The Order's Self-Denial Fund each year. I can't say that the trustees would have taken the money, but I felt God had a bigger plan. Hiring Steve Goodman helped The Order make the right decisions to protect and grow The Order's funds for many years. One added benefit was that I could sleep better knowing I had someone to help me with the investments, and Steve taught me how to handle The Order's growing funds.

THE BOLOGNA IN THE SANDWICH

One of the other struggles at the October 2007 council meeting made me feel like the bologna in a sandwich. I felt squished between my dear Episcopalian and Anglican sisters, loving those from both sides. Squished as I listened and witnessed the heartbreak and pain tearing at the fabric of our beloved order. Jacque Crosby, my Anglican friend, felt God was calling her to provide an alternative order for the Anglican Daughters who couldn't remain in The Order due to the split in the church. She presented her proposal first to Bishop Howe, who, after prayer, told her: "Jacque, the most loving thing you can do is give the Anglicans a place to go." She then presented the proposal to the National Council.

Jacque Crosby tells people I yelled at her when she asked the National Council's blessing to explore an alternative for our Anglican members who couldn't remain in The Order for various reasons. She was correct; I was very angry. I didn't understand why the Anglicans needed an alternative order. I loved The Order. Their prayers and support continued to strengthen and encourage me daily as The Order's national treasurer.

I had prayed and worked for many years to bring the Anglicans, Lutherans, and Roman Catholics into full membership. Finally, at Triennial 2006, it miraculously happened, and Jacque and I were elected to the National Council. So now, with the hard work of the bylaws committee, we were on the brink of having more precise guidelines on equality in our membership. At the October council meeting, the council appointed me as the representative to the Anglican formation committee, which was exploring starting a new order. I had mixed feelings but felt God was calling me to walk with them as Ruth did in the Bible story with Naomi.

At the first meeting of the formation committee in early 2008, I listened to the members for seven hours—hearing their pain at leaving their church and The Order and laying down their DOK crosses while faithfully living out their vow to Jesus. I respected their decisions. I didn't walk in their shoes. I loved each of them dearly. I saw that letting some of our sisters go with our love and support to a new order fashioned after DOK called The Order of the Daughters of the Holy Cross was the most loving solution for them. Forces outside The Order (bishops, priests, and lawyers) were much more powerful than our membership, making our commitment to a united sisterhood for some Anglicans difficult, if not impossible. I was thankful for Bishop Howe's guidance as he understood the situation better than I did. As I walked with the committee, an exceptional mystical experience happened.

We were meeting at one of the member's homes. She said that her husband traveled worldwide and always shopped in small second-hand stores in the cities he was in, looking for religious articles. He found an interesting store somewhere in South America on a trip. He asked the owner if they had any religious items. The owner brought out what looked like a Roman Catholic monstrance.[3] A small wood splinter was on the side where the Eucharistic Host was usually placed. He bought it and brought it home. When he opened the bottom, he found a very old German authentication that said the splinter was a piece of the true Cross of Christ.[4] I had some doubts

---

[3] The monstrance is one of the most essential elements of Eucharistic Adoration, besides the Eucharist host, of course. Eucharistic Adoration is the opportunity for faithful Catholics to pray to Jesus in His very presence through the Holy Eucharist, which is on display.

[4] St. Ambrose preached that when St. Helena found the true Cross, "she worshiped not the wood, but the King, Him who hung on the wood. She burned with an earnest desire of touching the guarantee of immortality." St. Cyril stated, "The saving wood of the Cross was found at Jerusalem in the time of Constantine . . . and the whole world has since been filled with pieces of the wood of the Cross." Catholic Straight Answers, *Did St. Helena find the true Cross of Christ?* https://catholicstraightanswers.com/did-st-helena-find-the-true-cross-of-christ/.

the splinter was an authentic relic from the Cross of Christ, so I took the monstrance into a back bedroom to be alone and pray.

As I prayed with the monstrance, I was overcome with Jesus' presence. Joy and divine love filled my being. I began to believe that the little sliver was from the Cross of Christ. I had been struggling with the Anglicans' invitation for the Roman Catholics to join them in the new order with full membership rights. I had been praying about whether or not this was God's will for the small group of Roman Catholic members I represented. While praying with the monstrance, God made it clear the Roman Catholics were to stay with The Order, as were some of the Anglicans. So I had my answer; I continued to walk this journey with Jacque and the committee while they developed the new order's structure. Then I resigned and wished them well on their path to holiness.

In the Spring of 2008, I attended Mass at my home church, crying over the division that caused some Anglicans to go to the Daughters of the Holy Cross. Suddenly, God gave me a vision. I saw a banner of blue satin with the DOK cross in the center and an under-girthing of strong silver metal cords. The banner was frayed on the edges and flapping in the winds but still held together because of the silver metal cords underneath. I understood God was giving me a sign that The Order would survive. We might be tattered, but we would hold together. Our silver cords, our lifelines of continuous prayer to Jesus, and those prayers of the Daughters who had gone before us would hold The Order together. God's peace filled my heart. I love all my sisters: Anglican, Episcopalian, Lutheran, Roman Catholic, and those who venture into a new order and beyond.

VISITING MERCY CENTER

One of the responsibilities of the National Council was attending gatherings in different provinces. Several members of the National Council, including President Joan Dalrymple, attended the Province VIII retreat at the Roman Catholic Mercy Center in Burlingame, California, in August 2008. I was apprehensive as some Province VIII Daughters opposed my election as national treasurer. I believe in treating everyone with respect and kindness, so I nervously moved among my sisters and greeted them with the divine love of Christ after I arrived. One of the blessings at Mercy Center was a beautiful outdoor labyrinth tucked in the trees surrounded by flowers. I walked the labyrinth several times and dwelled in the needed moments of intimacy with God, Who embraced me with His peace and gave me courage to return to the meeting through His presence.

On the last evening, after walking the labyrinth, I returned just in time for a beautiful Roman Catholic Mass. The procession was led by a five-foot-tall San Damiano Cross,[5] a copy of the cross that spoke to St. Francis of Assisi. The sisters sang many beautiful hymns during the service, including my favorite, "I Am the Bread of Life." After the service, we were invited to venerate[6] the San Damiano Cross.

---

[5] The San Damiano Cross is the large Romanesque cross before which St. Francis of Assisi was praying when he is said to have received the commission from the Lord to rebuild the Church. The cross is a crucifix of a type sometimes called an icon cross because in addition to the main figure of the Christ, it contains images of other saints and people related to the incident of Christ's Crucifixion.

[6] Adoration or veneration of an image or representation of Christ's Cross means that we adore what it represents. In kneeling before the Crucifix and kissing it, we are paying the highest honor to our Lord's Cross as the instrument of our salvation.

Attending a Roman Catholic Mass, singing my favorite hymns, taking Holy Communion, and having time to walk the labyrinth was healing for my soul and gave me the courage and energy to go on as national treasurer. I felt so at home at Mercy Center, and I returned often to Mercy Center when I was in the area.

I continued to receive letters from a small, vocal group of members asking for my resignation as treasurer. I found it depressing, but my family helped. My daughter, Susan, would read the letters first and tear them up if they were hateful so I didn't have to read them. I gradually just found the humor in their continuing attacks. Most of the Daughters supported me, and more importantly, I had given my all to serve my Savior through The Order. I vowed to honor the members' vote at the 2006 Triennial by staying and using my talents where God had directed me to go until God said to me, **"Well done, my good and faithful servant"** (Matthew 25:23a).

I went where God called me, even though retreating sometimes would have been easier. I felt passionate about fighting for my granddaughter Courtney, other Junior Daughters, and senior Catholic, Anglican, and Lutheran Daughters to have full membership rights. I saw prejudice in these negative letters and my sisters' hurtful actions. I prayed to have a heart of forgiveness. I put on the armor of God daily to continue the fight, as it says in Ephesians 6:11–13:

> Put on the armor of God so that you may be able to stand firm against the tactics of the devil. For our struggle is not with flesh and blood but with the principalities, with the powers, with the world rulers of this present darkness, with the evil spirits in the heavens. Therefore, put on the armor of God, that

you may be able to resist on the evil day and, having
done everything, to hold your ground.

I also faced prejudice in the Roman Catholic Church. The priests
I approached to start new chapters often opposed the Episcopalian
roots of The Order. The priests' reluctance was the reason for the
slow growth of the Roman Catholic DOK. Some members had said
that creating our own branch of The Order would help relieve the
prejudice; however, our roots would always be Episcopalian. Most
Catholic chapters were started by Daughters who left the Episcopal
Church and joined the Roman Catholic Church but wanted to stay
in The Order, including me.

TRIENNIAL 2009: ANAHEIM

One of the most challenging days of my life was at the 2009 DOK
Triennial business meeting. The meeting started with me on stage
with the rest of the executive board, Bishop Howe, and the parliamentarian. The main focus was on the bylaw revisions. In 2006,
the National Council and delegates interpreted the bylaws strictly
to mean that all members of The Order were allowed to seat, voice,
and vote at all levels, especially nationally. That decision was supported by the majority of the delegates but upset some members. The
small group of women who opposed the seating of delegates from
Anglican, Lutheran, and Roman Catholic chapters worked feverishly
for the next three years to get that decision reversed.

Meanwhile, the bylaw committee worked hard to create proposed
changes that would clear up any ambiguity, and Joan Dalrymple,
our president and National Council tried various means to calm

those who were upset without much success. The first move at the Triennial by those upset by the ruling in 2006 was to challenge the Credentials Report and unseat 17 out of the 299 delegates that didn't represent Episcopalian entities. A discussion took place by those arguing for the exclusion of these duly elected, dues-paying delegates. An equal amount of discussion happened by those who supported the continued inclusion of these delegates. The debate was hurtful to the seventeen, who were, of course, present throughout. Some delegates were absent because they were on an excursion with the Juniors. After the vote, those who wanted the women removed won by twelve votes. The vote meant that the affiliate delegates no longer had the right to vote or represent their chapters even though they paid dues and took the same vows as the Episcopal Daughters.

I remained composed while the events unfolded, quietly praying inside. The seventeen excluded delegates were deeply hurt. They left the floor in tears, sobbing as they went down the aisles to the back of the room. Ruth, the assistant directress of my Juniors Chapters, came forward in tears and laid her DOK cross on the front of the stage at President Joan Dalrymple's feet, basically resigning from The Order amid her pain. It was heartbreaking to watch, and I asked God: *Is this the train wreck you showed me in the vision in 2004? I trust you to help us reach the valley of exponential growth. It certainly feels like a train wreck to me!* It looked like we had lost the fight to give the other denominations full membership rights, but God wasn't done.

The next battle was over the first proposed bylaw amendment, which would officially give members from each denomination seat, voice, and vote. This bylaw was opposed by those wanting to ensure that only Episcopalians could vote and stand for office, so they proposed a substitute amendment. After much debate, both amendments failed.

We adjourned for lunch. Some approached me and wanted to meet to decide the next steps. I needed to change my clothes and focus on my final treasurer report that afternoon. My parting word was, "Pray!"

I returned to my room, and after giving in to a few tears, I changed into a suit, practiced my report, and spent the rest of the time praying. I found myself questioning God and reflecting on that night a few weeks ago when I stumbled out of bed and said, "Okay, God, I'm coming. Give me a minute to turn on the computer." I was used to God waking me to write, but that night was different. The only light was coming from the computer screen, but a fly hit me in the face as if trying to stop me from typing. Strange. Then the computer shut off while both my hands were on the keyboard. Hmm . . . I had an overwhelming feeling that night was different and the message more important, so I turned the computer back on and kept typing. As the words filled the page, I became aware of the importance of the prayer. I asked myself, *Could I deliver it as God called me to do? Just as He wrote it? I would need courage.* Some part of me hesitated and wondered, *Was this His powerful ending to the crusade I had been fighting for? An end to my persecution? Only time will tell.* I shut off the computer and returned to bed.

Now, here I was in my hotel room at Triennial, prepared to give one of the most important reports of my life, and my questioning of God began again. *Do you really want me to close with the prayer You gave me in the middle of the night a few weeks ago?* I remember the day after God gave me the prayer in the middle of the night, I was unsure about using it. I prayed for someone to read the prayer to, and then the phone rang. Father Tom called to tell me he couldn't go with me to Triennial. Odd, Father Tom never called me and especially never at 8:30 a.m. He is a night owl. I read him the prayer, and after a long silence, he said, "You must read it just as God gave it to you." That was my answer then, and now was the time.

So, with renewed determination, off I went to the ballroom. As I entered the ballroom to give my report, the keynote speaker had just finished. On the giant screens along both sides of the room was a picture of a bronze sculpture outside a Catholic church in Houston. I asked the speaker if she knew the location of the sculpture, and she said no. But I knew. The sculpture on the screen was a surprise from God!

The sculpture called "Christ the Beggar"[7] shows Jesus dressed as a beggar. Only His outstretched hands with the wounds from the nails let you know it was Him. The church, St. Cyril of Alexander Catholic Church, had a Roman Catholic Daughters of the King chapter that had pledged to pray for me for the three years I was national treasurer. Wow!! I knew this was another mystical sign from God that He was with me—carrying me through what I had to do. And others who disapproved of the prejudiced attacks against me also promised to pray for me. I felt like I was floating on a sea of prayer.

I gave my PowerPoint report, answering all the accusations with truth and facts one by one. The last slide showed an ice cream cone, and I said, "A priest told me to have an ice cream cone every time I got a negative letter asking for my resignation, and now my skirt is a bit tight." I laughed, and many laughed with me as I pulled on the

---

[7] The statue of Christ the Beggar, which was also created by Timothy Schmaltz, was placed outside the doors of St. Cyril of Alexandra Catholic Church, Houston, Texas, in 2004. Per the artist's instructions, the statue is placed on the ground to more readily resemble an actual person sitting and begging. The statue, in fact, is so realistic that the parish has received calls from people wondering who "the man sitting by the door" is!

side of my skirt. Then I said, "Let's pray," and bowed my head and began to read God's closing prayer slowly and with a steady voice, just as God had given to me to pray that mystical night.

Dear Heavenly Father: By the authority of my Baptism and in the name of Jesus Christ of Nazareth, I hereby bind all evil that is in this room and in this Order and send it immediately and directly to the foot of the Cross of Calvary, to be washed in the Precious Blood of our Lord and Savior, Jesus Christ.

I call on Margaret Franklin and all faithful Daughters of the King who have gone before to rush to the foot of Your throne to intercede on behalf of our Order. Dear Lord, pour down on us Your divine wisdom, power, and protection.

I implore You to send Saint Michael and all angels to this place to battle against any evil that may come against us and provide us with a wall of protection throughout this convention.

Thank you, Abba Father, for your continued blessings on our Order. Help us, Lord, to renew our focus and energy on the mission of this Order and give us a new, united spirit to carry the Gospel of Christ to all people throughout the world.

We ask all this in the power of the Holy Spirit and through the mercy of our Savior and

King, the Lord Jesus Christ, and For His Sake. AMEN! AMEN! AMEN!

After I finished, there were a few moments of silence, then thunderous applause and a standing ovation, except for the small group of Daughters in the middle of the room who had harassed me for three years. Amazing things started to happen throughout the room. The Province VII President, Missy Denny, said she felt chills as she saw the Holy Spirit descend on the room as I prayed, and then God spoke to her, **"What isn't of Me won't happen."** She started watching to see what God was going to do.

The national junior directress asked if two girls could address the Triennial Convention on behalf of the other Juniors. I was surprised by the request. The Juniors had gone on a field trip to the Mission of San Juan Capistrano, so I didn't understand how they knew what was happening in the business meeting. I was very concerned for my eleven Juniors who were there. The last thing I wanted my Juniors to hear about was strife in the Senior DOK. Ruth later told me that when the girls returned, some came into the back of the ballroom and sat with her, listening to the discussion. The girls were confused and had many questions, which Ruth tried to answer. The girls left during my report and talked with the other Junior Daughters. They decided to make their feelings known.

> As members of the Jr. Daughters of the King, we are shocked by the example that is being set by you all. Do you not teach us in the church to love thy neighbor as thyself and treat others as you would like to be treated? Is segregation of our Daughters

what God would want? God looked at us as His children and continues to love us no matter our denomination.

Out of the mouths of babes! Common sense, love, and acceptance. One of the Juniors who participated in the presentation of this statement was from my Roman Catholic Junior chapter. I was so proud of the Juniors for having the courage to speak up but saddened that they were aware of the actions that had taken place.

Then, a young woman came to the microphone. I knew she was a Roman Catholic, but she was representing an Episcopal chapter to which she belonged, so she hadn't been removed as a delegate. She moved to reseat the seventeen delegates because both amendments had failed. The 2006 existing bylaws were still in effect. Her motion elicited a strong reaction from those who had managed to unseat the seventeen delegates that morning! But, with the delegates back from the Junior excursion and some hearts and minds changed by the pain they had seen when the seventeen had to leave, the motion was passed by seventeen votes. I watched, speechless and so grateful, as God orchestrated this miracle. He was definitely in control.

Some of those on the losing side left the session and eventually left The Order to establish another organization. A dear friend and past national second vice president, Jean Marini, collapsed into heart-wrenching sobs. She had become an Anglican and wanted to stay in The Order desperately. The pain of the morning decision broke her heart, and she said, "It is done. Too much has happened to go back." She remained a lifetime member of The Order but did join the Daughters of the Holy Cross. I shed tears for her and others hurt too profoundly to stay. I continued my prayers and hoped for us to come back together. Later in the day, Joan Dalrymple gave Ruth her cross back.

Bishop Howe, who had served as our national chaplain during the past three years and suffered many attacks by his fellow bishops and members of The Order, expressed sadness to see how the turmoil in the Church had filtered into our Order and that bishops were putting pressure on their Daughters. These Daughters had to report to their bishops when they returned from Triennial. He was also grieved that some Daughters behaved so hatefully toward the elected leadership these past three years and toward their sisters in Christ that day. He was distraught that our Junior Daughters had been exposed to the day's events. He prayed for healing within The Order and strength to withstand the assaults against our prayer, service, and evangelism mission. We were blessed to have him as our chaplain as he listened to God and taught us to follow the love and do the loving thing.

There was a new joy in the room as the Glory Bound Singers closed the session with praise music. The evil that had been plaguing The Order was gone. Soon, the delegates and observers danced in the aisles to the song "We Are Marching in the Light of God,"[8] forming a conga line around the room. Watching from the stage gave me a beautiful view of the joy God had restored to our Order.

As I continued to watch, my life as a Daughter finally made sense, and the knowledge humbled me. God chose me to help bring His plan into fruition, first by calling me to join The Order as a

---

[8] "We Are Marching in the Light of God," Translated by Anders Nyberg into English. Source from South African Copyright: Words by permission of Walton Music Corporation.

young, battered housewife, then saving me from that marriage, and giving me a fantastic new husband to support me in my journey. I could see God's plan for my conversion to the Roman Catholic Church. By responding to His call, I served on the National Council with my sisters, Sharon Lundgren and Joan Dalrymple. God orchestrated my election to the National Council and National Treasurer. Only a charismatic Roman Catholic who prayed healing prayers, relied on St. Michael, and believed in the intercession of those who went before us could pray the prayer He gave me. What an incredible set of God's mystical encounters, miracles, and divine love led my stumbling in the direction of enabling God's plan for The Order.

In one of my other assignments, I saw in God's plan that I could lead without persecution and produce fruit for God that lasted. I was the spiritual formation chair during my three-year term. I introduced *Continuing the Journey: The Spiritual Formation Guide*[9] at the 2009 Triennial. God had prepared me for this position when He called me to be a spiritual director, and I was thrilled to use my training. I was inspired to create a project to bring Daughters across The Order together and help members develop a closer relationship with Jesus. I prayed and found DOK members representing all eight provinces across The Order to help create the guide. I enjoyed writing, editing, coordinating, and compiling the final guide. My faith increased by reading what others had written in their chapters. Different points of view made the guide more useful for all the Daughters. The guide celebrated life as a Daughter through prayer, service, and evangelism, giving members a better understanding of

---

[9] *Continuing the Journey: The Spiritual Formation Guide* is still available on the National DOK website.

God and His plan for our lives. As Daughters, we seek the Holy God in quiet daily prayer and rest silently in His presence. As Mother Teresa said in her book *A Gift for God*:

> We need to find God, and He cannot be found in noise and restlessness. God is the friend of silence. See how nature—trees, flowers, grass—grows in silence; see the stars, the moon, and the sun, how they move in silence . . . We need silence to be able to touch souls.[10]

I praise God for those dark and desert times when He was in the silence, even when I couldn't feel Him. And the dark and desert times helped me appreciate when the Light, our Lord Jesus Christ, returned to my life. One such time was in late 2008; shortly after I finished the spiritual formation guide, my adult son disappeared due to overwhelming stress. During rush hour, I found myself sobbing in traffic on I-10. I hadn't cried that hard in years. I felt utterly broken and abandoned by God. I was overwhelmed by the weight of my life! I felt helpless not being able to help my son. I was too broken even to pray. I reached out to my sisters to pray for me.

A couple of weeks later, when I had a better understanding of my son's problems and he was safe, I praised God for my sisters who prayed for me and for His divine love and the miracles He had been doing in my son's life to bring him to a better, healthier place. As Emilie Griffin tells us in her book *Simple Ways to Pray*:

---

[10] Mother Teresa of Calcutta, *A Gift for God: Prayers and Meditations* (New York: Harper & Row, 1975), 68–69.

> Prayer is the way we pursue a relationship with the
> God who made us and wants us to come close. This
> is no casual acquaintance, but a friendship that will
> change and develop over time.[11]

I have genuinely felt that my Triune God is my friend—God the Father, the architect of my life; God the Son; Jesus, my Savior and beloved; and God the Holy Spirit, my guide and inspiration. Going through the challenges of The Order and other areas of my life deepened and changed my friendship with God. Each trial I faced and came out better on the other side made me stronger. Continuing to stumble through God's plan taught me to trust Him in all things, suffering and joy.

WELL DONE, MY GOOD AND FAITHFUL SERVANT

After that 2009 Triennial, the Triennial Convention referred back all bylaw changes to the committee for discussion and revisions, and, finally, at Triennial 2015, the memberships moved past their fears and opened their hearts to full membership. The complete removal of the last discriminatory bylaws passed without one dissenting vote. All members were now equal. It was an incredible movement of the Holy Spirit to bring God's plan into existence—a miracle that ended a longtime problem in The Order. *Praise God!*

My term as national treasurer ended a few weeks after the 2009 Triennial with the successful completion of the last audit and the

---

[11] Emilie Griffin, *Simple Ways to Pray: Spiritual Life in the Catholic Tradition* (Lanham, MD: Rowman & Littlefield Publishers, Inc., 2006), 13–14.

transfer of all the accounts to the new treasurer. God provided many new activities to keep me busy.

During the move in 2017 into my new home, I found my records from when I was The Order's national treasurer and leader of the Roman Catholic branch. It just so happened that our past national president and historian and my good friend, Grace Sears, was in the process of writing the history of the Roman Catholic branch. We met up and had fun going through old pictures and other treasures from my time of service. Of course, she couldn't take my treasures on the plane but wanted me to mail them to her. A part of me held back for a few days, but then God said to me, **"Well done, my good and faithful servant"** (Matthew 25:23a). I knew it was time to send the treasures to the archives—to let go and move on.

Reflecting on my time as national treasurer, I felt God brought the Roman Catholics to The Order to smooth the Anglican split and save many members. Having survived heated discussions about opening The Order to the Roman Catholics made it much easier for The Order to say to the Anglicans, "We want you here as full members and to enfold the Lutherans in The Order gently."

Sadly, the Roman Catholic chapters faded away over time, leaving a few of us as Daughters at Large or members of Episcopal chapters. Still, God accomplished His purpose of opening The Order to the Anglican, Lutheran, and Roman Catholic members with full membership rights, love, and acceptance.[12] As for me, I'm still here honoring my lifetime vow in The Order as a Roman Catholic member of an Episcopal chapter and serving where God leads me.

---

[12] One last story, "A Radical Idea," that I wrote in 2008 can be found in the *Resources* chapter.

I continue to move on to other challenges and opportunities God has planned for me, with more growth through mystical encounters, miracles, divine love, and a new ministry.

CHAPTER TWELVE

TRUSTING IN JESUS

Increasing in God's Divine Mercy

The Three O'clock Prayer

You expired, O Jesus,
But the source of life gushed forth for souls
And an ocean of mercy opened up for the whole world.
O Fount of Life, unfathomable Divine Mercy,
Envelop the whole world and empty Yourself out upon us.
O Blood and Water,
Which gushed forth from the Heart of Jesus
As a fount of mercy for us, I trust in You.[1]
Amen.

---

[1] The Three O'Clock Prayer can be used to fulfill Jesus' request: "At three o'clock, implore My mercy, especially for sinners; and, if only for a brief moment, immerse yourself in My Passion, particularly in My abandonment at the moment of agony. This is the hour of great mercy for the whole world . . . In this hour, I will refuse nothing to the soul that makes a request of Me in virtue of My Passion." (*Diary* paragraph 1319–1320).

*M*y *introduction to the Divine* Mercy[2] came during a women's retreat in June 2005 when our priest, Father Tom Rafferty, and the retreat music group sang the Chaplet of Divine Mercy.[3] Father Tom, with his beautiful tenor voice, sang the lines: "Eternal Father, I offer You the Body and Blood." As I sang the response, "For the sake of His sorrowful Passion," alongside the music group, I realized the Chaplet was a beautiful intercessory prayer—perfect for my prayer order, the Daughters of the King. Our motto, "For His Sake," is close to the Chaplet's "For the sake," and my prayer order's emphasis on intercessory prayer for the whole world is precisely in line with the prayers of the Chaplet. I was so excited about the Chaplet that I introduced it to my prayer order—first at a council meeting and then as an additional prayer service that my Junior DOK helped lead at the beginning of the 2006, 2009, and 2012 Triennial Conventions. Many Daughters embraced the Chaplet and were excited to learn a new way to pray that focused on Jesus and intercessory prayer for the whole world.

The Chaplet of Divine Mercy became my favorite prayer. When we moved to St. Edith Stein Catholic Church in early 2007, I found that the church had just been given a large Divine Mercy Image for the Sanctuary. The Image came with the requirement that it be venerated. Eventually, it was hung in the back of the church. I expected the Image would be venerated on Divine Mercy Sunday in 2007 with a special service, but nothing happened. The following year, in

---

[2] For more information, see "St. Faustina and the Divine Mercy Story" in the Resources chapter.

[3] The Chaplet of Divine Mercy is a powerful prayer that asks for God's mercy and is prayed on Rosary beads. To learn how to pray the Chaplet: https://www.thedivinemercy.org/message/devotions/pray-the-Chaplet.

2008, I asked Father Bob if a special Divine Mercy service to venerate the Image would happen. He said, "You can plan something." I
was stunned for a moment but having grown in my love of Divine
Mercy and wanting to spread it to others in our church, I said yes.

The Divine Mercy Sunday service was a simple and beautiful
introduction to the Divine Mercy Ministry. After the service, several
people encouraged me, or maybe I should say *nagged* at me to start a
Divine Mercy group. With my busy work schedule, I wasn't excited
about taking on a weekly ministry. I prayed about it and waited on
God's direction.

Finally, after nudgings from God, I started a Divine Mercy
Cenacle, an apostolate of the Congregation of Marians of the
Immaculate Conception. The program is based on the *Diary of Saint
Maria Faustina Kowalska: Divine Mercy in My Soul*[4] and integrates
Scripture and the Catechism of the Catholic Church. A Divine
Mercy Cenacle is a group of people who meet weekly to discover
and share God's mercy in their lives, primarily through studying
the writings of St. Faustina. I felt the group was part of God's plan
for my life and a new opportunity to grow closer to Jesus. Over
the years, the group members and I have grown, healed, found a
closer relationship with Jesus, and developed a zeal to do ministry.
Group sharing is powerful. Miracles and mystical encounters have
accompanied God's divine love that He has showered on the group
members and me.

---

[4] Saint Maria Faustina Kowalska, *Diary of Saint Maria Faustina Kowalska:
Divine Mercy in My Soul* (Stockbridge, MA: Marian Press, 1981).

DIANA'S DISCOVERING THE DIVINE MERCY

In the fall of 2008, I invited my friend and spiritual mother, Diana, to share her story[5] with my local Daughters of the King at the Archdiocese of Galveston-Houston Assembly. God gave Diana the Chaplet of Divine Mercy when she needed it the most, and He used her testimony to bring many closer to Jesus, including me. I was familiar with her story, but I still shed a few tears as I listened to Diana.

> In early 2004, I was in Tennessee. I just found out my son Michael-Jon had fourth-stage cancer. The silence in the room was deafening. His eyes were looking at me as if saying, "I am sorry, Mom. I didn't mean to make you go through this pain." How could this be? He was a super young man. He didn't smoke or drink. He was a great son, husband, and father. He was crazy about his baby girl. He was only twenty-six years old. How would I handle this without breaking completely down? How could this happen? This was MY child.

As Diana spoke, I remembered the desperation she first felt when she found out about Michael-Jon's cancer. But then she started to share how God gave her strength and how she moved ahead with her life and prepared for whatever God had in store for them.

> I believed Isaiah 41:10: "Do not fear: I am with you; do not be anxious: I am your God. I will strengthen

---

[5] Used by permission of Diana Helms.

you." So I quit my job. I took early retirement to spend whatever time I had caring for him. One sleepless night as I was channel surfing, a song caught my ear. It was as if it was calling me. The Image seemed so familiar. Where had I seen it? I went to a drawer containing several prayer cards and booklets Mom gave me. There was the Image. It was beautiful, and I was transfixed by it. I fell in love with His Divine Mercy immediately. The more I prayed and understood the Chaplet, the stronger I began to feel. I wanted more and more to prepare Michael-Jon to be with our Lord, and God was preparing me for the day to come.

I was amazed at how strong Diana became, and her testimony of how the Divine Mercy Chaplet rescued her inspired me. I continued to listen with tears in my eyes as I knew she was coming to the most challenging part of her story.

December 5, 2004, at 3:00 p.m. in Knoxville, Tennessee, it was a very cold and dreary afternoon, and I was prostrated on the floor of the hospital chapel. I just finished praying the Chaplet of Divine Mercy. I asked God to forgive me for being selfish and thinking of only my pain instead of my son's suffering. I thanked God for my beautiful gift. After three miscarriages, God gave me the most beautiful, almost nine-pound miracle baby boy.

> Now, I was telling God I wanted to return my son to Him so He could take his pain and suffering away. Then, almost as if on cue, Michael-Jon's best friend, Brian, touched me on the shoulder and told me I was needed upstairs. I felt a pain shoot through my heart as if it were breaking. I knew my baby was gone. I went to his room and knelt beside him. He looked as if he was just sleeping peacefully. No more pain. He was surrounded by love. His loving wife, sister, dad, and multiple friends were there with him.

She started to cry, and most of us were already in tears. She paused to regain her composure, and I wanted to run to the front of the room and hug her. But I kept my seat. I taught my retreat teams not to disrupt emotional healing by interfering with people as they experience tears or other deep feelings like Diana's. Then, she took a deep breath and explained the mystical transformation that God did in her through the Divine Mercy Chaplet.

> Even though my body was numb and heartbroken, I felt at peace. My prayers had been answered. Through prayer, I learned to trust in Jesus Christ. Yes, I grieved for my son, but my faith and trust in God strengthened me. After my son's funeral, people would approach me and ask how I was not falling apart in grief. It was difficult for them to understand the mystical transformation in me. I told them, "Jesus is my Lord and Savior. I place

all my trust in Him and Him alone. He gave me the strength to carry on through the Divine Mercy Chaplet. He lifted me up when I was down, feeling helpless and hopeless. I hung on to His promise from the *Diary*: 'One act of trust at such moments [of suffering] give greater glory to God than whole hours passed in prayer filled with consolations.'"[6]

Michael-Jon's death and reliance on the Divine Mercy Chaplet gave her a new purpose in life. Her new ministry helped countless families whose loved ones were dying or ill and gave powerful testimony to her friends like me. Diana explained the reason behind her ministry when she shared more of her story.

I promised Michael-Jon and Jesus that I would continue spreading the word of His great mercy for us and the whole world. I have had the privilege and honor of being invited to pray the Chaplet for those in nursing homes and the sick and dying in hospitals. Several times, families have sent notes or called to tell me how their family members had passed away peacefully, some smiling after I had prayed the Chaplet for them. I always let them know it was Jesus Himself who performed the miracle of providing them with a peaceful death.

Diana always wore a lapel pin with the Divine Mercy Image on it, and after she prayed for someone, she gave them the pin. Such

---

[6] Kowalska,, *Diary*, paragraph 78.

a beautiful, humble gesture to help the sick or dying hold tight to Jesus throughout their journey. The Image on the pin was the Divine Mercy Image, and Diana loved sharing the Image with everyone, as she explained.

> My husband gave me a beautiful Image of His Divine Mercy. The Image is an open door to God's mercy, as the *Diary* says: "By means of this Image I shall be granting many graces to souls; so, let every soul have access to it."[7] I have been honored by many who have asked me to borrow my Image for their meetings and presentations—Have Image, Will Travel.

Diana brought the Image her husband gave her to the meeting, adding much to her story as she spoke. I had the idea when I heard her talk about borrowing her Image. I thought, *I could take the Image to the Triennial 2009 Convention and display it in the chapel when the Juniors and I once again lead the Daughters in the Chaplet. That would make the prayer time extra special.* She graciously let me borrow the Image, which added to the depth of the Daughters' prayers, with many of them commenting on the comfort the Image gave them when they prayed in the chapel during the convention.

Diana's incredible faith and peace after such terrible suffering helped me believe more in Divine Mercy and influenced many others. I'm so grateful to her for following God's plan and changing my life with her example of faithfulness. I followed her lead when my dad was dying from the effects of Alzheimer's. He was no longer able

---

[7] Saint Maria, *Diary*, paragraph 570.

to eat or speak. My sister-in-law and I prayed the Chaplet with Dad after my brothers had gone to bed. Just as Diana testified, I saw my dad go from restless, moaning, and thrashing to peaceful and quiet. My dad was raised in the Church of Christ and had fallen away from the church many years earlier. It was an incredible, mystical encounter in the quiet hospice room, watching Dad change. And I claimed for my dad what Jesus promised in the *Diary*: "When they say this Chaplet in the presence of the dying, I will stand between My Father and the dying person not as the just Judge but as the merciful Savior."[8]

I have led my Divine Mercy group at St. Edith Stein for several years. Many people have come and gone in those years, but some stayed the entire time and became family. One of them is Belinda. She had an extraordinary mystical experience with the Divine Mercy Jesus that has changed her life forever.

BELINDA'S BABY[9]

One Monday night in 2015, Belinda arrived upset. She shared she was pregnant. With three other children and over forty years old, another child was unexpected. She at least hoped it would be a boy since she had two girls and one boy; her youngest, Jonathan, was just three. Belinda said the new baby boy's name would be Samuel. We prayed for her and the baby during our intercessions at the end of the Divine Mercy Chaplet each week. Belinda's baby was our first baby in the group, and we were excited over the news but understood Belinda's feelings.

---

[8] Kowalska, *Diary*, paragraph 1541.
[9] Used by permission of Belinda Watson.

Two months later, Belinda arrived again, looking sad. The ultrasound showed the baby was a girl. We were all thrilled and said she should name the baby Faustina. But Belinda already had a Christina. Each week, we teased her about naming the baby Faustina. I started crocheting her a red and white baby blanket representing the rays in the Image of Divine Mercy. Then she came in and said they had decided on Samantha Faustina. We all hugged Belinda and continued to pray for baby Faustina's arrival.

As the baby's due date approached, Belinda arrived to say she had called the church to arrange for the baby's Baptism, and the next date for a group Baptism was Sunday, April 27, Divine Mercy Sunday, immediately before the Divine Mercy Sunday program. We all felt a mystical movement of the Holy Spirit in baptizing our little Faustina on Divine Mercy Sunday. A week or so later was Ash Wednesday.[10] I had the privilege of giving ashes and was so joyful at being asked to serve the Lord that way. I looked each person in the eyes and felt joy as I applied the ashes to their foreheads. Then Belinda came up, and I burst into tears when I touched her forehead. The feeling that our little Faustina was extraordinary and that God had a specific plan for her overcame me. In my heart, I knew I already loved the first baby in our Divine Mercy family as though she was my own.

Belinda missed a meeting. We didn't know if she had the baby, but we started our prayers of thanksgiving that night for her to have an easy labor and safe delivery of our little Faustina. We closed the meeting, as always, with our prayer of intercessions for Belinda and the baby. As we were packing to leave, her husband, Kirkwood,

---

[10] On Ash Wednesday, an ash cross is applied to peoples' foreheads and represents mortality and penance for the person's sins. It is applied with a small blessing such as "Repent and believe in the Gospel."

walked in. Faustina was born at 8:00 p.m. during our meeting. Belinda insisted that Kirkwood rush from the hospital to show us the first pictures. After all, we were family. We were thrilled and praised God that all went well.

Faustina's Baptism on Divine Mercy Sunday was joyful, and she was an angel with a sweet disposition and beautiful black ringlets. Faustina attended all our meetings during her first year of life with her mom and prayed with us, wrapped in her red and white prayer blanket. Faustina continues to attend many of our events and has grown into a delightful, intelligent girl who always smiles.

At the Divine Mercy movie and food drive family event in March 2023, I hugged her and told her she was anointed for something special.

She didn't hear me and asked, "I'm annoying?"

I said, "No, anointed means you are special and called by God."

She just smiled up at me with her angelic smile. When Faustina had her first Holy Communion in May, and I watched as she went forward to take Jesus for the first time. She was glowing and looked angelic. Tears of joy filled my eyes with love for this precious child who had grown up in our Divine Mercy family. I felt that Faustina has a unique mystical path that God has planned for her, even though, like me, many times, she may not be aware of where God is leading her.

OFF TO EASTERN EUROPE

A set of extraordinary Divine Mercy experiences happened in the spring of 2018 when George and I visited Poland and other Eastern European countries. In Poland, one morning, we got a call from home that Isaiah, our sixteen-year-old grandson, was having a crisis. Isaiah and my daughter Susan had lived with us since he was born, so he would tell people he had three parents. Isaiah attended a high school where he was in the minority and was often teased and picked on. Isaiah was a kind, sensitive boy who would take these attacks to heart. My husband and I didn't like seeing him hurt, especially when we were so far away. I was very upset as I reached the bus and asked Father Pat Garrett, who was leading our pilgrimage, to pray for Isaiah. The whole bus prayed for him on the way to St. Maximillian Kolbe's Shrine.[11]

At the shrine, I had some time on my own. I entered the church to light a candle for Isaiah and knelt to pray to the Blessed Mother. Then, as I looked up from my kneeling position, I saw a beautiful mosaic of the Divine Mercy Image of Jesus peeking at me. The Blessed Mother was in front of a curtain hiding the Image. As I peered around the curtain to gaze at the Image, I had a mystical glimpse of Jesus walking toward me with His hand raised to give me a blessing. As He blessed me, my heart filled with an overwhelming feeling of peace and the knowledge that God heard my prayers and Isaiah had gotten through the crisis. We got a call later confirming that message from God: The crisis was over, and all was well with Isaiah. Thank you, Lord, for watching over our special grandson when we are far from home.

---

[11] St. Maximilian Kolbe was a Franciscan priest and religious founder of the Monastery of Niepokalanów near Warsaw, operated an amateur radio station, and operated several other organizations and publications. He was arrested and martyred when he volunteered to die in place of a man named Franciszek Gajowniczek in the German death camp of Auschwitz.

Later that day, a miracle occurred in St. Faustina's home church, where she grew up. It is a sweet country church, small and cozy. We had Mass with our group, and I was chosen as the cupbearer serving Jesus' Precious Blood. When the sister gave me the cup she had filled, I noticed minimal wine, which disappointed me. I wanted all to take the cup, but there was only enough for three or four people. So I began giving the cup to my fellow travelers, and the amount in the cup never went down. I was amazed. Finally, at the end of twenty-four people taking the Precious Blood, the amount left in the cup remained the same. I couldn't believe my eyes as I drank the rest of the wine, as is the custom in the Roman Catholic Church.

As I knelt to pray after returning to my seat, I reflected on why God gave me this miraculous experience. I certainly experienced joy in providing all the travelers with the Precious Blood of Jesus. And the miracle reinforced my belief in the real presence of the bread, Jesus' Body, and the wine, His Blood. So increasing the wine would be easy for a God who made wine out of water and multiplied the fishes and loaves—a true miracle to strengthen my faith in today's times. I told George, who was third in line, about the incredible miracle, and he said he noticed the small amount of wine and was also surprised by how many people partook.

After Mass, one of the sisters gave us a private tour of St. Faustina's home which was a short distance from the church. I was overcome with awe that God raised a saint in such a small, humble home. I was asked to lead the Chaplet of Divine Mercy in her backyard. What a wonderful surprise and blessing. I felt humbled and grateful while leading the Chaplet where St. Faustina played as a child. Afterward, several other pilgrims asked questions about the

Chaplet and the group began praying the Chaplet daily on the bus while traveling to our destinations.

At our next stop, we saw the most beautiful icon, Our Lady of Częstochowa, at Jasna Góra Monastery in Częstochowa, Poland. Afterward, the group entered the side Chapel of the Sacred Heart of Jesus for Mass. I saw a stained-glass picture of St. Faustina at the top of the chapel. I felt like she was watching over us everywhere I went, which gave me peace.

One of my favorite stops was at the Archabbey of Pannonhalma on a hill in Hungary. From the moment I stepped off the bus, I felt peace and the Holy Spirit everywhere I looked. The simple yellow-and-orange-colored tulips lifted their petals to the sky in praise of God. The inner sanctuary of the church displayed simplicity with beautiful white onyx windows that glowed as the sun shone through them. A white onyx altar and a white onyx baptismal font were in the center, offset from the tall, dark grey stone walls. The simplicity of the church opened my heart to God. After our busy days of touring, I wanted to rest in silence. My soul longed for simplicity and the Holy Spirit. I sat in the quiet church while the group toured other areas. I just wanted to be alone with God and pray the Chaplet. Afterward, I asked Him through my journaling why I had felt so dry and lost since we left Poland despite the daily masses. I ended my entry with, "Jesus, I trust in You!" Then I listened in hope. In a few minutes, I heard God's voice in the stillness and began to write:

> **I love you, and I hear your prayers. You are my special child. Stay close to me, like St. Faustina. I am using you to reach others through the Divine Mercy Chaplet to help them grow closer**

to Me. My blessings are flowing to you and will sustain you as you serve My beloved children. Love, God.

My spirit felt refreshed and wrapped in God's divine love after our silent interlude. My time in prayer had brought me back to my center. It helped revitalize my spirit, which the busy days and too many sites without spiritual significance had drained. Thank you, God, for another beautiful mystical encounter. I walked out of the abbey silently to find George.

DIVINE MERCY DAY OF REFLECTION

Life went on as we returned home, but I pondered my mystical encounters in Europe. My heart longed to return to Poland and the beautiful abbey on the hill in Hungary. In January 2019, God surprised me with another miracle.

I had been very sick with a bad cold and cough for two weeks and was still coughing nonstop all day. I was nervous about giving the Day of Reflection, a one-day mini-retreat at my church, because I didn't want to cough through the day. I asked St. Faustina the day before to intercede for me. She had tuberculosis, so I knew she would understand my desire not to cough while bringing the message of Divine Mercy to the participants. The day started, and I coughed only once the entire day. After the Chaplet's closing prayer, I started coughing again for several more days. Praise God for a miracle of healing that day, and thank you for your prayers and intercessions, St. Faustina!

MYSTICAL GLIMPSES FROM THE *DIARY*

My Divine Mercy group has read a few pages in the *Diary* each week. Over the years, I have been amazed at how many mystical glimpses God gave me when the *Diary* passages reflected what was happening in my world or the larger world in general. For example, Father Mike Gemignani, a longtime friend and spiritual director, read the messy first draft of my first book in November 2018 and said:

> You do, indeed, have a powerful story to tell. I'm already convinced you could write a book that is well worth reading and inspiring to other women, all too many, who have endured traumatic childhoods and abusive marriages.

Father Mike's words gave me the strength to move ahead. I read the *Diary* at our weekly meeting the following Monday and was surprised by its direct instructions to me:

> When, over a long period of time, a soul has received much light and many inspirations, and when the confessors have confirmed the source of these inspirations . . . Jesus now makes it known that it is time to put into action what it has received. The soul recognizes that God is counting on it, and this knowledge fortifies it.[12]

---

[12] Kowalska, *Diary*, paragraph 145.

I had put writing the book off for years but had finally started. This latest message from God in the *Diary* encouraged me that since my confessor, Father Mike, had confirmed the source of my inspiration, I was moving in the right direction. So I moved forward, and I published my first book on September 28, 2020, on the anniversary of my divorce from my abusive husband. I had such a feeling of accomplishment at finishing an action that God was counting on. And I thanked Him for all the people He put in my life to help me and bring the book to completion. I couldn't have done it alone.

God gave me another message in October 2021 from the *Diary*, where St. Faustina's feelings were the same as how I have sometimes felt in parts of my life. I kept Jesus with me, whether as a lonely teenage girl sitting by the river years ago, eating alone in the evening in countless restaurants after work on the road, or standing for fiduciary responsibility and ecumenical membership in The Order of the Daughters of the King. Her words soothed my hurt, lonely places deep in my heart because I knew she understood.

> But I am not alone because Jesus is with me, and with Him, I fear nothing . . . Suffering, contempt, ridicule, persecution, and humiliation will be my constant lot . . . My Jesus, my strength, and my only hope, in You alone is all my hope.[13]

Having a saint like St. Faustina send me messages I could relate to gave me inner strength and encouragement to continue God's plan for book two. I had struggled with three false starts before I got on the right track, or so I thought. Then God sent a message in April

---

[13] Kowalska, *Diary*, paragraph 746.

2022 through the *Diary*. I quickly read the last three paragraphs assigned that night as we ran out of time. I started with paragraph 895, where St. Faustina says: "I didn't feel like writing today. Then I hear a voice [Jesus] in my soul: **My daughter, you don't live for yourself but for souls; write for their benefit . . .**" I hadn't felt like writing that day either, but as I read the paragraph, I knew Jesus was talking to me. Confirming that I, too, should keep writing for others' benefit.

Now, how I suffered through a nine-month desert time spiritually, during which I was looking for an answer from God as to where I should go to serve Him. I heard nothing. Feeling lost, I was grateful to have other people's faith and the sacraments to lean on, which helped me eventually find my way to God's plan in His anointed time.

CHAPTER THIRTEEN

LEAVING THE DESERT FOR PERFECT JOY

Finding Peace with St. Francis of Assisi

If we do not forgive perfectly,
Lord, make us forgive perfectly,
so that we may really love our enemies for love of you,
and pray fervently to you for them,
returning no one evil for evil,
anxious only to serve everybody in you.
—St. Francis of Assisi

Unbeknownst to me, two significant losses were coming my way, causing me to enter a desert time for many months. A time of spiritual dryness when my heart longed for God's presence, but He felt far from me and my prayers were unanswered. The first heartbreak came in April 2010 in the form of an email from my spiritual director.

> Dear directees, Before it gets out via the rumor mill,
> I wanted to tell you that I have been diagnosed with
> a cancerous tumor in my esophagus. If any of you
> would like to continue with a different director,
> please don't hesitate to let me know. I know you
> will keep me in your prayers. I will keep you posted.
> Peace, John.

I was surprised but not particularly worried. John had been my spiritual director for ten years, so I decided to pray and await his return. Life moved on at its normal, busy pace. A few weeks later, my sweet husband, George, gave me a unique birthday gift: a Franciscan pilgrimage to Italy. I was so excited. Life was so good.

Late one night, a few days after my birthday, I got a call from John's wife. John was dying. The cancer had spread rapidly throughout his whole body, and his heart was failing. The next day, I was worried and went to see him. Eight days later, the email came from his wife: "It is with sadness that I write this. John has passed from this world to the heaven that awaits us all. He died at home today." John was only sixty-nine, just a year older than my husband at the time. I was in shock and heartbroken.

The second heartbreak came less than twenty-four hours later. The day after John passed away, I was called into a special meeting with eight members of the Secular Franciscan Fraternity[1] where I belonged. I had been studying with them for two years. They accused

---

[1] The Secular Franciscan Order is an order in the Roman Catholic Church, founded by St. Francis of Assisi third order over 800 years ago and canonically established by Pope Honorius III. St. Francis desired that ordinary people be able to join his new order.

me of many things I hadn't done and dismissed me from the fraternity. All I could say throughout the forty-five minutes of verbal abuse was: "I don't understand?" I became more and more hysterical until I finally ran out of the room. My heart was utterly broken. I was left in total confusion. Had I misunderstood God's call to the Secular Franciscan when I met with Brother Robert Lentz and he told me about them? Then, talking to a friend, she said she planned to attend their next meeting and invited me along. I felt both incidents were God's glimpses that came out of nowhere, directing me to follow St. Francis of Assisi, whom I had always admired for his simplicity and incredible faith.

On a Franciscan retreat in May, just a month before, I prayed and discerned God's will for me while sitting by the beautiful, tree-lined Louisiana bayou. I realized that God was calling me to membership in the Franciscans, but He didn't want me to leave my prayer order. God made it clear to me that there was no conflict in belonging to the two groups. He gave me a beautiful analogy. He told me that the Daughters of the King were my family of origin, growing me to spiritual adulthood. Now, as a spiritual adult, it was time for me to move into a new family (sort of like leaving home to get married). But getting married didn't mean leaving my original family behind. God's analogy was a mystical moment for me. I was relieved because I loved the Daughters and felt called to be a Franciscan.

I tried to explain the analogy to the fraternity members in the meeting during the forty-five minutes of confrontation. Still, in hindsight, I think I brought confusion into the process. They wanted me to belong only to the Franciscans, but that wasn't good enough when I offered to resign from the Daughters. I was confused and deeply hurt. I went home and immediately wrote notes asking for forgiveness from all I was accused of hurting. Sadly, it would be many months before others confirmed what I knew in my heart: that truth hadn't been spoken that day.

These two events, both losses—without warning and so close to one another—left me in the desert spiritually. God seemed distant, and my prayers were unanswered. I came to rely on the Holy Eucharist for my comfort and support. Two days later, at the Rosary for John, I shared with my friend Sue Ellen that something terrible had happened, and I needed a new spiritual director right away. When I saw her the following day, Sue Ellen said God had given her the name of someone who would be an excellent spiritual director for me: Tom Peery. She said she would introduce me to him after John's funeral if he was there.

Later, I went to the church a bit early for the funeral to visit with John's widow and have some quiet prayer time. A couple was walking into the church just ahead of me. The man graciously stopped to hold the door for me. Then he turned and asked me if I, too, was a friend of John's. I said, "Yes, he was my spiritual director." The man then said he was also a spiritual director; he introduced himself, and you got it: Tom Peery. I laughed, which made him step back. I quickly explained that Sue Ellen planned to introduce him to me after the funeral because she felt God was calling him to be my next spiritual director. He was quite surprised but agreed to meet with me.

John's body was donated to science, so we had a beautiful memorial Mass for him. The celebration of the Holy Eucharist helped to soothe my grief, and the homily fed me spiritually. John left a message for us. He said, "I didn't have faith in Jesus; I knew Jesus. And we weren't to blame God for not healing him. He is in a beautiful place, praying for us." I thought, *Was it John's prayers that helped put Tom's name on Sue Ellen's heart or a mystical encounter moving me toward God's plan for my life?* As it turned out, Tom had recently written and published a book, so God knew Tom was a perfect spiritual director to encourage me to write my first book. Like John, he was also kind and intelligent, and I felt blessed to have Tom as my spiritual director for many years.

SEARCHING FOR ANSWERS

I started spiritual direction with Tom the following week. At our first session, Tom suggested I look at what God was trying to teach me in the dismissal from the fraternity. I prayed, cried, and journaled for several weeks and still wasn't getting clarity from God.

So I turned to the Sacrament of Reconciliation.[2] Two weeks later, I saw Father Ed, a retired priest, at the Cenacle Retreat Center. I spent an hour with him, talking through my dismissal. I cried as I told Father Ed the story. I was still bewildered and looking for answers to why my path with the Franciscans abruptly ended when God had called me. "Did I misunderstand God's call?" I asked. He couldn't give me an answer but summed it up like this: "Kathy, you have to accept that sometimes people just don't like you." People not liking me was hard to hear for someone who has been a people pleaser all her life. Reconciliation helped me accept that God had

---

[2] The Sacrament of Reconciliation was established so sinners can obtain forgiveness for their sins and reconcile with God and the Church. The priest gives a penance for the penitent to do and asks them to say an Act of Contrition. Then the priest grants absolution, using the power that Christ entrusted to the Church and by which he pardons the sins of the penitent in the name of the Father, and the Son, and the Holy Spirit.

forgiven me, but the dryness in my prayer life and my search for answers continued.

As my pilgrimage to Italy drew nearer, I became increasingly apprehensive. One of the fraternity members who participated in my dismissal also signed up for the trip. I didn't relish spending ten days with her. I kept praying to God for an answer. Should I cancel the trip and lose George's money or go? No answer came.

Then, in August, a month before my trip, I went for a routine cardiac checkup. I had developed pain in my side under my arm. I'd had heart problems for many years and a history of fatal heart attacks in my family, so my cardiologist, Dr. Selim Sekili, was concerned and ordered an immediate nuclear stress test. The test showed something in the bottom left corner of my heart, so he immediately worked me into the schedule for a heart catheterization with the plan to put in a stint if needed. A stint would mean I couldn't go to Italy because flying would be too dangerous so soon after heart surgery.

I thought, *Was this an answer from God? Would this be the excuse I needed to cancel the trip for medical reasons and get George's money back?* Two days before my heart catheterization, I went to Mass at St. Edith's to receive the Sacrament of the Anointing of the Sick. As soon as Father Leszek, a visiting priest, placed his hands on my head and prayed for me, I felt a surge of the Holy Spirit flow through my body like electricity. Then, Deacon Leonard placed his hands on my head and prayed for me. Again, the same surge of the Holy Spirit went through my body. I returned to my seat and told George I had just been healed.

When Dr. Sekili came into the operating room two days later, I told him to go ahead, but he wouldn't find anything because I had been healed. He patted my arm, smiled, and said, "We'll see." Well, he didn't find anything. Dr. Sekili was surprised that my heart was healthier than eight years earlier when he did my first heart catheterization—a miracle that he couldn't explain. And yes, I went to Italy in September.

MY FRANCISCAN PILGRIMAGE

My pilgrimage to Assisi was a challenging but healing ten days. I prayed for several weeks for all the members of my fraternity who deeply hurt me with their dismissal, including my traveling companion. Now, I had to put my prayer into action by completely forgiving her and showing her the kindness and the divine love of Christ as instructed in Luke 6:27–28: "Love your enemies, do good to those who hate you, bless those who curse you, pray for those who mistreat you." When I saw her at the airport, I greeted her as a dear friend, hugged her, and acted like nothing had happened. It was hard to forgive her and move forward, but it did calm my anxiety. Throughout the pilgrimage, I was respectful to her but didn't spend time with her. I made many new friends among the other pilgrims.

Our tour guide, Bret Thoman, surprised me when he added a visit to Gubbio, which wasn't on our itinerary. One of my favorite stories of St. Francis is taming the wolf[3] and saving the town. In the story, St. Francis convinced the wolf to stop killing animals and people in exchange for the townspeople feeding him. Reflecting on the story in the city of its origin made me think about how we sometimes hurt others because of our needs. I wondered, *Was that*

---

[3] Murray Bodo, OFM, "St. Francis and the Taming of the Wolf," in *St. Anthony Messenger,* February 2020, https://www.franciscanmedia.org/st-anthony-messenger/st-francis-and-the-taming-of-the-wolf/.

what happened in the fraternity? Did the leader need to be in control of the fraternity because her life at home was out of control? Maybe this was part of the answer for my dismissal.

Despite such clarity, the dryness in my prayer life continued and followed me to our next stop—the Chapel of the Stigmata.[4] This chapel lies on top of the spot where St. Francis received the stigmata—the wounds of Christ—in 1224. On the drive to Mt. Laverna, Bret asked me to share my story, but I was still too hurt to open up in front of my traveling companions. As I entered the Chapel of the Stigmata, I saw the beauty of the large crucifix in porcelain over the altar, which was part of the Della Robbia *maioliche* (glazed ceramic) behind the altar. At the bottom was a verse written in Latin from Lamentations 1:12:

> Come, all who pass by the way, pay attention and
> see: Is there any pain like my pain, which has been
> ruthlessly inflicted upon me, with which the LORD
> has tormented me on the day of his blazing wrath?

A small glass vase of flowers and the flickering oil lamp marked where St. Francis received the stigmata. The stunning beauty of the ceramic scene, plus the Bible verse, spoke deeply to me of Christ's suffering for me—pain ruthlessly inflicted on Him. The memory of the pain that I experienced caused me to start crying. I had stayed in the chapel long after the others left, praying and listening for God's voice, hoping to hear anything, but my desert time continued.

---

[4] The stigmata is the spontaneous appearance of the wound marks of our crucified Lord on a person's body. These marks include the nail wounds at the feet and the hands, the lance wound at the side, the head wounds from the crown of thorns, and the scourge marks over the entire body, particularly the back.

Here at the Sanctuary of La Verna, I spent more time in tears than joy. In my thoughts, I continued to question God: *Lord, why can't I stop crying? When will my broken heart and the feeling of rejection be healed? I need to hear Your voice and feel Your divine love.*

Intellectually, I knew that Francis and Christ endured far more rejection and suffering than mine, but my human heart still hurt. Being dismissed from the fraternity shattered my dream of being a Secular Franciscan. Not hearing God's voice or His answers to my prayers through months of my desert time made me feel hopeless and lost. I desperately desired God to give me a clear path to follow His will.

Later, I joined all the pilgrims following a relic of St. Francis in the procession from the main church back through the chapel and around the square in the bright Italian sunshine. My soul found joy in the beautiful singing and the ringing of the church bells. Afterward, I was the last one in line as we finally started down the mountain so I could talk to Bret alone. I was thankful for this special time to share my story with him and pour out my broken heart. He had been through his own trials, so he understood, and his words were comforting. Bret shared times God had helped him and encouraged me to continue to search for God's answer. The day ended with Mass. Again, the sacrament of the Holy Eucharist, even in Italian, was soothing.

THE STORY OF PERFECT JOY

During my desert time, I reflected on St. Francis' story, specifically when he told Brother Leo that perfect joy came from being rejected and falsely accused. The following is an abbreviated version of this story:

> Once, in a conversation with Brother Leo, Francis explained what he called "perfect joy." Francis responded by describing the possibility that they would arrive at their destination after walking in the rain and cold and, upon presenting themselves as fellow brethren, were accused of lying and turned away. That, Francis said, would be perfect joy. He went on to add, "And if we knock again, and the porter comes out in anger to drive us away with oaths and blows, as if we were vile impostors, saying, 'Begone, miserable robbers, for here you shall neither eat nor sleep!' But, if we accept all this with patience, joy, and charity, O Brother Leo, write that this indeed is perfect joy."[5]

This story is a clear example of how St. Francis found joy in suffering like Christ—who was falsely accused and rejected. The concept of perfect joy seemed confusing and counterintuitive to me. How could I find joy in false accusations and being turned away? Yet I accepted my dismissal with forgiveness in my heart for those responsible and learned that joy comes from inside. Joy reminds me that even when I'm devoid of happiness, God is still with me and will always love me. And maybe my desert time was God's plan to teach me patience. That was a virtue I had struggled with most of my life.

---

[5] Susan Hines-Brigger, "Editorial: The Gift of Perfect Joy," *Franciscan Media*, December 6, 2023, https://www.franciscanmedia.org/news-commentary/editorial-the-gift-of-perfect-joy/.

In learning St. Francis' story, I came to understand his pain when he lost his order to the rules imposed by others. I could relate to his experience—when the rules become more important than the person and the person's dignity. As I descended the mountain, one of my travel companions told me I could join another fraternity in my area. I had been unaware of that possibility, and finally, I had hope. I prayed that if I got to join another fraternity, I would remember that everyone who comes needs to be loved and accepted, and love should come before the rules. I'm so grateful to some of my travel companions who taught me that acceptance and understanding are part of being a true Franciscan, like St. Francis.

After my return from Assisi, I continued to search for answers and understanding. Despite my new knowledge and hope, my desert time continued. I contacted a canon lawyer who referred me to Canon 307 of the Roman Catholic Church, which encourages people to belong to more than one association of the faithful, the term that describes The Order of the Daughters of the King. He supported my discernment: I could be a DOK and a Secular Franciscan fraternity member.

In November 2010, a friend invited my daughter, Susan, to a women's retreat, and Susan asked me to accompany her. I was still praying to God for an answer. At one point in the retreat, we all sat in a circle, and people shared the feelings they were experiencing. Suddenly, a woman who was new to the retreat got up, started moving around the circle, and shared what God told her about each person. From the other retreatant's reactions, I could tell she was correct in what she said, but it was frightening to many who weren't used to people prophesying about their lives. As the woman moved around the circle, I prayed that she would skip Susan as I saw how frightened Susan was. God answered my prayer, and after she skipped Susan, she reached me; I put up my hand to tell her to stop. Spiritual gifts aren't to be used to frighten people but for the upbuilding of the church, as it says in Ephesians 4:8b,12: "He gave gifts to men . . . to equip the holy ones for the work of ministry, for building up the body of Christ." Our eyes met, and she paused. Then she told me, "God knows you want an answer, but it isn't time." Afterward, she sat down. Wow! This mystical message from God shook me. I realized I needed patience as my desert time wasn't over. My life went on.

Early in January 2011, I taught a two-part workshop on the spiritual gifts that we are all given at Baptism and are enlivened through the Sacrament of Confirmation. During the workshop, I shared the story of my dismissal and my continuing desert time. One of the parishioners came up after the session and said, "You have been given such a gift!" I was surprised and didn't feel that my desert time or the pain of my dismissal was a gift. But as I thought about his comment, I realized he was bringing me a message from God. In the following days, I began to count all the blessings that had come during my desert time and the healing of my broken heart. I had grown in my faith, learned to wait on the Lord with a new depth of patience, and understood St. Francis' story of perfect joy, which brought me closer to Christ. I also examined my path. I realized God was leading me on His path, even if I didn't understand where we were going. As it says in James 1:2–3: "Consider it all joy, my brothers, when you encounter various trials, for you know that the testing of your faith produces perseverance." My joy was slowly returning.

THE END OF MY DESERT TIME

In January 2011, I received an email from the woman involved in my dismissal from the fraternity. She asked Jeff, the regional formation director, if it was right for her fraternity to dismiss me because of my membership in The Order of the Daughters of the King. Jeff told her that the fraternity misunderstood my membership in The Order—an association, not a third order in the Roman Catholic Church—so it didn't conflict with the Secular Franciscan Order. Jeff asked her to convey an invitation to me to attend his fraternity.

I felt this was a miracle from God confirming my call to the Secular Franciscans and to come through the person who had participated in my dismissal. Wow! My kindness toward her and the healing love of Christ had transformed her spirit and flowed back to me as a blessing! My desert time was ending, As Lamentations 3:25 promises: "The LORD is good to those who trust in him, to the one that seeks him."

In February 2011, I met with Father Page Pope—the priest who had been the spiritual assistant for my first fraternity. I asked him if he knew of any reason why I shouldn't accept the invitation to Jeff's fraternity after being dismissed from the first one. I didn't want to be dismissed again and wanted to be sure there wasn't a flaw in me that others saw, but I didn't. He was confused, and as I went back over what happened in my dismissal, I could tell he was angry but didn't say anything. I suspected he didn't know about my dismissal. He finally told me to go ahead and join the new fraternity. Two weeks after meeting with Father Pope, the leader who dismissed me resigned. Sadly, I learned later that I wasn't the only one hurt during this time in the fraternity.

In March 2011, my desert time ended, and my new life began. The discernment during my desert time helped me say a definite yes to the new fraternity, but I also knew in my heart that I was to continue my lifetime membership in The Order of the Daughters of the King. I had grown spiritually and understood the meaning of perfect joy. I studied with my new fraternity for several months. In August 2011, my new fraternity felt I was ready to make my profession.[6]

On the first of September in 2011, two weeks before my profession, I received a call from a dear friend, Connie. I hadn't seen her since my dismissal. She asked me to return to my old fraternity for her profession ceremony the next week. We had studied together, and Connie wanted me there for her special day. After some prayer, I decided to go, although I was nervous how the other members would greet me. I arrived a bit early, and as each fraternity member arrived, there was genuine love and joy on their faces as they saw me. They greeted me with smiles and hugs and said they missed me. I greeted them with a smile and hug as if nothing had happened. I had truly forgiven them and was joyful to be there for Connie. I was indeed able to celebrate with her. I stayed for the reception and had a great time renewing old friendships. It was a wonderful day of healing and renewal.

My new fraternity selected September 17, 2011, as my profession date. As soon as I heard the date, I knew God had orchestrated it for my profession because September 17 is the Feast of the Stigmata of St. Francis Assisi. When the formation director selected the date, she didn't realize it was special. I found such healing and joy at the

---

[6] Profession signifies a candidate's desire to become a member of the order and to make a permanent commitment to the Gospel life of Jesus Christ by following in the steps of St. Francis of Assisi.

Chapel of the Stigmata that I knew it was part of God's plan for my life to profess that day! As I finally fulfilled God's call to the Secular Franciscans Order (OFS)[7] during a beautiful Mass, I sang God's praises like St. Francis. Perfect joy replaced my desert time as the minister placed my Tau cross around my neck. Without God allowing my many months of desert time, I wouldn't have realized how vital my profession was to me and that I was ready to make a permanent profession. My new fraternity was a much better fit for me. God knew all along where I belonged! Thank you, Lord.

One lasting lesson my desert time taught me was although I couldn't hear God, He was always with me. The most essential part of traveling through the desert time was to continue to do the practices that kept me connected: Sacraments, community, and prayer. Most important is prayer if only to listen and to be there, as this simple poem reminds us.

How to Pray[8]

Prayer is so simple.
It is like quietly opening a door and slipping into
the very presence of God
there, in the stillness,
to listen for His voice,
perhaps in petition
or only to listen,
it matters not,
just to be there,
in His presence
is prayer.

---

[7] OFS: Ordo Franciscanus Saecularis is the official name in Italian for the Secular Franciscan Order.
[8] Often attributed to Brother Lawrence, this simple poem is used as a guide to discover the presence of God.

As my desert time ended and prior to my profession, God again entered my prayer time with His still, small voice. He sent me to a new ministry where I would serve for seven years in three different Roman Catholic churches while experiencing more mystical encounters, miracles, and divine love. God's plan involved me growing in leadership and presentation skills, but most importantly, learning how to build community.

CHAPTER FOURTEEN

GROWING INTO COMMUNITY

Guiding ACTS Retreats[1]

The Pilgrim's Map

Mainly it's the stories we carry with us,
the tales of those who've gone before,
those who've made their own map, as we will make ours.
The stories and rituals passed down from generation to generation.
They will help us make our map.
The stories, rituals, the Spirit of God.
Of these shall we be created anew.
Of these three is pilgrimage: story, ritual, Spirit.
How we listen and do and pray
becomes the map we make.
—Murray Bodo[2]

---

[1] An ACTS Retreat (Adoration, Community, Theology, Service) is a parish-based event which offers parishioners an opportunity to experience the love of Jesus Christ. This, in turn, fosters a desire for intentional discipleship. ACTS Retreats are given by parishioners for parishioners, and in this way, serve to build Christian community at the parish.

[2] Bodo, *The Road*, back cover.

In April 2011, God kicked me through the next door to serve Him, surprising and exciting me. The spiritual companion (director) for my church's first ACTS retreat at St. Edith Stein suddenly took a job at another church. I was asked to take over as a spiritual companion for her. Over five years had passed since I served as a spiritual director for a retreat team, and I missed the camaraderie and growth that came with being a part of a team. I hadn't attended an ACTS retreat, so I knew nothing about this type of retreat. I thought, *How hard can it be? After all, I had served as spiritual director on many other retreats and attended even more.* So I said yes and thought, *Piece of cake!*

Attending an ACTS retreat was a prerequisite for serving on the team, so I signed up immediately for a retreat with another church. I was the only person from another church on the retreat. My tablemates were in various stages of grief from losing a spouse, including our facilitator, so the small group sharing time was a time of tears. I had long since healed my grief over my failed marriage, so I spent much of the time listening and empathizing with my tablemates. I needed to practice my spiritual direction skills to serve my ACTS team since the retreat had a different format than my previous retreats. I felt God blessed me by placing me in this group.

Later in my retreat, I sat in the chapel, praying the Rosary with the other retreatants. I realized I finally felt comfortable praying this important Catholic prayer. I had struggled with the Rosary since converting to the Catholic Church in 1994. Part of my problem was the speedy way folks often prayed the Rosary—too fast for a newbie to follow or learn. But gradually, I did learn it and, on this retreat, realized I enjoyed praying the Rosary—finding peace and comfort with the Blessed Mother. What an extraordinary mystical glimpse God gave me. I felt like the Blessed Mother was there with me, holding me like her child. Maybe I was finally Catholic.

At the final retreat activity, my prayer partner revealed that she had prayed a particular verse for me before and during the retreat, John 15:16: "It was not you who chose me, but I who chose you and appointed you to go and bear fruit that will remain." Wow! I was amazed. The verse reflected what I believed: that God chose me specifically to take on essential challenges—the challenges in Daughters of the King, my work with Oracle, serving as a spiritual director, and now serving in ACTS. This is why I have written my books with God's help, to leave fruit that will remain.

PREPARING THE ACTS TEAM

As the spiritual companion of the ACTS retreat, one of my responsibilities was helping the team members prepare their talks. This responsibility taught me that everyone has a faith story—even if they don't know it. I also learned that sharing their story on the ACTS retreat was healing, especially if they were honest with their feelings and experiences. It is hard to share embarrassing and hurtful experiences, but such healing comes from that sharing, not just for the speaker but also for the retreatants and other team members.

I also learned the importance of praying for the right team members to be called to give the talks. On the second retreat in 2013, God pointed me to one woman in particular. When I invited her to tell her story, she said, "I don't have a story to share." I kept questioning and encouraging her to write whatever God gave her when she prayed about her story. Finally, she brought two handwritten paragraphs to our first mentoring session. As I questioned her about her life, I learned her husband had died suddenly. It was a painful time for her. We explored the story and developed that sad time into a sharing that touched others who had lost someone special. I felt honored and humbled to help her heal a painful part of her life.

Each of my ACTS teams was a unique community, and I experienced mystical encounters and more during the team preparation, retreat days, and follow-up sessions after the retreat. Later, the retreatants joined the community. In his book *Can You Drink the Cup*, Nouwen perfectly describes the community that ACTS teaming and retreat experiences create and how important it is to be part of a mutual care fellowship. He says:

> Community is a fellowship of people who do not hide their joys and sorrows but make them visible to each other in a gesture of hope. In community we say: "Life is full of gains and losses, joys and sorrows, ups and downs—but we do not have to live it alone. We want to drink our cup together and thus celebrate the truth that the wounds of our individual lives, which seem intolerable when lived alone, become sources of healing when we live them as part of a fellowship of mutual care."[3]

The C in ACTS stands for community, and as the spiritual companion, it was my job to help instill the feeling of sisterhood and mutual care within the team and then in the retreatants. Usually, the retreatants open up after the Friday evening talks and events and begin deep sharing, but not on my second St. Edith retreat, and I

---

[3] Nouwen, *Can You Drink*, 57.

felt helpless. I knew that only the Holy Spirit could move the hearts of the retreatants. The next morning one of the talks opened the retreatants' hearts to honest sharing. Watching the Holy Spirit moving in an extraordinary way so late in the retreat was amazing. He moved through their hearts, helping them to open up during sharing and created an unexpected unity that bonded the retreatants, which was evident in their afternoon activities. Instead of individual table activities, all the retreatants created an outstanding activity together. The mystical movement of the Holy Spirit brought tears to my eyes. Truly, God had a unique plan for the retreat.

SPREADING ACTS

After my first two ACTS retreats at St. Edith Stein, I was asked by the ACTS Missions Houston Chapter to help spread the ACTS ministry to St. Justin Martyr, my former church, where I still had many friends. I felt like I had come home to be with them again. I got many hugs and had great fun catching up with friends and changes in their lives. My memories of the St. Justin women's retreat years ago came flooding back with the joy and lessons learned. I was excited to work with some of the same women on the ACTS team. While preparing for and throughout St. Justin's ACTS retreat in 2014, God's mystical glimpses offered me moments to reflect on and search for the meaning of His messages.

One message from a particular Bible verse popped up on that retreat many times. Several of the team members had the verse in their talks. When the third team member read her talk, the verse appeared again. I knew God was trying to get my attention. The verse wasn't the theme of the retreat. I knew in my heart that God was trying to tell me something, and I needed to listen, but I was struggling to understand what He was telling me. Sometimes, He is too mystical! The verse was Jeremiah 29:11: "For I know well the plans I have in mind for you . . . plans for your welfare and not for woe, so as to give you a future of hope." I was still at a loss as to what God was trying to tell me. One of my teammates gave me the verse in a beautiful frame. After the retreat, I placed it on my piano, where it still sits today, and I have read it many times. The verse helps me to remain hopeful when suffering or trials enter my life. I knew that God was watching over me each day planning for my welfare and that good things would happen in the future. It has helped me hang on through hurricanes, illnesses, and unexpected changes. The verse became my inspiration as I continued with hope to stumble along His sometimes broken, sometimes smooth path.

THE COLOR PURPLE

Each ACTS retreat is a unique event. The many weeks of teaming where the team grows and bonds as sisters in Christ makes the retreat go smoothly. In some years, this process was more successful than in other years. Usually, the team discerned a theme, artwork, and color for folders and other items to match. St. Justin's second ACTS retreat team in 2015 started as usual. The theme picture was by an unknown artist. A beautiful picture showed many things representing the path to spiritual life, including a cross that formed a bridge crossing a ravine to let us walk the road to heaven. The path was a reminder of the love and suffering of Jesus and our path to salvation. The journey's ultimate goal was to experience the abounding joy in His presence in heaven, which reflected perfectly our theme for the weekend from Psalms 16:11a: "You will show me the path to life, abounding joy in your presence."

The picture also reflected our ACTS team as we traveled together as sisters on the path—some people helping one another, some trying to pull others from the flames, and still others holding people back to keep them on the path. We help each other through the darkness and stay in the light as we walk on life's paths. If we fall, other sisters are there to support and encourage us. We, in turn, can be there for them as we strive to obtain the goal we all desire: to experience the abounding joy and divine love in the presence of our Father in Heaven.

The retreat team took on a mystical essence that revolved around the color purple and created a powerful and successful team bond that became the team's identity as Daughters of God. Purple wasn't in the theme picture, but it became our color. We became royal princesses on a journey to God's presence. Purple combines the calm stability of blue and the fierce energy of red. Purple is often associated with royalty, nobility, luxury, power, and ambition. Purple represents wealth, extravagance, creativity, wisdom, dignity, grandeur, devotion, peace, pride, mystery, and independence. Purple is in the Bible in many places. Roman soldiers clothed Jesus in purple before beating him and crucifying Him. They mocked His supposed royalty, but it was ironic since Jesus was, in fact, royalty. As Mark 15:17–18 says: "They clothed him in purple and, weaving a crown of thorns, placed it on him. They began to salute him with, 'Hail, King of the Jews!'"

Interestingly, the team started to identify with a woman in the New Testament in Acts 16:14: "One of them, a woman named Lydia, a dealer in purple cloth, from the city of Thyatira, a worshipper of

God, listened, and the Lord opened her heart to pay attention to what Paul was saying." As we prepared week after week for the upcoming retreat, we all became like Lydia, with God opening our hearts to pay attention to His divine love. The team began wearing purple. We found purple scarves and shawls for the events on the retreat weekend. We asked everyone, team and retreatants, to wear purple on Sunday when we returned from the retreat to Mass. As we sang our theme song before Mass, we praised our awesome God as though we had already arrived in heaven at the end of our life paths and were celebrating in the abounding joy in His presence as His beautiful Daughters."

MY LAST TWO ACTS TEAMS

Many of us from St. Edith's ACTS ministry came to Epiphany of the Lord Catholic Church to help them start their ACTS ministry. I was the spiritual companion, and my good friend Penny Whited was the director. I faced many challenges from a representative of the ACTS Missions Houston Chapter, who was there to ensure the team's preparation happened adequately. She didn't like what I had always done and kept challenging me, causing me to have anxiety. She questioned my handouts and meeting preparation. I spent more time studying the official director's manual, trying to do everything perfectly, but nothing seemed good enough. The stress often brought me to tears on the way home from the meetings. Exacerbating the situation, I was dealing with serious health issues. I worked hard with the team for months in 2017. The team was ready, and the retreatants had started registering. A little over three weeks before the retreat, on August 25, Hurricane Harvey made landfall.

Heading toward Houston, Harvey eventually destroyed the Cenacle Retreat House where the retreat was to be held. The whole team was devastated, but many were dealing with more significant problems as many of their homes or those of family and friends experienced severe damage or total loss.

In the meantime, St. Justin Martyr was also to have their third retreat at the Cenacle in November 2017 and had to cancel. I had helped train their new spiritual companion, a special friend, and gave the team a Day of Reflection. I was heartbroken for them, too, at having to reschedule their retreat. After scrambling, they found a new retreat center and rescheduled for February 2018.

The St. Justin's 2018 ACTS retreat experience began much like my first one at St. Edith in 2011. Their spiritual companion suddenly stepped down for health reasons. I got a call from Mary Lou, their director, in December 2017. St. Justin's ACTS team had been on my mind and heart for several weeks, and I had been praying very hard for them after Hurricane Harvey caused the cancelation, but I was unsure why. When she called and asked me to finish the teaming and serve as their spiritual companion on the retreat, I knew in my heart God wanted me to say yes. Mary Lou told me she felt God had given her my name because it was the first thing she saw when she opened the previous spiritual companion's files. God had a plan! Mary Lou told me she was so relieved I said yes. She felt my yes was a divine answer to her urgent prayers. Since I served on two retreats with them before and gave their Day of Reflection for the 2017 team, I knew most team members and bonding would be easy.

As I hung up the phone, I thought back to the first St. Justin's retreat when the verse from Jeremiah 29:11 kept popping up. *I needed that verse right now before I started Epiphany teaming again. For I know well the plans I have in mind for you . . . plans for your welfare and not for woe, so as to give you a future of hope.* I needed to know that I was following God's plan and He was in control, growing me through the stressful situation when I first teamed with Epiphany. Rather than fight, I humbled myself, forgave each incident and co-operated, but it was a difficult teaming time, which left me drained. Going home to St. Justin's again, where I could teach as I love to do without worrying about someone criticizing my every move, was a welcome reprieve. I worked hard to learn solid team-building methods during the successful ACTS retreats I led. I wanted St. Justin's to have a wonderful retreat.

St. Justin's third retreat, where I had many loving friends, was healing. Also, the women who helped me with the spiritual part of the program were young, enthusiastic, eager to learn, and full of joy. I called them my "Little Angels"! Their joy and energy were a saving grace for me. I praised God for them many times during the retreat as they did an excellent job and took some of the work from me. When I finished my talk sharing a story from my life, they all surrounded me with big hugs and giggles, and one said, "How do you do a talk like that?" It was awesome. God's divine love came through St. Justin's retreat and restored my heart and soul. I experienced so much joy sharing the team's joy at a successful retreat. Thank you, Lord, for healing my heart and for my dear St. Justin Martyr ACTS family.

I returned with renewed energy and took Epiphany through their second teaming experience and first retreat in November 2018. As an extra blessing, I was able to help Epiphany use the same retreat center that St. Justin's used. Since I had already led one retreat there, I could better prepare Epiphany for their retreat. Also, the woman from the ACTS Missions Houston Chapter didn't attend our meetings so I could relax and enjoy teaching and interacting with the women. Their retreat went well, and I was relieved when it was over. I did have joy at their success, and I was energized by their enthusiasm at finally having their retreat.

My ACTS experience taught me much about building a team into a community, trusting the Holy Spirit to fill in areas where I lacked, coaching women to find, write, and deliver their stories, and realizing the powerful healing God can bring from an ACTS retreat and through the teaming experience. Retreats took every bit of my energy and more to finish the weekend, plus the twelve weeks of team preparation, the Day of Reflection and the follow-up sessions also required a lot of preparation. I retired from the ACTS ministry after Epiphany's retreat. My job promoted me to manager, requiring more hours, and my ongoing physical problems were causing fatigue, so it was time to move on.

God's path for my life had other lessons and experiences, which I learned and became a reality through traveling the world. One of the most critical lessons God taught me was the importance of preparing my heart to receive God's mystical experiences, miracles, and divine love in places I visited.

CHAPTER FIFTEEN

MY STUMBLING CONTINUES

Traveling the World

"Truly, the LORD is in this place and I did not know it!"
. . . "How awesome this place is!
This is nothing else but the house of God, the gateway to heaven!"
—Genesis 28:16–17

In the Celtic world that gateway is present everywhere.
In every place is the immediacy of heaven.
In every moment we can glimpse the
Light that was in the beginning
and from which all things have come . . .
We can step over this threshold
and back again in the fleeting span of a second.
In a single step we can find ourselves
momentarily in that other world,
the world of eternal Light, which is woven
inseparably through this world—
the world of matter that is forever unfolding like a river in flow.[1]

---

[1] John Philip Newell, *The Rebirthing of God: Christianity's Struggle for New Beginnings* (Woodstock, VT: Skylight Paths Publishing, 2014), 32.

In March 2009, we went on a cruise to the Holy Land (Israel) and surrounding countries—Egypt, Greece, and Turkey—for our fifteenth wedding anniversary. I learned that preparing my heart was more important than my luggage! After planning the contents for weeks, I carefully packed our two large suitcases, which didn't arrive in Cairo. We waited over six hours for the next flight, but still no luggage. I was exhausted when we finally got to the hotel.

Our tour started in Egypt, where we rode camels, saw the pyramids and the Sphinx, and experienced the sights and sounds of an Arab country. Having lived in Saudi Arabia for three years with my first husband, I was familiar with the sights and sounds of an Arab country, and it brought back memories. Overcrowded, barren, lots of honking cars all day and night, bargaining with merchants, and the call to prayer five times a day. And I was ready to leave almost as soon as we got there. Moving on to Israel and Turkey and seeing all the places where Jesus walked, Peter preached, and Mary lived after Jesus' Ascension was awesome.

Once I realized the luggage wasn't coming, I accepted God's plan and realized that my heart and soul mattered on this pilgrimage, not my clothes. God simplified my wardrobe very quickly, and no one cared. I had worried about the wrong things in getting ready for the trip. I learned a valuable lesson that has helped me better prepare for other trips. The tour company provided a car and guide after our day of touring the River Jordan and the Sea of Galilee. We went shopping at the local market, and in ninety minutes, we got most of what we needed and maxed out two credit cards! Having shopped in Saudi while I lived there prepared me for the markets in

Israel so I could bargain with the merchants. I was determined to make do and fully experience the journey God had planned for us.

I had several amazing mystical experiences that I'll always treasure. My first was when we visited the Mount of Olives. George stayed on the bus because the walk down was steep. But I got off the bus to take the path down to the Garden of Gethsemane, and a storm blew in with rain and wind. I quickly fell behind the others. The wind shredded my umbrella and almost stripped off my shawl. I found myself surrounded by male vendors trying to sell their wares. Money changers! I was scared.

As I approached the Garden and came around the wall, I saw a single purple iris in full bloom. I was immediately filled with peace and comfort, replacing my fear and chaos. The purple iris was my late mother's favorite flower; she grew rows of them every spring when I was a child. I knew she was surrounding me with her love. I suddenly felt safe and warm in her embrace. This mystical encounter wasn't the first time my mom had come into my life after her death. The first time was in 1993 at her funeral when the pianist surprised me by playing one of my upcoming wedding songs, followed by a rainbow on the way to the cemetery. I felt reassured that she would be at my forthcoming wedding in spirit.

I didn't know how or why these mystical encounters with my mom happened. God gave me clarity years later while at the Ruah Center[2] in 2019. My mom came to me in a dream, directing me to add something to my first book about her domestic abuse. I was

---

[2] Ruah Spirituality Center, a ministry of the Sisters of Charity of the Incarnate Word located in Houston, Texas, focuses primarily on promoting the re-creation of the human spirit.

surprised by the intimate encounter and prayed to God to help me understand how these mystical encounters happened.

Later the same weekend, I had a nudging from God I should read a book open on the retreat center's hall table for my grand-daughter's birthdate, November 4th. I was so surprised when the book *You Are the Beloved* explained my mother and my after-death relationship.

> Relationships are a mystery. It is possible to have intimate relationships with loved ones who have died. Death sometimes deepens the intimacy . . . [I do believe,] though, that after separation, certain people continue to be very significant for us in our hearts and through our memories . . . I am a human being who was loved by God before I was born and whom God will love after I die. This brief lifetime is my opportunity to receive love, deepen love, grow in love, and give love. When I die, love continues to be active, and from full communion with God, I am present by love to those I leave behind.[3]

I finally had clarity on my mystical encounters with my mother. Each encounter gave me a feeling of closeness I hadn't shared with my mom during my adult life. I was isolated from my family by my first abusive husband. Nouwen's passage also helped me understand what happened after my dad died in 2013. A few weeks after his death, I attended a Christian rock concert. I was standing, clapping

---

[3] Henri Nouwen, *You Are the Beloved: Daily Meditations for Spiritual Living* (London: Hodder & Stoughton, Ltd., 2018), 338.

my hands, and singing with the musicians when suddenly, I had a vision of my dad's face zooming toward me from the ceiling. He had a brilliant light around him and was glowing and smiling. The vision gave me peace that he was now in heaven and joyous, happy, and free of Alzheimer's disease, which took him from us for over ten years before he died. Thank you, God, for the mystical glimpses and encounters with my parents and the knowledge to understand.

Now, back to the Garden of Gethsemane. The storm continued, so I quickly moved to the Church of All Nations next door. Some of my group helped me dry off and find a seat to regain my composure during the rest of Mass. The harassment by the vendors visibly shook me, and then I saw the iris and felt my mom; I needed to sit in silence and process what had just happened. The Mass was in English and packed with tourists, but I was able to block out the noise around me and concentrate on God and His divine love. He had taken good care of me in what could have been a dangerous situation and simultaneously gave me a mystical glimpse. Thank you, God, for loving me so much.

The next day, we walked the Via Dolorosa that Jesus walked on the way to Calvary. Now it was a winding path through many noisy small shops with shopkeepers peddling their wares loudly on both sides of the path. I wore a long scarf one of my shipmates gave me when she found out we had lost our luggage. The scarf helped me to block out the noise and people as I walked. I envisioned Jesus walking after being severely scourged, weak, bleeding, exhausted, and moving forward slowly, each step more painful than the last. I saw the drops of blood dripping on the dirt path as He stumbled up the hill to Calvary. At the top of the hill, there was more jeering, angry voices, and tremendous pain for Jesus as I watched them nail

Him to the Cross and hoisted the Cross into the air. As I reached the end, I paused with my eyes closed, completely experienced His Passion, and wept.

As we slowly moved on to the Church of the Holy Sepulchre and waited in line to see the massive anointing stone Jesus' body laid on to be prepared for burial and His tomb, my tears continued to fall at all Jesus suffered for me. When we reached the altar that covered the top of the hill of Golgotha, I knelt and placed my hand under the altar. There was an opening in the glass that encased the rock of Calvary. As I touched the rock, the Holy Spirit overcame me immediately, and I froze in time and place. I felt like I was electrocuted. A warm sensation of ecstasy filled my body as I started shaking and couldn't let go of the rock. Others behind me were pushing me to get me to move, but I couldn't. I'm unsure how long I knelt under the altar attached to the rock. Once released, I stumbled to a nearby chair, still shaking and dazed. I sat there until I could get enough strength to walk down the stairs. George was helping people down the stairs at the bottom. George looked at me and knew something had happened. I was still shaking and couldn't speak. He took my arm and led me out of the church. It was many hours before I could tell him what happened, and even then, I couldn't explain it. It was a miraculous event beyond my human understanding or words that left me humbled and wrapped in God's divine love.

Years later, the moment still makes me tingle and pause to thank my Savior for His sacrifice on Calvary for me, His daughter. His divine love continues to surround me when I meditate on His Passion, which is now so real to me, having walked where He did and touched the stone where He died. I often shared the story to encourage others and help them deepen their faith. I feel truly blessed.

The next day, our tour continued in Peter's Cave in Antioch, Turkey, where St. Peter and the other disciples hid from the Roman soldiers and preached the Gospel, converting many to Christianity. I again felt overcome by the Holy Spirit and started to cry. I felt fear and holiness, both at once, in the cave's atmosphere. I realized that the power of faith surrounded by threats from the outside made the cave a temporary hiding place for Peter and others.

The following day, I walked the ruins of Ephesus, which was incredible. Walking in Saint Paul's steps made the Acts of the Apostles come alive. I could see him preaching and healing happening as described in the Acts of the Apostles:

> So extraordinary were the mighty deeds God accomplished at the hands of Paul that when face cloths or aprons that touched his skin were applied to the sick, their diseases left them and the evil spirits came out of them (19:11–12).

Next, we drove up the mountain to Mary's House,[4] where she hid with the disciple John and, upon her death, ascended to heaven. I put a prayer request for Isaiah on the wall. It was a beautiful, sunny day; suddenly, it began to snow as we finished Mass—big, soft flakes that melted as they hit my face. What a blessing. Like kisses from God.

George caught the terrible virus spreading throughout the ship and was still very sick as we boarded the bus at 4:00 a.m. to return

---

[4] The House of the Virgin Mary is a Catholic shrine located on Mt. Koressos in the vicinity of Ephesus. The house was discovered in the 19th century by following the descriptions in the reported visions of Blessed Anne Catherine Emmerich (1774–1824), a Roman Catholic nun and visionary.

home. I was apprehensive as he seemed seriously ill, but George slept on both flights, and we made it home. As we walked in the door, we were greeted by our two suitcases, just as I had packed them. The trip had been extraordinary, and I pondered and shared the mystical encounters and glimpses I had for many years to come. God changed me, deepened my faith, and protected me. I was so grateful for God's divine love for providing me with this incredible trip.

CONTINUING MY QUEST

I felt drawn to my mother in the Garden of Gethsemane; I also felt drawn to my grandmother in Ireland. Our trip to Ireland began in the fall of 2014; I was on a quest that began years ago at a retreat taught by Brother Robert Lentz. He said, "You need to find your Celtic roots." Celtic roots? What did that mean? His words sent me on my quest, first to books on Celtic spirituality, then to my family tree, where I found my paternal grandmother. Grandma Mola Wolfe[5] was Irish and Celtic. Unfortunately, she died when my dad was only seven, so I never met her. My cousin said her mother described Grandma Mola as quiet, easy-going, and hard-working. She liked pretty things like flowers, working in the garden, and quilting. My cousin's description helped me feel closer to my grandma and maybe explained my love of flowers and creating beautiful things.

We had visited several places in Ireland, but a rainbow appeared when we were near where my ancestors lived and farmed outside of Cork. I felt it was a message from my grandmother confirming that I had come home. My ancestors had to leave to save their lives in the mid-1850s during the potato famine in Ireland that killed over one million people. But I still had a longing to know more.

---

[5] Wolfe was her maiden name.

I drove alone to a retreat at Ghost Ranch outside of San Antonio taught by John Philip Newell in the summer of 2016. I had read his book, *Listening for the Heartbeat of God: A Celtic Spirituality,*[6] and hoped to quench the yearning still in my heart to know more about my Celtic ancestors. His teaching and the beautiful, earthy Celtic music were salve to my soul. The music and the prayers especially touched me on a deeper level. The simple, earthy refrains resonated with my Franciscan spirit, further confirming my Celtic ancestry. Like Saint Francis, I felt one with the earth as I listened and absorbed their beautiful rhythms. But still, I thought I needed to go further.

MY PILGRIMAGE TO IONA

In May 2019, I went on a spiritual pilgrimage led by John Phillip Newell to Iona off the coast of Scotland to continue my quest. Iona is a tiny island of remarkable beauty that holds a unique place in the story of Scotland. It is where people have lived, worked, and worshipped for centuries. To and from its shores have come monks and friars, clan chiefs and kings, artists and craftsmen, farmers and fishermen, and now pilgrims.

The second day of the pilgrimage was Divine Mercy Sunday. As I walked to the White Sand Beach of Martyrs Bay on Iona with the other pilgrims, my thoughts drifted home to St. Edith Stein and the celebration without me happening at home for the first time in many years. My co-leader, Penny Whited, led the beautiful service with the support of the Divine Mercy Group. I was sad not to be at my church but was enjoying the silence and beauty of Iona. I needed this pilgrimage to refresh my soul.

---

[6] Phillip J. Newell, *Listening for the Heartbeat of God: A Celtic Spirituality* (Mahwah, NJ: Paulist Press, 1997).

John Philip Newell told the story of the sixty-eight monks killed by Vikings on the beach, turning the white sands red in 806. As he talked, I started to see the scene in vivid color, with the mysticism of the historical event overtaking my senses. The colorful longboats of the Vikings rowing to shore. Then, the fierce and terrifying Vikings ran through the surf, yelling and swinging their weapons of war: axes, lances, and spears. I watched as they massacred the defenseless monks. The monks' blood flowed from their robes and turned the white sand red around my feet. I drifted away from the group and wandered alone around the dunes of white sand, meditating on those martyred so many years ago. I tried to make sense of the scene I saw in God's latest mystical glimpse. Why had they died? For what little wealth they had? To satisfy the Vikings' greed? I cried at the Vikings' cruelty to others who lived in peace.

The scene reminded me of the red and white rays emanating from Jesus' heart in the Divine Mercy Image, representing His suffering on the Cross when the lance pierced His side, and His blood and water turned the ground red. The beautiful, sunny day suddenly turned cold, windy, and cloudy. We walked quickly for the mile back to our hotel. I pondered what mattered in life. I often felt like my life was a merry-go-round I couldn't get off—too busy, too noisy, versus the life of the monks on Iona, who had a life of quiet, peace, and simplicity until the greed of others took away all they had, including their lives. I continued to pray for simplicity, quiet peace, and God's divine love in my life.

The beauty of Iona was mesmerizing, with the deep blue water, off-white sheep with baby lambs on green pastures, hills covered in purple heather, unique rock formations, and various beautiful sand and rock beaches. I hiked the hills in my Irish-green-trimmed hat for the week, walked the shoreline, and participated in spiritual exercises in the eleventh-century Oran chapel and the twelfth-century Benedictine abbey. The spiritual practices opened my heart to more profound ways of prayer through singing, silence, and times of praying with others.

As the only Roman Catholic, I made the trek safely through the pasture where a bull lived and up a long hill alone on Sunday to the little Roman Catholic chapel. The windows behind the altar look at the water across the green fields. After Mass, I visited with the priest and the few visitors staying in the home adjoining the chapel. It was so peaceful and beautiful that I thought, *Maybe I should return one day and stay here.*

Saint Columba, an Irish priest and a prince, brought Christianity to Iona in 563. The bay bears his name and is where historians believe he and his fellow monks landed. We made a four-mile hike over the hills and down valleys, through rocky paths, and down steep slopes to get to Columba Bay. It was a tough day, where the male pilgrims had to push some of us women literally up the steep slopes. We had a picnic on a hillside not far from the sheep. Some pilgrims went on for another five more miles of hiking. It was a miracle that I made four miles with my artificial hip. My heart was full of God's creation, joy, and the satisfaction of finishing a challenge.

One afternoon, our group sailed across the bay to an uninhabited pillar island called Staffa. Staffa was named for the natural beauty of the unusual basalt columns created by three volcanic eruptions millions of years ago. Set alone in the ocean, Staffa is also a safe breeding ground for puffins, small black-and-white seabirds with colorful bills. The birds return to Staffa from May to August yearly to lay their eggs and raise their little ones. We watched thousands of birds as they surrounded us, came up to us, and sat on their eggs. It was a beautiful statement of God's unique plan to care for even the smallest of His creatures. I enjoyed snapping pictures and laughing at the birds' shenanigans. On the ride back, I stood at the rail and watched Staffa fade away in the distance. Suddenly, I felt a mystical glimpse of God begin. I asked, "How much more do you care for me than these beautiful small birds for whom you created this special home?" I waited. God filled my heart with His love, and He answered:

> **My dear daughter, I have created the perfect home for you with a wonderful husband. Enjoy and love where you live. Serve your family as the birds care for their little ones. Fly out to meet others with the abandonment of the puffins. Soar above the cliffs in your life and enjoy the highs. I will take care of the lows. Offer up the times of suffering and pain to Me. Remember, I know the plans I have for you, so trust Me as the puffins do, and have hope. It is time to go home and live fully. Love, God.**

As I pondered my time on Iona, I realized it was mystical and life-changing, leaving me with a deeper faith and unity with God, but not where I belonged. I had found God's answer to my quest for my Celtic roots, and the answer wasn't in Iona or Ireland. It was at home. I just needed to be me and connect with those I love. And He gave me the understanding of the verse from Jeremiah that had confused me for so long. I needed to return home and have hope for the future—soar sometimes and trust God completely at other times. I felt refreshed and was grateful for the simplicity of the Celtic prayers, with their focus on nature and everyday life, which helped me deepen my mystical connection with God. A few days later, as I left Iona behind to travel home, a beautiful Celtic prayer we prayed during the week from *Sounds of the Eternal: A Celtic Psalter* rang in my ears, speaking of my new vision for my life—to be grateful for each new day and the gift of the present moment.

On This Day

In the gift of this new day,
in the gift of the present moment,
in the gift of time and eternity intertwined
let us be grateful
let us be attentive
let us be open to what has never happened before,
in the gift of this new day,
in the gift of the present moment,
in the gift of time and eternity intertwined.[7]

ADVENTURES IN THE CARIBBEAN

Over the years, I have continued to see God's intimate care for the smallest creatures and the beautiful, varied flowers He has planted in different parts of the world. George and I took a cruise to rest in January 2023. I went on several excursions alone because George was having trouble walking. I experienced grace on an excursion

---

[7] Used by permission of John Phillip Newell, *Sounds of the Eternal: A Celtic Psalter* (San Antonio: New Beginnings, 2012), 53.

to Honduras's Gumbalimba Preservation Nature Park. We had to cross a suspension bridge, a few people at a time. The two young men behind me thought it was fun to make it rock, not realizing I had vertigo and was already scared. They caught up to me as I got off, so I said, "I'm slow; you can go ahead." Instead, Adam, one of the two young men, said he would go before me if I fell on the steps, and his friend would stay behind. They helped me down the rock steps, and he and I discussed art, spirituality, and other topics. My excursion became a surprising, grace-filled encounter amidst the tall trees, thick shrubbery, and beautiful tropical flowers. The experience reminded me of an explanation of grace I had read recently:

> Grace, like mist in the mountain air, hangs in our midst each morning, there to enjoy and experience—to sense, to savor, to swim within. As the fog fills the valley, may we know we, too, are being filled, abundantly loved, fully accepted, and perpetually filled with divine [love].[8]

Too often, I'm unaware of God's grace until a mystical encounter happens. Then I stop and ponder, *God, why do you love me, a sinner, so much that you provide grace-filled moments, mystical glimpses during which I feel your divine love fill my heart and soul? Thank you, Lord, for Your grace and for being mindful of me.*

Later in the same cruise, I stepped outside our cabin onto the balcony. I was overwhelmed by God's wondrous world. Clouds of different shapes and sizes filled the sky, with patches of blue sky

---

[8] Stephen Copeland, "Grace Is Always Here," *Franciscan Media Praise+Pray*, September 27, 2023, https://www.franciscanmedia.org/pausepray/grace-is-always-here-2/.

here and there. The ship's beautiful white-capped wake followed us, trimmed in aquamarine and glowing white. Hanging over parts of the sea was the heavy air from the night of rain. The immense sea surrounded us, as far as I could see, no land anywhere. On the horizon, there was just dark grey water and white caps. The breeze gently blew my hair, a gentle caress of a mighty God for His beloved daughter. I was overwhelmed by God's mystical presence and the feeling of being completely surrounded by His love in the midst of His awesome creation. I lifted prayers of praise and thanksgiving to my God before reentering my cabin.

God has blessed me with many other trips. I have grown in so many ways on each trip, from the people I meet to the places I have seen to the mystical glimpses God has given me. I find spiritual places everywhere I go because God is always with me, but sometimes, the sites and activities distract me. God has a way of always bringing me back to Him, to the silence where He and I communicate best, to His plan for my life, to lessons I need to learn, and to the suffering that refines me and gives me ways to help others. Traveling also makes me appreciate my home and family when I return. Speaking of home, let's move on to the story of God's plan for a new home, His saving grace, and a special angel who came to visit me with a promise from God.

CHAPTER SIXTEEN

SURVIVING HARVEY AND THE PANDEMIC

Living through Changes

Prayer During Pandemic by Pope Francis

O Mary, you always shine on our path as
a sign of salvation and of hope.
We entrust ourselves to you, Health of the Sick,
who at the Cross took part in Jesus' pain, keeping your faith firm.
You, Salvation of the Roman People, know what we need,
and we are sure you will provide so that, as in Cana of Galilee,
we may return to joy and to feasting after this time of trial.
Help us, Mother of Divine Love, to conform to the will of the Father
and to do as we are told by Jesus,
who has taken upon Himself our sufferings
and carried our sorrows to lead us, through the Cross,
to the joy of the resurrection.
Amen.[1]

---

[1] On March 11, 2020, in the midst of the COVID-19 pandemic, Pope Francis entrusted the world to Mary.

In 2016, God gave me a message, another mystical glimpse redirecting my life. I was sitting in our home of ten years on a Tuesday when George walked across the living room, and I heard God's powerful voice clearly say, "**You need to move**." George, my sweet husband, was losing the use of both his ankles, struggling more and more with the ravages of arthritis and too many years on his feet working outside in Houston heat. I started looking at houses we could modify for him, but the modifications were too expensive, so I moved on to new homes.

God guided me to a new home center nearby, and I made an appointment for Saturday. I hesitated to tell George because he said he never wanted to move again after we bought our current house. But when I told George the day before our appointment, he said it sounded good. We invited our regular realtor to go with us, and he helped us get the price lowered. We looked at a couple of models and floor plans, and within five days of God's message to move, we signed the paperwork to build a house with the features that would be good for George. God also blessed us with a $40,000 reduction in price for the home builder's fortieth-anniversary sale. We were excited and went by the site of the new home often, saying prayers and blessing each part of the building with holy water.

The move in March 2017 was stressful and exhausting. I was excited to have the home of our dreams, one story with a three-car garage, but the move took all my energy. It took six movers and three trucks for all our treasures and two additional weeks to finish the move. We had been cleaning out for several weeks and donating a van full of items to our local Boy Scouts garage sale each week, but that didn't make a dent! In addition, I had a hip replacement in August of 2016 and got a severe infection in the hospital. It took months of antibiotics to get over it, and we were well into the move before I recovered. In my weakened condition, I cried often. I loved my new home, but it was such a mess, and with my job taking most of my energy, I had nothing left to put things in order. In August 2017, I was still exhausted, and a few boxes remained unpacked. Then the weather changed.

SURVIVING HURRICANE HARVEY

On August 26th, 2017, I watched the continuing weather warnings showing Hurricane Harvey making a slow move on Houston. The bands of rain had started the day before, and we didn't know what to expect. We renamed our street the "Tonkawa River" as the water ran down the street with the speed of a river. The water was over my sidewalk in places and coming closer to the sidewall of my new house. In my fear, I turned to the Bible and started praying scriptures to calm the storm, especially Mark 4:39: "He woke up, rebuked the wind, and said to the sea, 'Quiet! Be still!' The wind ceased and there was great calm." I prayed this prayer loudly from the backyard under the cover of the patio, begging for the rising water to stop, for the storm to be quiet and still, and for God's mercy. I felt I was "praying blood" as Jesus did in the Garden of Gethsemane. Finally, after an hour, I moved to the front yard, where I had a better view of the "Tonkawa River," as it was creeping ever closer to my house. I continued praying aloud into the storm for it to be still, but its fury continued as sheets of rain taunted me.

Then I saw something white float by. Strange. A few minutes later, a neighbor from up the street came running up to me with a beautiful, two-foot-tall white marble guardian angel. He asked if it was mine. I said no, and he said, "It is now." We were on the corner, and the other side of my house was now an impassable lake, so he

couldn't go further with his quest to find its owner. The statute was heavy, and the storm was still pouring rain down on us, so he put it in front of my tree for me. I instantly felt peace despite the torrents of rain that continued. I knew God had sent the angel because He heard my prayers. In my heart, I knew we would be okay. I was trusting in Jesus. So I went into the house, and shortly after that, the rain slowed and finally stopped.

George and my then nineteen-year-old grandson, Isaiah, took the lull in the storm to wade across the "Tonkawa River" to a house under construction with a sand pile.

They filled many garbage bags with sand and piled them in front of doors, hoping that even a few inches of protection would hold back the rising water when the rain began again.

In the meantime, I watched the weather. The weatherman said he was amazed and couldn't explain the phenomenon that had started to happen. A warm wind from the west had started to blow into the center of Harvey, calming the storm and slowing the rain. The rain slowed to the point that our street started to go down and continued to drain until morning. I knew the warm wind was a miracle from God and praised Him.

The rain began again, but not as strong, and it rained for two more days. The "Tonkawa River" continued to flow outside its banks, otherwise known as curbs. We were prisoners in our house, but the water never touched the angel as she stood guard in my front yard. I continued to praise God as He protected us and spared us the tragedy of water in our home. We got only thirty-five inches of rain in those three days, less than others in the area that saw fifty-six to sixty-five inches.

A few days later, my best friend, Millie, who lives in Michigan, called to check on us and told me her husband had died three weeks earlier from a brain aneurysm. I told her I would have come for the funeral if she had told me. She said he was cremated and invited me to come to the memorial service the following week. I hesitated for a moment and then said yes. I was so tired of the stress of Houston, of seeing piles of debris everywhere, of empty grocery store shelves and gas pumps. Of closed streets and heartbreaking stories from friends and strangers who had lost everything. Of the guilty feeling of not doing enough because of my weakened health as so many others were giving their all. Isaiah and Susan went to clean houses, and George helped collect cleaning supplies at our church. And I gathered supplies to send with them and gave financial support where I could.

After flying to Michigan, I jumped into helping Millie set up for the funeral. As we walked by a small table in the church's foyer, two issues of *The Royal Cross*, the newsletter for my prayer order, caught my eye. I asked the lady who was helping us why they were there. She didn't know where they came from. I was surprised because the funeral was at an Assembly of God church, and my prayer order was primarily Episcopalian. I picked up the issues and was even more surprised to see they were from the Spring of 2007 and Spring of 2008. My picture with the National Council was on the front of one of them! I thumbed through the issues to see what stories I had written back then. I showed both stories to Millie, who needed encouragement, and she said, "See, God knew you were supposed to be here." He always guided my stumbling with His mystical glimpses because He had a plan!

It was a lovely service. Millie chose many praise songs, such as "Eye of the Storm,"[2] which healed my broken heart from the losses in my city after Harvey. After the service, I shared my Harvey story and the picture of my angel with those at the reception. I learned from my neighbors that over fifty items had floated two blocks and around three corners from the cemetery behind our subdivision to travel down the "Tonkawa River." My angel was the largest and heaviest of the items, and I was still amazed she could float so far. After she protected my house, I sadly returned her to her special place in the cemetery.

For the next few days, Millie and I shared many memories with her two grown sons of how we met forty-two years ago in 1975 at a bus stop in Saudi Arabia. With tears in my eyes, I left her these words before boarding my return flight, "We have come a long way from those two young, naive housewives." The trials of broken marriages and abusive husbands had grown and shaped us into strong women of God. We had survived much suffering. It was such a blessing to pray and heal with her, to experience God's presence, and to be surprised by His mystical glimpses throughout the visit. God, by giving me longtime friends who intimately know my story, has helped me follow God's plan. These special friends sometimes hear His voice clearer than I do during times of trials and help keep me on the right

---

[2] "Eye of the Storm" music and lyrics written by Ryan Stevenson and Bryan Fowler.

path. Millie is one example, as she helped me with my first book by listening to the manuscript while we were on pilgrimage on Iona. Millie helped me with edits and shared a story of how God rescued her from an abusive marriage with a message from an angel. I cried as I listened to her story and added it to the book. I'm grateful to God for Millie and others' continuing friendships.

ENCOUNTERING THE EMPTY CHURCH

On March 15, 2020, the pandemic hit us all, suddenly closing down everything. But Father Kulma, our priest, still wanted me to do the Good Friday St. Faustina's Stations of the Cross. He was so excited as he unveiled his new camera to livestream the event. The church was cool and so still. I stood at the ambo while he videotaped me introducing the event. Penny, my co-leader, and I followed Butch, her husband, as he carried the Cross. The words of the *St. Faustina's Way of the Cross* DVD[3] played, and I stopped reverently at each station, bowing, praying, and experiencing each station in my heart and soul. Father followed us with his camera. I was consumed with the words, Jesus speaking and then St. Faustina answering.

I sang each verse as the Cross moved ahead in a steady, beautiful rhythm to the next station. Tears started to flow as my heart was more deeply touched. Watching our Savior walk to His death, falling under the weight of the heavy Cross, I felt I was alone with Him in the still church. St. Faustina's voice reminded me of my sins, failings, and shortcomings. At station four, we met Mary, Jesus' sorrowful mother, watching her son on His way to His death. I was

---

[3] *St. Faustina's Way of the Cross*, DVD, Directed by David and Joan Maroney, Mother Mercy Messengers, Stockbridge, MA: Marian Press, 2004.

heartbroken, just as I would have been if I watched Bill, my son, go to his death. In the quiet of my heart, I heard St. Faustina's voice:

> I saw the Blessed Virgin, unspeakably beautiful. She held me close to herself and said to me, "I am Mother to you all, thanks to the unfathomable mercy of God. Most pleasing to me is that soul that faithfully carries out God's will. Be courageous. Don't fear apparent obstacles, but fix your gaze upon the Passion of my Son; this way, you will be victorious."[4]

Victorious? In death? How hard was that to do? Mary showed courage when she followed her Son and watched until the end. Later, He was placed in her arms one last time. The baby she cradled, the child she comforted, the man she watched Him become, the Savior of the world was still her little boy. More tears, sharing one mother's love with another, knowing the pain of losing a child, whether to the Cross or miscarriage or our modern world of evil, drugs, alcohol, or violence. I thought, *Yes, I lost two babies early into each pregnancy, but after the losses, God gave me the incredible miracle of being able to carry my daughter, Susan, to full-term.* We moved on in silence, only the voices on the DVD reverberating through the empty church, bouncing off the walls in an echo that seemed to come from the depths of eternity.

St. Faustina's words of the closing prayer from paragraph 304 of the *Diary* touched my soul:

---

[4] Kowalska, *Diary*, paragraph 449.

My Jesus, my only hope, I thank You for this book, which You opened to the eyes of my soul. This book is Your Passion, undertaken out of love for me. From this book, I learned how to love God and souls. This book contains inexhaustible treasures. O Jesus, how few souls understand You in Your martyrdom of love. Happy the soul that has come to understand the love of the heart of Jesus.[5]

In the silence of the empty church, we reached the end, the empty tomb, the knowledge of the Resurrection, of joy, of life beyond death, with love that continues beyond the grave, with the promise of so much more. As I sang the words of the Chaplet to close the session, my soul lifted from the empty church to the choir of heaven. I joined all the angels and saints in praise, forgot the camera, and was filled with joy. It was the perfect joy of the risen Christ, knowing that the Passion wasn't the end but the beginning, just as my journey through the empty church to the empty grave to the heavenly gates is full of new beginnings as I stumble through God's plan.

THE MIRACLE OF TECHNOLOGY

As the pandemic dragged on, I was so tired of the virus and quarantine, of being afraid and careful, of others being careless and spreading it. I was brokenhearted at missing events like my friend and coworker Barbara's funeral. She died so quickly, unexpectedly. Watching Barbara's funeral on Zoom helped me heal after her death.

---

[5] Kowalska, *Diary*, paragraph 304.

I almost felt like I was there with my friend Wally and Barbara's daughter and grandchildren; I felt included and prayed, "Thank you, Lord, for the miracle of technology."

I was also brokenhearted that I didn't get to attend my great-grandson Conner's Baptism. My granddaughter, Courtney, sent me pictures—he was so cute—and a video that made me feel like I was almost there. Conner kept looking at the other baby to find out why the other baby was crying. The look of questioning on his face was so cute, and then he started crying in unison. It was too funny, as though they had a secret communication method. I wanted to see him and the rest of the family, and the video cheered me up and made me feel like I was there. Again, I prayed, "Thank you, Lord, for the miracle of technology."

I continued to pray for all and held my Divine Mercy group and Franciscan fraternity meetings on Zoom, which helped with my loneliness and isolation. Plus, so many prayer requests needed our attention, which made each session a blessing. Many prayers were said for those who were ill, including my daughter-in-law Sara, who almost died and was sick with COVID-19 for over three months. The technology kept my groups going, and I even trained a new Franciscan candidate via Zoom. All my attendees and I prayed, "Thank you, Lord, for the miracle of technology."

Using technology during the pandemic made my life complete and kept me moving forward. The conversations and seeing friends and family's faces made me feel connected and stimulated. I have used what I learned about communicating via technology since the pandemic as new opportunities have come along, such as bad weather, illness, or when talking from home is more convenient. "Thank you, Lord, for the miracle of technology."

A HEALING MIRACLE

The pandemic left me, like many others, bruised, hurt, disappointed, frightened, and uncertain. But the biggest disappointment of the pandemic stemmed from my second hip replacement delay. About a year and a half after my first hip replacement and recovery from the longtime infection, I started having allergies to everything! Celery, balsamic vinegar, drugs I had taken for years, and more. My face swelled up, and I had a constant, itchy, blistered rash on my chest and face. The dermatologist was stumped. So was my allergist. In addition, my thigh hurt below my hip replacement, especially after I exercised. I went to several doctors who did X-rays and said nothing was wrong. I was frustrated and kept praying to God for an answer.

Finally, in late 2019, after almost a year and a half of suffering, an acquaintance at the gym ran up and said she had been watching for me. Her sister had found a doctor who had finally solved her ongoing hip problem—a miracle for her sister. She thought he could help me. I was excited and hopeful. I waited two months for an appointment. He listened to me and took me seriously, a miracle in itself. He said he wanted to put me to sleep, draw out the fluid in the hip, and send it to a lab in Pennsylvania with a special microscope that can see even tiny problems. He thought the ongoing infection had spread to the replaced hip joint.

Well, he and I were both surprised when the result showed metal poisoning. The particles were too tiny to be seen on an X-ray. The metal ring over the ceramic ball was loose and flapping when I exercised or moved a lot, producing metal particles to enter my system. I was anxious to have a second replacement to fix the problem, end my pain, and stop all the allergic reactions and the terrible itching. I had all the tests done, got medical clearance, and was scheduled for surgery in a few days when the pandemic shut down all elective surgeries. I was crushed and asked God, "Why?" I was so tired of suffering.

Five weeks later, I got a call from my doctor's office. The hospital was opening up a separate surgery wing, sealed off from COVID patients, and they wanted to do surgery immediately. My medical clearance was still good; I just needed a COVID test, which I passed. The following day after the surgery, it was amazing that my thigh no longer hurt. And all my allergies and itching started to disappear. What a miracle! I learned that God could direct me to a knowledgeable doctor who explored options for my symptoms. I also realized that our bodies are connected and that metal poisoning in one area can affect many others. And finally, I learned to keep searching and praying for an answer. God wants us to be whole, healthy, beloved children. Thank you, Dr. Stefan Kreuzer, for going the extra mile, and thank you, God, for guiding me to the right doctor.

THE LIGHT IN THE DARKNESS

Another bright spot during the pandemic was publishing my first book. It was a long process that came together with the help of many others. The launch date, initially scheduled for August 1, was moved to September 28, 2020, because of production delays. That was a WOW moment for me as my divorce from my abusive husband was finalized on September 28, many years ago! God surprised me with perfect planning and timing!

Despite this big win, the rest of the pandemic was difficult, but God comforted me with Micah 7:8b. It says, "I will arise; though I sit in darkness, the LORD is my light." I could relate to this prayer, for God was everywhere in my life during the pandemic. He was in the miracles, the videos and pictures of my great-grandsons, the new modes of communication with my brothers through shared messages, the phone calls, the increased time to play games with Isaiah and Susan, the small family dinners at home, Susan bringing us take-home food from our favorite restaurants, watching Mass on YouTube, meetings with my Franciscan fraternity and Divine Mercy groups on Zoom, and more prayer time to deepen my faith.

The Gospel of John praises the enfleshed Word of God, who dares to bring light into the world where darkness lingers like an unwelcome intruder at a banquet—just like the pandemic.

> All things came to be through him, and without him nothing came to be. What came to be through him was life, and this life was the light of the human race; the light shines in the darkness, and the darkness has not overcome it (John 1:3–5).

Into my fears of waning health from COVID-19, God came as light. Into the uncertainty and loneliness of a pandemic, God came as light. Into the commotion of family life, God came as light. Into the stress of going places with masks and hand sanitizer, God came as light. When light arrives in a space, darkness flees. Christ, our Light, continues to shine brightly, inviting me to illuminate places where shadows linger and find hope in His mystical encounters, miracles, and divine love.

CONCLUSION

WRITING GOD'S PLAN

Prayer

Creator of the beginning Word,
Author of the unturned page,
Poet,
Wordsmith,
Storyteller of life,
You inscribe us on the palms of your hands
And every breath we breathe
Is written on your scroll.
Our gratitude is indelible;
Our hope in you cannot be described.
[Divine] Love, O God, is your first language
And life is our shared story—
Begun, continued, and unending in You
For by your hand we are,
In truth and forever,
Woven together in [Divine] love.
Amen.[1]
—Pamela C. Hawkins

---

[1] Prayer written by Pamela C. Hawkins and featured in the January 2017 edition of *Weavings: A Journal of the Christian Spiritual Life* (32, no. 1).

When I finished the final draft of my first book in April 2020, I had another of God's surprising encounters. After Mass one night, our good friend's daughter asked George and me to join them for dinner at a nearby Mexican restaurant. We got sidetracked, conversing with others after Mass, and were the last to arrive. The only chair left on the women's side of the table was across from our friend's daughter. I didn't know her. The conversation turned from small talk about my dogs and children to my book.

I told her I was writing a book about my abusive marriage. Immediately, she began to open up to me about her divorce, reconciliation, and the death of her spouse. I could see her pain. She shared that she had no one who understood her situation, which brought her to tears. I understood and sympathized with her. I had been there, so I encouraged her by sharing my journey of escape from my abusive marriage and recovery. By the end of the evening, I asked her to read a current draft of my book, and she said yes. I hoped it would help her heal and grow as she recovered. I wrote the first book to help others and was amazed that God was already bringing people into my life whom my book might positively impact.

A few days later, I received a card from George's son and his family for my seventieth birthday. The card touched my heart and made me think of our friend's daughter and my book and how it had touched her. The words reminded me of what I have come to believe: A life well lived is measured by those your life has touched and those who have touched your life, as well as the dreams that you have achieved and those yet to be fulfilled. Life can be full of joy if God's divine love directs the path and helps you stumble through the tough times to accomplish His plan.

I pray that I will touch more lives in person and through my books and teachings. My dreams of being a spiritual writer and teacher—reaching more people—seem within reach as I continue fine-tuning my completed dreams. I am committed to bearing fruit by ministering to others and following God's plan for my life as He reveals it through many mystical encounters, miracles, and divine love.

MY DREAMS COMING TRUE

My first book continued to bring blessings and extraordinary mystical glimpses. I met a new friend on a cruise in January 2023 and gave her a copy as a birthday gift. When she learned that I taught workshops, she asked me if I would consider doing a presentation for her church's Saturday morning women's group. Of course, I said, "Yes. I love to teach." We decided on "Simplifying Your Life" as the topic, and I started to feel excited that I was fulfilling my dream of being a speaker even though the date was months away in September.

As I prepared, I felt honored to be asked and increasingly motivated to do a good job. I was looking forward to meeting the women and visiting a new church. I was nervous and excited when I arrived, but I found a large Image of Divine Mercy Jesus next to the podium, which made me feel God's divine love surrounding me. As I started my presentation, I called attention to the Divine Mercy Image of Jesus and shared that the Image had been life-changing for me and that I often simply pray, "Jesus, I trust in You," when I am too stressed or heartbroken to find other words. Several times, I turned and referred to Jesus during the presentation. I felt like I had a faithful friend beside me, keeping me calm and giving me confidence and courage. I enjoyed teaching and the women's active participation. The teaching concluded with the following quote from Claire Cloninger's book, *A Place Called Simplicity*, which gives her answer to achieving simplicity in our lives:

> The simple beauty of this One who walked with fishermen and lovingly touched the skin of lepers and laughed with little children is available and waiting to be poured out in us, filling us with all the serenity and [divine]love we have been seeking. With His life at the center, we really can be simpler . . . in every part and particle of our lives can flow simply for the deep center of the One who abides there.[2]

Yes, I have learned that I could have serenity and divine love by letting every particle of my being focus on Jesus. Even during suffering and desert times, God's abiding love in my deep center has carried me through and filled me with perfect joy and hope for the future, simplifying my choices and leading me to trust Him completely.

After the presentation, several women approached me. One said, "When I saw the topic was simplifying your life, I hoped there would be at least some small spiritual content, but instead, the whole presentation was spiritual!" I just laughed, as my "Simplifying Your Life" teaching consists of eight biblical concepts based on the Scriptures. Another woman asked for a copy of one of my quotes,

---

[2] Claire Cloninger, *A Place Called Simplicity* (Eugene: Harvest House, 1993), 181–182.

allowing me to talk about God's latest mystical revelation to write a third book. I explained that during one of our late-night encounters a few months ago, He surprised me when He revealed that I am to write a third book on my teachings, and "Simplifying Your Life" will be one of the chapters. God's surprise helped me realize that this second book was also part of His plan to help me reach my dreams of writing and teaching spiritual topics. Through this book, I hope to reach more people and help them grow spiritually by finding and accepting the mystic inside of them.

My friend who invited me to speak approached and asked me to lunch. She said that I had glowed throughout the presentation. Such a nice compliment, although I knew it wasn't me, but the light of Jesus showing through me just as Thomas Merton said: "This little point of nothingness and of absolute poverty is the pure glory of God . . . blazing with the invisible light of heaven."[3] A mystical light from the Triune God, the Father who created me, Jesus, my companion and beloved, and the Holy Spirit, who gives me peace and mystical guidance.

As I have stumbled through God's plan, I have learned to live each moment and to stop to recognize when God gives me a mystical encounter, a miracle, or an embrace with His divine love. Being aware of God at all times and in all circumstances has helped me find a deeper, more intense relationship with Him. Sometimes, He reveals more of His plan for my life. Sometimes, He wants my attention. Other times, He just wants me to spend time with Him in silence.

---

[3] Thomas Merton, *Conjectures of a Guilty Bystander* (New York: Image, 1965), 155.

I have had an incredible journey, made many wonderful friends, and spent many hours in prayer with my Triune God. Through my stories, I hope you have found the mystic inside you, that unique God-given center we all have. As Brother David explained: "The mystical experience is an [often sudden] awareness of being one with the Ultimate—a sense of limitless belonging to God."[4] I praise my awesome God, who had helped me experience the limitless belonging to God, the embrace of His divine love, and the many mystical encounters and miracles through my journey. And I pray that each of you experiences your limitless belonging to God as you travel through God's plan for your life. Blessings . . .

---

[4] Steindl-Rast, *The Way*, 20.

RESOURCES AND OTHER STORIES

The Loom of Time[1]

Man's life is laid in the loom of time
To a pattern he does not see,
While the Weaver works and the shuttles fly
Till the dawn of eternity.

Some shuttles are filled with silver threads,
And some with threads of gold,
While often but the darker hue
Is all that they may hold.

But the Weaver watches with skillful eye
Each shuttle fly to and fro,
And sees the pattern so deftly wrought
As the loom moves sure and slow.

God surely plans the pattern—
Each thread, the dark and fair,
Is chosen by His master-skill,
And placed in the web with care.

---

[1] Grant Colfax Tullar, *Written Because—: And an Autobiography, Some Stories and Poems* (Orange, NJ: The Tullar Studio, 1937), 48.

He, only, knows its beauty,
And guides the shuttles which hold
The threads so unattractive,
As well as the threads of gold.

Not till each loom is silent,
And the shuttles cease to fly,
Shall God unroll the pattern
And explain the reason why.

The dark threads were as needful
In the Weaver's skillful hand,
As the threads of gold and silver
For the pattern which He planned.
—Grant Colfax Tullar

MERTON'S EXAMPLE OF MYSTICISM

One final passage from *Conjectures of a Guilty Bystander*, by the great mystic Thomas Merton, beautifully describes a similar example of the mystical encounter I experienced at the airport.

In Louisville, at the corner of Fourth and Walnut, in the center of the shopping district, I was suddenly overwhelmed with the realization that I loved all those people, that they were mine and I theirs, that we could not be alien to one another even though we were total strangers. It was like waking from a dream of separateness . . . I have the immense joy of being [hu]man, a member of a race in which God Himself became incarnate . . . And if only everybody could realize this! But it cannot be explained. There is no way of telling people that they are all walking around shining like the sun . . . Then it was as if I suddenly saw the secret beauty of their hearts, the depths of their hearts where neither sin nor desire nor self-knowledge can reach, the core of their reality, the person that each one is in God's eyes. If only they could all see themselves as they really are. If only we could see each other that way all the time. There would be no more war, no more hatred, no more cruelty, no more greed. . . At the center of our being is a point of nothingness which is untouched by sin and by illusion, a point of pure truth, a point or spark which belongs entirely to God . . . This little point of nothingness and of absolute poverty is the pure glory of God in us . . . It is like a pure diamond, blazing with the invisible light of heaven. It is in everybody, and if we could see it, we would see these billions of points of light coming together in the face and blaze of a sun that would make all the darkness and cruelty of life vanish completely.[2]

Merton's explanation of a love affair with God leads us to our true selves and is the secret to peace. If only all the people could embrace each other—Heaven on earth! It is a deep desire of this all-too-human mystic.

---

[2] Merton, *Conjectures*, 153–156.

The Forgiveness Prayer[3]

The following prayer covers most of the significant areas of forgiveness. Often, such a prayer will bring to mind areas that need forgiveness. Let the Holy Spirit move freely and guide your mind to persons or groups you need to forgive.

[Skip over sections that do not apply to your life. A good practice is to pray the prayer for thirty days (for example, during Lent) and then once every few years.] The prayer is a paraphrasing of the original.

Lord Jesus Christ, I ask today to forgive **everyone** in my life. I know that You will give me the strength to forgive. I thank You that You love me more than I love myself and want my happiness more than I desire it for myself.

Father, I forgive **You** for the times death has come into the family, hard times, financial difficulties, or what I thought were punishments sent by You. People said these times were "God's will." I became bitter and resentful toward You. Purify my heart and mind today.

---

[3] Betty Tapscott and Father Robert DeGrandis, SSJ, *Forgiveness & Inner Healing: Prayers of Forgiveness and Healing of Memories* (Houston: Self Published, 2007), 5–10.

Lord, I forgive **myself** for my sins, faults and failings, for all that is bad in myself or that I think is bad, for what I have done or failed to do. I forgive myself, and I accept Your forgiveness.

I further forgive **myself** for not worshipping You by attending church, for hurting my parents, husband, and friends, for sins against purity, adultery, and fornication, for abortion, stealing, lying, and hurting others with gossip. You have forgiven me today, and I forgive myself. Thank you, Lord, for your grace at this moment. Fill me with Your Holy Spirit.

I truly forgive my **mother**. I forgive her for all the times she hurt me, she resented me, she was angry with me, and for all the times she punished me. I forgive her for the times she preferred my brothers or sisters to me. I forgive her for the times she told me I was dumb, ugly, stupid, the worst of the children or that I cost the family a lot of money. For the times she told me I was unwanted, an accident, a mistake or not what she expected, I forgive her. I forgive her for the times I felt abandoned.

I forgive my **father**. I forgive him for any non-support, any lack of love, affection or attention. I forgive him for any lack of time, for not giving me his companionship, for his drinking, arguing and fighting with my mother or the other children.

For his severe punishments, for desertion, for being away from home, for divorcing my mother, or for any running around, I do forgive him.

Lord, I extend forgiveness to my **sisters and brothers**. I forgive those who rejected me, lied about me, hated me, resented me, competed for my parent's love, those who hurt me, or who physically harmed me. For those who were too severe on me, punished me or made my life unpleasant in any way, I do forgive them.

Lord, I forgive my **spouse or significant others** for lack of love, affection, consideration, support, attention, and communication; for faults, failings, weaknesses and those other acts or words that hurt or disturb me.

Jesus, I forgive **my children and other children** for their lack of respect, obedience, love, attention, support, warmth, and understanding; for their bad habits, falling away from the church, and any bad actions that disturb me.

My God, I forgive **my relatives**, my grandmother and grandfather, aunts, uncles, cousins, in-laws, and other relatives by marriage, who treat my family with a lack of love. For all their words, thoughts, actions or omissions, which injured and caused pain, I forgive them.

Lord, I forgive **my friends** who have let me down, lost contact with me, do not support me, were not available when I needed help, borrowed money or possessions and did not return it, or gossiped about me.

My neighbors need to be forgiven, Lord. For all their noise, letting their property run down, not tying up their dogs who run through my yard, not taking in their trash barrels, being prejudiced and running down the neighborhood, I do forgive them.

I now forgive **my priest, deacon, and church** for their lack of support, affirmation, bad homilies, pettiness, lack of friendliness, not providing me or my family with the inspiration we needed, for any hurts they have inflicted on me or my family, even in the distant past, I forgive them today.

Jesus, help me to forgive **my coworkers and fellow members of groups** I belong to who are disagreeable or make life miserable for me. For those who push their work off on me, don't show up, gossip about me, won't cooperate with me, or try to take my job, I do forgive them.

Lord, I forgive **my employer or supervisor** for not paying me enough money, for not appreciating my work, for being unkind and unreasonable with me, for being angry or unfriendly, for not promoting me, and for not complimenting me on my work.

Lord, I forgive **my schoolteachers and instructors** of the past as well as the present. For those who punished me, humiliated me, insulted me, treated me unjustly, made fun of me, called me dumb or stupid, and made me stay after school, I truly forgive them today.

Lord, I forgive all those who are of **different persuasions**, those of opposite political views who have attacked me, ridiculed me, discriminated against me, made fun of me, and economically hurt me.

I forgive those of **different religious denominations and beliefs** who have harassed me, attacked me, argued with me, and forced their view on my family and me.

Those who have harmed me **ethnically,** discriminated against me, mocked me, made jokes about my race or nationality, and hurt my family physically, emotionally, or economically, I do forgive them today.

Lord, I forgive all **professional people** who have hurt me in any way: doctors, nurses, lawyers, judges, politicians, and civil servants. I forgive all service people: policemen, firemen, bus drivers, hospital workers and especially repairmen who have taken advantage of me in their work.

Lord Jesus, I especially pray for the grace of forgiveness for the **one person** in life who has **hurt me the most**. I ask to forgive anyone whom I consider my greatest enemy, the one who is the hardest to forgive or the one who I said I would never forgive.

Lord, I beg pardon of all these people for the hurt, especially my mother, father, and marriage partner. I am especially sorry for the three greatest hurts I have inflicted on each of them, for things I have done to them or not done for them, for the times I was unkind, unloving, controlling, demanding, rude, or distracted.

Thank You, Jesus, that I'm being freed of the evil of unforgiveness. Let Your Holy Spirit fill me with light and let every dark area of my mind be enlightened. Amen.

ST. FAUSTINA AND DIVINE MERCY STORY

A brief introduction to St. Faustina, a modern-day saint, and the devotion given to her, Divine Mercy. Saint Faustina was born Helena Kowalska in a small village in western Poland on August 25, 1905. Saint Faustina was called to sanctity at a very early age and entered religious life with the Congregation of the Sisters of Our Lady of

Mercy, whose members devoted themselves to the care and education of troubled young women in Poland in 1925 at the age of twenty. The following year, she received her religious habit and the name Sister Maria Faustina, to which she added: "of the Most Blessed Sacrament."

In the 1930s, Sister Faustina received a message of mercy from our Lord Jesus that she was to spread worldwide. She was asked to become the secretary of God's mercy, a model of how to be merciful to others, and an instrument for reemphasizing God's plan of mercy for the world. In imitation of Christ's life, her entire life was to be a sacrifice, a life lived for others.

At the Lord's request, St. Faustina willingly offered her personal sufferings in union with Him to atone for the sins of others. She became a doer of mercy daily, bringing joy and peace to others. By writing about God's mercy, St. Faustina encouraged others to trust in Him and thus prepare the world for His second coming. She wrote and suffered in secret, with only her spiritual director and some of her superiors aware that anything special was taking place in her life.

On November 10, 1937, when St. Faustina's superior showed her the first booklet ever published with the prayers she provided regarding devotion to Divine Mercy, Jesus told her: "Already there are many souls who have been drawn to My love by this Image. My mercy acts in souls through this work."[4] Saint Faustina wrote:

> Today, I saw the glory of God, which flows from
> the Image. Many souls are receiving graces . . .

---

[4] Kowalska, *Diary*, paragraph 1379.

In spite of Satan's anger, The Divine Mercy will triumph over the whole world and be worshipped by all souls.[5]

After St. Faustina's death from tuberculosis on October 5, 1938, at the age of thirty-three, even her closest associates were amazed as they began to discover what great sufferings and profound mystical experiences had been given to this sister of theirs, who had always been so cheerful and humble. In the years following her death, the Image of Divine Mercy and the Chaplet of Divine Mercy were distributed on prayer cards, just in time to give strength to those citizens of war-torn Poland sent to the concentration camps during the German occupation in World War II.

The message that Sister Faustina received is now being spread throughout the world through her *Diary: Divine Mercy in My Soul*, which has become the handbook for devotion to Divine Mercy, including doing deeds of mercy as Jesus commanded in the *Diary*:

> I demand from you deeds of mercy, which are to arise out of love for Me. You are to show mercy to your neighbors always and everywhere . . . I am giving you three ways of performing mercy to your neighbors: the first, by deed; the second, by word; the third, by prayer. In these three degrees is contained the fullness of mercy, and it is unquestionable proof of love for Me. By this means, a soul glorifies and pays reference to My mercy.[6]

---

[5] Kowalska, *Diary*, paragraph 1789.
[6] Kowalska, *Diary*, paragraph 742.

A RADICAL IDEA

In 2008, while I was national treasurer for The Order of the Daughters of the King, I had the following mystical encounter. God woke me in the middle of the night with a radical idea. Here is the letter I wrote to the national executive board and the national chaplain:

Dear Sisters and Bishop Howe,

Well, I should be in bed. I was there once tonight, but when God starts talking, I know I must get up and write because He won't leave me alone until I do. So please read this with an open heart and the Holy Spirit's guidance. I can't believe I'm writing it, but it feels right.

The wildest vision popped into my head tonight! I saw myself at the council meeting tearing up the bylaws and guidelines and saying it is time for love, not rules, to take over The Order. So, what if we tore up the bylaws and policies, etc.? Do we abandon them, stop trying to regulate who can belong under what circumstance and by whose authority, and simplify The Order? Stop fighting? And go to the following simplified structure:

1. A church that has three baptized and confirmed women who have the permission of their clergy can form a chapter.

2. All chapters within a particular geographical area would belong to the same entity. The entity would follow our current geographical structure of Episcopal dioceses but without a connection to the Episcopal Church. Just using their boundaries for all chapters. Episcopal, every flavor of Anglican, Roman Catholic, Methodist? Whatever? I would belong to this entity as an equal and full member with no restrictions or prejudice. Then, the entity would roll up to a province with the same theory. Open to all, all are equal. Again, we can use our current geographical structure or design a new structure.

Each president would select her chaplain as her spiritual adviser. The chapters would look to their clergy for their spiritual counsel. The Order would be a free and transparent entity.

3. The national level would continue with a representative from each province (if that is what the entity is called) and fifteen elected by ALL chapters equally. In addition, the USA and each country would add their representatives to an international council.

This is a radical idea to consider by those raised in an ecclesiastical church with rules and hierarchy. Many are tolerant as long as things are done their way but become protective and prejudiced when differences arise. And yes, the Eucharist would be a problem. Maybe we would have to unite with prayer services and save the Eucharist for our private church services.

Still, we could do that if we are indeed sisters in Christ. It would also solve the problem of some Juniors who belong to the wrong denomination and can't become Senior Daughters. It would also open the doors for those going to more Protestant faiths to continue as Daughters. It would make everything much more straightforward! More loving! And more like heaven. No denominations.

In summary, we all need to take the advice someone gave us at the Province VII meeting two weeks ago: 2 Chronicles 7:14:

> If then my people, upon whom my name has been pronounced, humble themselves and pray, and seek my face and turn from their evil ways, I will hear them from heaven and pardon their sins and heal their land [The Order]."

I'm sure you are all thinking of 100 reasons why this isn't a good idea. I have been, too, but God's divine love speaks louder to my heart than my brain. It is worth considering. So please pray, pray, pray! And maybe I can sleep now. Blessings and the peace of Christ . . . Kathy.

Well, the letter was too radical for a time of upheaval. However, years later, seeing how the Daughters have split into other groups, I still think it was a good idea and would like to see all of us come back together as Daughters first, denomination second. I miss my sisters who went in other directions.

Note: As I was finishing this book, I received a call from the first vice president of The Order. She told me she didn't know where the bylaws committee for Triennial 2024 got the bylaw revisions. Curious, I went out and read the proposed bylaws. Wow! They align closely with my suggestions above, but no one from my days on the council had any input. That tells me the time is right for God's plan. I'm looking forward to seeing what happens at Triennial 2024: Louisville.

BIBLIOGRAPHY

Every effort has been made to contact all copyright holders of the materials herein; no required credits have been intentionally omitted or overlooked; corrections will be made in the next edition if needed.

Abrahamson, Wendy K., "Holy Women," in *Echoes of the Spirit: Women's Prayers and Meditations*, Margaret Graham Beers, editor. Cincinnati: Forward Movement Publications, 2000.

Artress, Lauren. *Walking a Sacred Path: Rediscovering the Labyrinth as a Spiritual Tool.* New York: Riverhead Books, 1995.

Babinsky, Ellen L, translated and introduced. *Marguerite Porete: The Mirror of Simple Souls, The Classics of Western Spirituality.* Mahwah, New Jersey: Paulist Press, 1993.

Bodo, Murray, OFM. *The Road to Mount Subasio: Spiritual Pilgrimage as a Path to God.* Phoenix: Tau Publishing, 2004.

—. "St. Francis and the Taming of the Wolf." *St. Anthony Messenger*, October 2017. https://www.franciscanmedia. org/st-anthony-messenger/st-francis-and-the-taming-o f-the-wolf/.

Burke, Dan. "A Mystical Encounter with God." *Spiritual Direction*, November 14, 2014. https://spiritualdirection.com/2014/11 /14/a-mystical-encounter-with-god.

Catoir, John. "A Spiritual Goal Will Give Your Life Purpose." In *Uplifting Thoughts for Every Day*. NJ: Catholic Book Publishing Corp., 2007.

Catechism of the Catholic Church for the United States of America, English Translation. Libreria Editrice Vaticana: 1994.

Cloninger, Claire. *A Place Called Simplicity*. Eugene: Harvest House, 1993.

Copeland, Stephen. "Grace Is Always Here." *Franciscan Media Pause+Pray*. September 27, 2023. https://www.franciscan-media.org/pausepray/grace-is-always-here-2/.

Fonck, Benet A. *Called to Build a More Fraternal and Evangelical World: A Concordance to the SFO Rule*. Quincy: Franciscan Press, 2002.

Graham, John K. *Graham Crackers & Milk: Food for the Heart and Soul*. Nashville: Dimensions for Living, 2003.

Griffin, Emilie. *The Reflective Executive: A Spirituality of Business and Enterprise*. New York: The Crossroad Publishing Company, 1993.

—. *Simple Ways to Pray: Spiritual Life in the Catholic Tradition*. Lanham, MD: Rowman & Littlefield Publishers, Inc., 2006.

Hawkins, Pamela C. *Weavings: A Journal of the Christian Spiritual Life* 32, no. 1, January 2017.

Hines-Brigger, Susan. "Editorial: The Gift of Perfect Joy." *St. Anthony Messenger,* December6, 2023. https://www.franciscanmedia.org/news-commentary/editorial-the-gift-of-perfect-joy/.

Hume, Basil (Cardinal). *The Mystery of the Cross.* Brewster, MA: Paraclete Press, 1998, 2000.

Kelly, Mike. "9/11's First Casualty Mychal Judge Is a Legend—Can He Be a Saint?" *NorthJersey.com,* Sep. 10, 2021. https://www.northjersey.com/in-depth/news/columnists/mike-kelly/2021/09/10/father-mychal-judge-911-attacks-fdny-catholic-saint/4939813001/.

Kowalska, Saint Maria Faustina. *Diary: Divine Mercy in My Soul.* Stockbridge, MA: Marian Press, 1981.

Lentz, Robert, and Edwina Gateley. *Christ in the Margins.* Maryknoll, NY: Orbis Books, 2003.

Lewis, C.S., and Walter Hooper, editor. *God in the Dock: Essays on Theology and Ethics.* Grand Rapids, MI: William B. Eerdmans Publishing, 1970.

Lundgren, Sharon. *Revive Us Again: A Daughter's Spiritual Journey.* Self-Published, Sharon Lundgren, 2015.

McGuinn, Bernard, editor. *Meister Eckhart and the Beguine Mystics: Hadewijch of Brabant, Mechthild of Magdeburg, and Marguerite Porete.* New York: Continuum, 1997.

Merton, Thomas. *Conjectures of a Guilty Bystander.* New York: Image, 1965.

—. *Thoughts in Solitude.* New York: Farrar, Straus and Giroux, 1958, 1999.

Mother Teresa of Calcutta. *A Gift for God: Prayers and Meditations.* New York: Harper and Row Publishers, 1975.

The New American Bible, Revised Edition: The Leading Catholic Resource for Understanding Holy Scripture, © 2010, 1991, 1986, 1970 Confraternity of Christian Doctrine, Washington, DC. From website: https://bible.usccb.org/bible.

Newell, J. Phillip. *Listening for the Heartbeat of God: A Celtic Spirituality.* Mahwah, NJ: Paulist Press, 1997.

—. *The Rebirthing of God: Christianity's Struggle for New Beginnings.* Woodstock, Vermont: Skylight Paths Publishing, 2014.

—. *Sounds of the Eternal: A Celtic Psalter.* San Antonio: New Beginnings, 2012.

Newman, Saint John Henry. "Learning Christ," in *The Father Gilbert Prayer Book*, Father Gilbert Hay, M.S.SS.T. Silver Springs, MD: Trinity Ministries, 1965.

Newman, Saint John Henry, "Light of the Soul," in *Meditations and Devotions of the Late Cardinal Newman*. New York: Longmans, Green, and Co., 1893.

Nouwen, Henri J. M. *Can You Drink the Cup*. Norte Dame: Ave Maria Press; Tenth Anniversary Edition, 2012.

—. *Life of the Beloved: Spiritual Living in a Secular World*. New York: The Crossroad Publishing Company, 1992.

—. *You Are the Beloved: Daily Meditations for Spiritual Living*. London: Hodder & Stoughton, Ltd., 2018.

—. *The Wounded Healer: Ministry in Contemporary Society*. New York: Image Books, 1979.

Perrin, David B. "Mysticism." In *The Blackwell Companion to Christian Spirituality*, edited by Arthur Holder. West Sussex, UK: Wiley-Blackwell, 2011.

Pope Benedict XVI. "Prayer at Ground Zero." *EWTN*, New York, April 20, 2008. https://www.ewtn.com/catholicism/library/prayer-at-ground-zero-6613.

Pratt, Lonnie Collins, and Daniel Homan, OSB. *Radical Hospitality: Benedict's Way Love*. Brewster: Paraclete Press, 1952.

Rice, Helen Steiner. "On The Wings of a Prayer." In *A Collection of Love Gifts*. Uhrichsville, Ohio: Barbour and Company, Inc., 1995.

Steindl-Rast, David, OSB. *The Way of Silence: Engaging the Sacred in Daily Life.* Cincinnati: Franciscan Media, 1989, 2016.

Tapscott, Betty, and Father Robert DeGrandis, SSJ. "The Forgiveness Prayer." In *Forgiveness & Inner Healing: Prayers of Forgiveness and Healing of Memories.* Houston: Self-Published, 2007.

The Way of the Cross with Text from the Scriptures. Baltimore: Barton-Cotton, Inc., 1965.

Tullar, Grant Colfax. *Written Because—: And an Autobiography, Some Stories and Poems.* Orange, NJ: The Tullar Studio, 1937.

Warren, Rick. *The Purpose Driven Life: What on Earth Am I Here For?* Grand Rapids, MI: Zondervan, 2002.

The Order of the Daughters of the King, Inc.® Publications:

- Handbooks: 2003, 2006.
- *Continuing the Journey: The Spiritual Formation Guide*
- *The Royal Cross: The Quarterly Magazine of The Order of the Daughters of the King* issues: All Print:
    - Volume 2, October 1892
    - Volume 70, Issue 2, Spring 2002
    - Volume 74, Issue 2 & 3, Summer-Fall, 2006
    - Volume 74, Issue 4, Spring 2007
    - Volume 75, Issue 1, Spring 2008

ABOUT THE AUTHOR

Kathryn M. Wohnoutka, OFS, is a member of the Secular Franciscan Order and the Daughters of the King. She presents workshops and days of reflections on spiritual gifts, simplifying your life, forgiveness, and Franciscan joy, and she has served as the spiritual director and speaker at numerous women's retreats.

Kathryn retired from a twenty-four-year career at Oracle Corporation, where she was a member of the Leadership Circle, recognizing her excellence as an instructor and in customer service. A CPA, she has served on boards and finance committees of several nonprofit organizations.

Now a great-grandmother, Kathryn and her husband, George, live in Katy, Texas, and are active at St. Edith Stein Catholic Community. As Kathryn continues her journey with God, she embraces her life with joy, healing, and following His plan. Connect with Kathryn at her website: kathrynmwohnoutka.com or email: kmwohnoutka.books@gmail.com.

Other Books by Kathryn M. Wohnoutka
Whole, Single, Free, ME! An Escape from Domestic Abuse

·

Made in the USA
Las Vegas, NV
03 December 2024

13296210R00178